The Palgrave Lacan Series

Series Editors

Calum Neill
School of Psychology and Sociology
Edinburgh Napier University
Edinburgh, UK

Derek Hook
Duquesne University
Pittsburgh, USA

Jacques Lacan is one of the most important and influential thinkers of the 20th century. The reach of this influence continues to grow as we settle into the 21st century, the resonance of Lacan's thought arguably only beginning now to be properly felt, both in terms of its application to clinical matters and in its application to a range of human activities and interests. The Palgrave Lacan Series is a book series for the best new writing in the Lacanian field, giving voice to the leading writers of a new generation of Lacanian thought. The series will comprise original monographs and thematic, multi-authored collections. The books in the series will explore aspects of Lacan's theory from new perspectives and with original insights. There will be books focused on particular areas of or issues in clinical work. There will be books focused on applying Lacanian theory to areas and issues beyond the clinic, to matters of society, politics, the arts and culture. Each book, whatever its particular concern, will work to expand our understanding of Lacan's theory and its value in the 21st century.

More information about this series at
http://www.springer.com/series/15116

Diana Caine • Colin Wright
Editors

Perversion Now!

palgrave
macmillan

Editors
Diana Caine
Department of Neuropsychology
National Hospital for Neurology and Neurosurgery
London, UK

Colin Wright
Department of Culture, Film & Media
University of Nottingham
Nottingham, UK

The Palgrave Lacan Series
ISBN 978-3-319-83696-6 ISBN 978-3-319-47271-3 (eBook)
DOI 10.1007/978-3-319-47271-3

Cover image: A re-staging of installation by Hephzibah Rendle-Short + Eve Sprague, London, August 2015. Installation title: 'uncompanionable right now–TABLE.FACE.VESSEL'. Photo: Michael Traynor

Printed on acid-free paper

This Palgrave Macmillan imprint is published by Springer Nature
The registered company is Springer International Publishing AG
The registered company address is: Gewerbestrasse 11, 6330 Cham, Switzerland

Acknowledgements

This book is evidence of a rich collaborative enterprise which would not have been possible without the generous and thoughtful work of translation by: Siavash Bakhtiar, Ariana Cziffra, David Eckersley, Denis Echard, Thomas Harding, Ben Hooson, and Kristina Valendinova.

"Human vs. mechanical in Lacan: fetishistic strategies of death and intensity" by Željka Matijašević makes use of material that previously appeared in an article entitled "Human vs Mechanical in Lacan's 'Borderland': Fetishistic Strategies" in the *Journal of the Centre for Freudian Analysis and Research*, 2016.

Introduction to the conference 'Perversion et Modernité/Perversion Now', London, 15–17 September, 2015

To introduce this symposium on perversion and modernity, London is really a good place!

First, because globalisation is a characteristic of modernity, and London is one of its capitals—and there are not so many. Then, because globalisation is being fulfilled before our eyes, mainly under the impetus of capitalism, whose engine is still the "fetishism of merchandise". All stock exchanges operate on this model: the movement of goods overrides the interests of their producers, who are thus "reified", objectified, as Marx wrote in Book I of *Capital*. Goods are the fetish that the capitalist uses to obtain a *jouissance* from their producers because the financial interest of the capitalist is significant only because it is a way of taking *jouissance* from those who make them. The "added value" of capitalism is actually a "more of *jouissance*" as Lacan has written.

It is really striking that, almost during the same period that Marx established his theory of the "fetishism of merchandise", Freud was developing a theory of fetishism in a fairly similar way, since for Freud perversion involves taking pleasure from a partner by imposing on her a dress or a certain object. Of course, it is the violence of this imposition that triggers excitement, not the fetish in itself, which is significant only because of childhood reminiscences of infantile sexuality, since there is a *jouissance* without a sexual relation in perversion. There is an amazing parallel between Marx and Freud on this point. This is yet another reason to say that the conference "Perversion and Modernity" should take place in London, because as you may know, Marx and Freud are buried in this city and it is under this double patronage that we are speaking.

I would like to say now why perversion has a special importance in our globalised modernity. I do not intend to argue that our age is the time of a generalised perversion: before Krafft-Ebing, and Freud there existed no criteria for a diagnosis of perversion, no statistics to predict such an apocalyptic judgment. But at a first glance, the cruelty of the circus games in Rome does not seem worse than pornography on the internet in our time, to speak only of what can be called a "mass perversion". I leave aside the question of whether, at all times, political power has practiced what I have just called "mass perversion", on the model of merchandise fetishism.

Psychoanalytic anthropological studies are just beginning, psychoanalysis is a very young science, and before making hasty generalisations, it is cleverer to deepen the concept of perversion in respect of the structure of the subject. There is still some work to do before we understand how the child's polymorphous perversion extends—only sometimes—into adult perversion. That implies a complete sexual *jouissance* without sexual relations. It is not so easy to understand how the denial of castration that produces perversions, is the usual remedy of psychotics and neurotics to overcome difficulties of their eroticism. Jean-Jacques Rousseau, for example, a prestigious paranoiac, found it hard to get along with a woman if she did not really mistreat him. He has written, in his *Confessions,* of how a good spanking triggered his first erection. So I cannot sustain the view that there is an extension of perversion in our age. But I still would say that perversion is more likely to become a universal Ideal than psychoses and neuroses; as a kind of globalised ideal.

Regarding psychoses, first of all, it is a mistake to believe that psychotics are all just good enough to finish up in asylums. Only those who are crushed by a terrible father, fantasmatic or real, end up in psychiatric hospitals. But, on the contrary, there are also many psychotics who identify themselves with a father, terrible or not. They invent ideals or new religions, and it is often easy to see that these are delusions. They are able to manage very large masses of neurotics, who are so thirsty to find a father that they are ready to repeat complete delusions without any critical mind, even on a small detail. With what I have just said, it is clear that the various delusions of different religions are contradictory amongst themselves and cannot be useful to modern globalisation. They can just be useful for war, as we can see.

And now about neurotics, when their symptoms do not make them too sick, they are too busy adjusting their daily relationship to sex, they are too bothered by sexual intercourse to think at all seriously of political matters. They are not cowards, but the question of the other sex just cuts them down, and they require only one thing: that a political leader offers them an ideal. And later they can cut off his head as soon as possible. Neither psychosis nor neurosis are able to offer a global model. It is rather the case of perversions. Fetish fashion is globalised. The criminal heroes have a worldwide success. Fetishism, violence against women, speculators, are very rigid ideal models that do not oppose each other, but are in mutual accordance. And I could conclude this short introduction with a paraphrase of Marx. Marx says: “Workers of the world, unite yourselves!” and I will not say: “Perverts of the World, unite yourselves” but “Perversions of the world, unite us!”

Gérard Pommier
Paris, France

Contents

List of Contributors

Jean-Claude Aguerre is a psychoanalyst and member of Espace Analytique. He studied philosophy with successively François Chatelet and Gilles Deleuze as thesis supervisors. Originally he was a physicist and worked on the structure of matter.

Diana Kamienny Boczkowski is a psychoanalyst and psychiatrist. She is author of articles about mourning and melancholia, and psychosis; Director of "Psychanalyse et Transferts Culturels", http://psychanalyse-et-transferts-culturels.com/about/; member of the Association Lacanienne Internationale and of Aleph-Savoirs et Clinique. She is also a founder member of Association Franco-argentine de Psychiatrie.

Gorana Bulati-Manenti is a psychoanalyst and author of numerous articles. Her most recent book is *Comment fonctionne une cure analytique* (Eres, 2012). She is secretary-general and treasurer of the Fondation Européenne pour la Psychanalyse and research associate at University of Paris VII. She is member of the editorial board of the review *La Clinique Lacanienne* and of *d'Espace analytique*. She lives and teaches in Paris.

Luigi Burzotta is an Italian psychologist and psychoanalyst, with a Master's Degree in Modern Literature. He is former President of Fondation Européenne pour la Psychanalyse, and lecturer at Laboratorio Freudiano, Institute of Rome. His most recent published work was *Lo sguardo della maschera—psicanalisi e arte poetica* (Armando Editore, Rome, 2013).

Diana Caine is consultant neuropsychologist and Lacanian psychoanalyst at the National Hospital for Neurology & Neurosurgery in London. In her published work, she draws on psychoanalytic theory to rethink the implications of neurological damage for human subjectivity.

Roland Chemema is a psychoanalyst in Paris, has been president of the Association Lacanienne Internationale (ALI) and of the Fondation Européenne pour la Psychanalyse. His last published work was *La Psychanalyse comme Ethique* and, in collaboration with Christiane Lacôte-Destribats and Bernard Vandermersch, "Le métier de psychanalyste".

Ariana Cziffra is an affiliate member of the Centre for Freudian Analysis and Research. She launched a psychoanalytic practice in Mauritius in 2008 and has run a seminar of psychoanalysis for eight years at the Institut Français de Maurice. She is also an artist, a poet and a translator.

Xavier Fourtou is a London-based psychoanalyst. He has participated in the opening of Maison Verte-UK and is co-founder of Bubble & Speak, the first psychoanalytically oriented drop-in centres in the United Kingdom, for children under four years old and their carers.

Astrid Gessert is a practising psychoanalyst and a member of the Centre for Freudian Analysis and Research (CFAR) and of the College of Psychoanalysts UK. She is a regular contributor to CFAR's public lecture and training programme and she lectures and facilitates seminars at other psychoanalytic organisations and writes on psychoanalytic subjects.

Hélène Godefroy is a psychoanalyst in Paris and has a Doctorate in psychology, psychopathology and psychoanalysis. She is a member of the Espace Analytique and of the Fondation européenne pour la psychanalyse and a teacher (Études psychanalytiques) at the University of Paris VII. She is an associate researcher at Centre de recherches psychanalyse, médecine et société (CRPMS), University of Paris-Diderot and author of numerous articles, most notably "Perversion between neurosis and psychosis", Ed Lédoria, Madrid, 2014.

Gyorgyi Koman is a Romanian-born Hungarian national who works in London as a Lacanian psychoanalyst in private practice. She is also a linguist with the Chartered Institute of Linguists, UK. Before moving to the UK (in 2009), she worked in Budapest as a counsellor with children in foster care, facilitating groups for victims of hate crimes, and as a movement therapist with autistic children. She has an MA in philosophy and psychology.

Patrick Landman is a psychiatrist, child psychiatrist, psychoanalyst, and lawyer. He is a former Chairman of the Espace Analytique, and Chairman of STOP DSM. He is author of *Le refoulement* with Gérard Pommier (Erès, 2014), *Tristesse Business* (Max Milo, 2014), and *Tous Hyperactifs* (Albin Michel, 2015).

Monique Lauret is a psychiatrist and psychoanalyst, member of the association Espace Analytique (Paris) and member of the Fondation Europeenne pour la Psychanalyse. She is author of *L'énigme de la pulsion de mort* (Puf, 2014), *Lectures du rêve* (Puf, 2011) and *Mélanie Klein, une pensée vivante* (Puf, 2008).

Željka Matijašević is Professor of Comparative Literature, Faculty of Humanities and Social Sciences, University of Zagreb and member of the Croatian Philosophical Association, the Croatian Psychiatric Association and La Fondation Européenne pour la Psychanalyse. She has a PhD from Cambridge University and is the author of three books in Croatian, *Lacan: The Persistence of the Dialectic* (2005), *Structuring the Unconscious: Freud and Lacan* (2006), and *Introduction to Psychoanalysis: Oedipus, Hamlet, Jekyll/Hyde* (2011).

André Michels is a psychoanalyst and psychiatrist (Luxembourg, Paris), a member of the Espace Analytique and the Fondation Européenne pour la Psychanalyse, and editor of *Actualité de l'hystérie* (Eres, 2001), *Les limites du corps, le corps comme limite* (Eres, 2006), *Norm, Normalität Gesetz* (Turia & Kant, 2012).

Michael Newman is Professor of Art Writing at Goldsmiths, University of London. His doctorate in philosophy on the trace was at KU Leuven, where his research also included psychoanalysis. He has published numerous essays on modern and contemporary artists, as well as thematic essays on the wound, the horizon, contingency, memory, drawing, and nonsense. He is the author of *Richard Prince Untitled (couple)* (2006), *Jeff Wall: Works and Writings* (2007), *Price, Seth* (2010) and co-editor of *Rewriting Conceptual Art* (1999) and *The State of Art Criticism* (2007). Curated exhibitions include Tacita Dean at York University, Toronto, Revolver2 (contemporary artists) at Matt's Gallery, London, and 'Drawing after Bellmer in Europe, North America and Japan' will be at The Drawing Room, London. The first volume of his selected writings, *'I know very well... but all the same': Essays on Artists of the Still and Moving Image* is forthcoming with Ridinghouse.

Dany Nobus is Professor of Psychoanalytic Psychology and Pro-Vice-Chancellor for External Affairs at Brunel University London, where he also directs the MA Programme in Psychoanalysis and Contemporary Society. In addition, he is the Chair of the Freud Museum London, and the author of numerous books and papers on the history, theory and practice of psychoanalysis.

Ian Parker is co-founder and is co-director (with Erica Burman) of the Discourse Unit (www.discourseunit.com). He is a member of the Asylum: Magazine for Democratic Psychiatry collective, and a practising psychoanalyst in Manchester. His books include *Revolution in Psychology: Alienation to Emancipation* (Pluto, 2007) and *Lacanian Psychoanalysis: Revolutions in Subjectivity* (Routledge, 2011).

Arlette Pellée is a psychoanalyst practising in Paris, member of the Fondation Européenne pour la Psychanalyse and has directed the association Supervision et Analyse Psychanalytique des Pratiques Professionelles (SAPP). She has notably published with Isabelle Foc'h *L'Inconscient est-il politiquement incorrect?* (Erès, 2008), *Ce que nous enseignent les ruptures majeures* (L'Harmattan, 2011), *Le Cerveau et l'Inconscient: Neurosciences et Psychanalyse* (Ed. Armand Colin, 2015).

Gérard Pommier is a psychiatrist, psychoanalyst, university professor, member of the laboratory of Paris VII and honorary professor of the University of Rosario, Argentina. His most recently published book is *Féminin, révolution sans fin*, published by J.J. Pauvert.

Hephzibah Rendle-Short is a painter with a practice-led PhD from the Royal College of Art, London. The PhD program employed Lacanian psychoanalysis as a theoretical lens, which soon after became her object of study. Now in her sixth year of training at the Centre for Freudian Analysis and Research, she works as a Lacanian psychoanalyst in London.

C. Edward Robins is Director of the Dr Robins Treatment Center, New York City.

Maria Izabel Oliveira Szpacenkopf is a psychoanalyst and member of the Espace Analytique de Paris, the Psychoanalytical Society of the City of Rio de Janeiro (SPCRJ), the International Society for Psychoanalysis and Philosophy (SIPP) and the Fondation Europeenne pour la Psychanalyse. She has a PhD in Communication and Culture at the Federal University of Rio de Janeiro, and is researcher at the Laboratory of Social Theory, Psychoanalysis and Philosophy of the University of São Paulo.

Estela Welldon is founder of the International Association for Forensic Psychotherapy, a Fellow of the Royal College of Psychiatrists, Honorary Consultant Psychiatrist at Tavistock Portman NHS Clinics, and a member of the British Psychoanalytic Council. She works privately as a psychoanalytical psychotherapist. She is the author of *Mother, Madonna, Whore: The Idealization and Denigration of Motherhood* (1988), *Sasomasochism* (2002), and *Playing with Dynamite: A Personal Approach to the Psychoanalytic Understanding of Perversions, Violence, and Criminality* (2011).

Anne Worthington is a psychoanalyst practicing in London. She is a member of the Centre for Psychoanalysis, Middlesex University, the Centre for Freudian Analysis & Research and the College of Psychoanalysts UK.

Colin Wright is Associate Professor of Critical Theory at the University of Nottingham, UK. He is a member of the Centre for Critical Theory there, and is the Director of the MA in Critical Theory and Cultural Studies. He is also a Lacanian analyst with a private practice in Nottingham.

1

Introduction: Mapping Perversion in the Contemporary World

Diana Caine, Xavier Fourtou, Gyorgyi Koman, Hephzibah Rendle-Short, and Colin Wright

A child is seated on a throne, imagining that he is king and master of all he beholds; at the same time his unconscious fantasy appears on a screen, but in another place. With no hint of subtlety, this is followed by the title of Freud's famous text 'A Child is Being Beaten', flashed across the screen. This emblematic scene from Todd Haynes' short film *Dottie Gets Spanked* (1993)—deeply rooted in popular culture, with its nod to *I Love Lucy* and the mesmerising power of the mass media—succeeds in conveying a profound equivocation with regard to the place of conscious and unconscious fantasy, transgressive desire, sexual identity, and between the

D. Caine (✉)
National Hospital for Neurology & Neurosurgery, London

X. Fourtou • G. Koman • H. Rendle-Short
Psychoanalyst in private practice

C. Wright
University of Nottingham

D. Caine, C. Wright (eds.), *Perversion Now!*,
DOI 10.1007/978-3-319-47271-3_1

affects of humour and pathos. The film's creation as such, as well as its provocative content, points in different ways to the on-going problematic of perversion in contemporary life, as also to the central place of psychoanalysis in that problematic. It is on this 'other scene' of perversion today that this book attempts to shine a light.

While always present within culture and society—albeit in the shadows—perverse behaviour seems to surge up in different ways at different times. It raises difficult issues, challenging the status quo, the judicial and moral law, always provoking responses even as it somehow slips away. This is echoed within the field of psychoanalysis, where we sense perversion both everywhere and nowhere: everywhere because the constitutive 'abnormality' of human sexuality continues to be a core tenet of Freud-derived psychoanalytic theory, a certain reading of which has played its part in the liberalisation of sexual mores during the 20th century; and yet nowhere because, precisely as the *spectacle* of perversion becomes prevalent in the media, in literature, in film, and online, its diagnostic counterpart is much more rarely seen by psychoanalysts in the clinical setting. As the pages that follow will show, this paradox is prompting urgent questions about the category of perversion amongst practicing psychoanalysts.

What form must the pervert's fantasy take today when TV and other media already seem so saturated with perverse imagery, as if *The Dottie Show* itself pre-empted all the work of erotic elaboration? What is the fate of transgression in such an apparently permissive age (the main character in Haynes' film clearly develops his spanking fantasy partly because his 'modern' or 'progressive' mother declares 'we just don't believe in hitting')? And, crucially, how does psychoanalysis, as a theory but also a clinical practice, keep up with these changing times without coinciding entirely with them?

1.1 Part I: The Backstory

1.1.1 A Cartel on 'Perversion'

This book, like any patient in analysis, has a backstory. For several of the writers of this introduction, questions such as those just raised, questions to do with perversion's paradoxical place in psychoanalysis and in the world at large, became the impetus for the formation of a 'cartel'.

With some inspiration from Wilfred Bion, Jacques Lacan introduced the idea of the cartel in 1964.[1] He conceived of it as a group of just three to five people who agree to work together on a particular aspect of psychoanalytic theory or practice, and to produce, singly or together, some sort of outcome that helps to advance and renew psychoanalysis. According to Lacan's original text on the subject,[2] a cartel should also have a 'plus one', an outsider who supports the work of the group. Inherent in the idea of a Lacanian cartel is opposition to orthodox notions of education and training, to related forms of dogmatic knowledge, and to the conventional hierarchical arrangements of groups.[3] The 'plus one', then, is a function that can be enacted in many different ways, but always with the intention that it will provoke the members of the group to work towards some outcome, not necessarily by any means a shared production (or 'output', as the academic world is inclined to say these days).

The particular cartel in question here formed in London in 2013, and comprised Hephzibah Rendle-Short, Xavier Fourtou, Gyorgyi Koman and Diana Caine. After meeting regularly for a few months to work on Freud's writings on perversion, Xavier encountered Hélène Godefroy at a conference organised by the *Fondation Européenne pour la Psychanalyse* in Toledo, Spain. She expressed an interest in finding a way to work in some way in the UK. Her response to our invitation to join us as our 'plus one' was immediately positive and enthusiastic.

The cartel took as its starting point the text 'Freud et la Perversion',[4] written by Patrick Valas—psychiatrist, psychoanalyst, and analysand of Lacan, who also supervised Valas' work as analyst—which thoroughly reviewed Freud's work on perversion. This survey began with Freud's

[1] Lacan, J. (1990)[1964]. "Founding Act" (*Acte de foundation)* in *Television/A Challenge to the Psychoanalytic Establishment.* D. Hollier, R. Krauss, & A. Michelson (Trans.). London and New York: W. W. Norton & Company, pp. 97–106. For a commentary on this text by Lacan, see Gallagher, C. (2010). The Founding Act, the Cartel and the Riddle of the PLUS ONE. *The Letter: Irish Journal for Lacanian Psychoanalysis*, 44 (Summer): 1–31.

[2] Lacan, op. cit.

[3] Parker, I. (2005). Cartels in Lacanian Psychoanalysis, paper given at the founding meeting of Manchester Psychoanalytic Matrix, 1 June 2005.

[4] Valas, P. (1986). Freud et la Perversion. *Ornicar? Revue du Champ Freudien*, Oct–Dec: 9–50.

letters to Fliess[5] and his *Studies on Hysteria*.[6] Still influenced by the notion that perversion was a function of being insufficiently civilised, Freud regarded it at that time as a manifestation of the originary bestiality of human beings, the product of a constitutional brain abnormality in comparison with the healthy brains of hysterics, consistent with the medical and sexological epistemologies of the era. It was only with the 'Three Essays on the Theory of Sexuality'[7] (1905) that Freud began, in a startlingly and doubly radical way, to lay out the fundamental themes of psychoanalytic discourse regarding perversion. Here he asserted on the one hand that sexuality is intrinsic to the experience of infancy and childhood—an idea still considered outrageous and subversive relative to a dominant discourse which holds to the essential innocence of children, even within some psychoanalytic circles—and on the other hand, that sexuality as such is fundamentally perverse, the evidence for which is precisely the polymorphous sexual perversity of the infant.

Guided by Valas, the cartel then traced Freud's elaboration of perverse human sexuality and its place in human subjectivity; what a child does with the real of anatomical sexual difference, the paths open to a child in relation to the castration complex and its associated interdiction. These sexual histories are mapped in a number of Freudian texts including: 'Instincts and their Vicissitudes' (1915)[8]; 'A Child is Being Beaten' (1919)[9]; 'Some Psychical Consequences of the Anatomical Distinction Between the Sexes' (1925)[10]; 'Fetishism' (1927)[11]; 'Splitting of the Ego

[5] Freud, S. (1897). Letters 55, 69, 75, 125 from Freud's correspondance with W. Fliess. In *Pre-PsychoAnalytic Publications and Unpublished Drafts*. S.E. 1. J. Strachey (Trans.). London: Hogarth, 1953.

[6] Freud, S. and Breuer, J. (1895). *Studies in Hysteria*. N. Luckhurst (Trans.). London: Penguin, 2004.

[7] Freud, S. (1905d). *Three Essays on the Theory of Sexuality*. S.E. 7: 123–242. J. Strachey (Trans.). London: Hogarth, 1953.

[8] Freud, S. (1915). *Instincts and their Vicissitudes*. S.E. 14: 109–40. J. Strachey (Trans.). London: Hogarth, 1957.

[9] Freud, S. (1919). *A Child is Being Beaten': A Contribution to the Study of the Origins of Sexual Perversions. S.E.* 17: 175–205. J. Strachey (Trans.). London: Hogarth, 1955.

[10] Freud, S. (1925). *Some Psychical Consequences of the Anatomical Distinction Between the Sexes*. S.E. 19: 248–258. J. Strachey (Trans.). London: Hogarth, 1961.

[11] Freud, S. (1927). *Fetishism*. S.E. 21: 147–157. J. Strachey (Trans.). London: Hogarth, 1961.

in the Process of Defence' (1938)[12] and 'An Outline of Psychoanalysis' (1938).[13] In the last, published after his death, Freud describes the splitting of the ego as 'essentially topographical or structural.' He claims that the ego defends itself either by disavowing a portion of the external world or by rejecting an instinctual demand from the internal world. Both solutions result in a rift within the subject's mental life.

In the light of this last discovery, the cartel wondered if further reading might shine new interpretative light. We turned from Valas to Joël Dor who reads Freud through Lacan, arguing that already in Freud perversion is conceived structurally. In his book *Structure and Perversions*[14] Dor shows that Freud distinguished between two psychic processes of negation—disavowal and repression—resulting in two different structural organisations, perversion and neurosis respectively. More centrally than Valas, he emphasises a distinction between such a perverse structure predicated on disavowal, and the perverse traits found in obsessional neurosis and hysteria. While our move towards Dor demonstrated that alternative guides might have generated different figures of perversion, it also confirmed our original hypothesis—which motivated the cartel's inauguration—that perversion is both pervasive and singular. It is the engine of the fantasies of each singular subject from the starting point of polymorphous perversion; it is a constant if discomforting thread in cultural production; and it is a forbidden, secretive but somehow core facet of society as a whole. As the texts that follow demonstrate, it thus offers itself as an unexpectedly rich well-spring from which to consider what it is to be a speaking being.

1.1.2 From Cartel to Conference

Hélène was a very welcome addition to the cartel meetings for which she generously travelled to London. Meetings with her were always carried

[12] Freud, S. (1938). *Splitting of the Ego in the Process of Defence*. S.E. 23: 271–278. J. Strachey (Trans.). London: Hogarth, 1964.

[13] Freud, S. (1940)[1938]. *An Outline of Psychoanalysis*. S.E. 23: 139–207. J. Strachey (Trans.). London; Hogarth, 1964.

[14] Dor, J. (2001). *Structure and Perversions*. S. Fairfield (Trans.). New York: Other Press.

out in both English and French. At one of those meetings, Hephzibah said it seemed to her that 'the French are like natives in the Lacanian world, while we Anglophones are more like immigrants there'. That remark underlined the extent to which the encounter with Lacan, in the context of the cartel, has also been an encounter with French itself. It was not always easy. Ideas often flowed more quickly than they could be translated. Sometimes there was more attention to words than to ideas. And it also meant wrestling with a sometimes impossible divide, words and expressions that simply do not translate, or ambiguities in French that can only be rendered with more specificity and less nuance in English: *jouissance*, *le desir de l'autre*, *objet petit a*, *angoisse*. In spite of the difficulties, maybe in part because of the very challenge of translation, a space for thinking, rich with possibility, seemed to open up.

The cartel focused on the work of Freud, yet notwithstanding our historical perspective it soon became apparent that it was impossible not to read Freud through Lacan, unearthing the seeds of Lacanian ideas embedded in the Freudian texts. Throughout our reading we were puzzled to find that although the idea of 'normality' is rigorously interrogated, it is at the same time persistently evoked. We encountered a recurrent tension between the idea of perversion as a universal feature in the mental life and the fantasies of neurotic subjects, and perversion rather as a distinct and particular psychic structure which manifests in the acts rather than the fantasies of the subject. In each case there is the question of a response to the problematic—the threat—of castration, of loss.

After some months Hélène proposed the idea of a conference in London on behalf of the *Fondation Européenne pour le Psychoanalyse*. The *Fondation*, an organisation which is dedicated to the transmission of psychoanalysis, comprises members from a constellation of Lacanian psychoanalytic groups in France, Italy, Spain and elsewhere. It holds conferences each year in one or another major city, sometimes more than one, on a theme of import to psychoanalytic theory and practice. But it is little-known in England and it had never held a conference there before.

The possibility of collaborating with the *Fondation* on the topic of perversion, the work of the cartel, seemed like an opportunity to explore in greater depth both the subject and the inter-linguistic/inter-cultural space that had opened up in our work with Hélène. But it was a risk on all sides. We did not really know one another, and we certainly had not worked together on a project like this before. There was a need for trust and confidence across the Channel, a stretch of water often more associated with mistrust and incomprehension. It required a great deal of good will and co-operation. Firstly, on the part of the speakers, especially the English participants who in the main did not know of the existence of the *Fondation* and so were not sure to what they were committing themselves; then on the part of the *Fondation* in entrusting the organisation of an event in its name to a small group of foreigners; on the part of all the speakers, English and French, who were asked to submit their papers in time for them to be translated, by they knew not whom; and finally, on the part of seven translators who enthusiastically responded to the request to participate and who worked with commitment and speed, to have the papers ready on time.

It needs to be said as well that on the English side, the conference was only possible because of the association of some of us with the *Centre for Freudian Analysis and Research* (CFAR), a London-based organisation which is deeply committed to the transmission of Lacanian theory and practice, and which functions in part as a kind of hub around which many different groups and activities circulate in the pursuit of this aim, of which our cartel was just one. A number of members and trainees from CFAR were involved in every aspect of the conference: as speakers, organisers and translators.

The task of organising the conference, undertaken on the English side largely by Diana Caine and on the French side by Hélène Godefroy, required unexpected negotiation around everything: the hours of starting and of finishing, the cost of registration and hospitality, the work of translation itself and how it would be done, even how long the lunch break should be and at what time. It turned out that, quite apart from any issues of meaning and translation, on either side of the Channel we do very similar things but in rather different ways, and with curiosity and puzzlement about the other on both sides.

1.1.3 Towards Publication

The resulting conference 'Perversion et Modernité/Perversion Now', was held over three days in London in September 2015. The collection you hold in your hands comprises entirely papers written for and presented at that event. Notwithstanding all the complexities involved in its organisation, the conference represented an extraordinary coming together of Lacanian analysts from the UK, Europe and elsewhere. It was conducted in French and English, with the translation of each presentation projected for concurrent reading so that everyone had access to all of the papers.

This publication emerged from the general feeling that here was a collection of texts of depth and quality, in two languages, in which many people in different disciplines might be interested. Many conference registrants, having had their appetites whetted by hearing the papers, asked whether they would be available to read, the better to contemplate their content. Colin Wright, who had participated in the scientific committee organising the conference and as a speaker, kindly agreed to join us in the production of the book.

Bringing the texts together in written form has again exposed unexpected cultural differences. To an English eye it appears that the Lacanian community in France holds meetings and conferences with astonishing frequency, with the consequence that the move between spoken and written production is made relatively lightly. Some Francophone authors made no changes to the texts of their original verbal presentations at all, others only very few. Academic referencing seemed to be at a much lower premium for them than it tends to be in the Anglophone world where the move into the written—and, therefore, more enduring form—seems to be subject to a stronger sense of the need to bend to the demands of the academic rule-book.

This difference has produced variability in texture and tone amongst the papers, one we have deliberately chosen to preserve. Some have remained, more or less, as spoken. Others have become more formalised for reading. We took the decision not to try to camouflage that difference, in part because it captures cultural differences that lie beyond words, in part because it means that the text retains some of the immediacy and spontaneity of the spoken event (who if not psychoanalysts should insist on the value of speech?). And finally, because in itself it conveys something of the richness of the collaborative process that the resulting book has benefitted from.

1.2 Part II: The Structure

Although the term 'perversion' conjures the idea of something aside, something hidden, the texts comprising this volume demonstrate that perversion indeed pervades every aspect of our lives, from the very intimate privacy of the clinic to the very public discourses and conduct of our politics. Here, perversion becomes a revealing lens through which to view life in our time. While the range of material covered by the papers is remarkably diverse, certain salient themes emerge, reflected in the five sections into which the book is divided.

1.2.1 Part I: Clinical Reflections from Freud to Lacan

If the title *Perversion Now!* presupposes that perversion has a history, it is not in the sense that it is a fixed nosological category 'discovered' at a particular historical moment, but rather that it is a term that responds to, perhaps even prompts, historical, social, cultural, and moral shifts. This history is by no means the monopoly of psychoanalysis of course, since 19th century psychiatry had already focussed on the perversions in various ways before Freud. Yet if the Freudian 'revolution' implied a critique of that work by breaking the assumed link between sexual aim and sexual object, it also transformed ideas of 'normal' human sexuality, moving it away from questions about heredity and reproduction towards questions about libido and fantasy.

As well as reflecting an historical arc to changing meanings and uses of the term 'perversion' in the evolution of psychoanalytic theory, Part I foregrounds *the clinic* as the foundation of both Freud's and Lacan's theoretical innovations. At the same time, although often lost in its academic uses as a literary or cultural theory, these papers demonstrate that psychoanalysis as a praxis also has history.

With this in mind, the collection begins with Xavier Fourtou's provocative challenge to the 'father of psychoanalysis' regarding his famous case of 'Little Hans'. Is there something perverse, Fourtou wonders, in Freud's apparent reduction of Hans to a 'case' of phobia, which happened conveniently to fit with his evolving Oedipal theory? This desire for theoretical knowledge; the relationships between analyst and patient, supervisor and friend; the apparent erasure of Hans as subject, all lead him to conclude that the treatment of Hans infringed many of the rules and recommendations Freud made as to analytic practice, raising the question of whether there was not something transgressive in its conduct.

Tracing the dramatic reformulation of perversion from Freud to Lacan, Astrid Gessert notes the shift from a focus on perversion as a transgression against some kind of norm to the question of how a subject manages their desire. While neurotic subjects suffer desire, reluctantly embracing substitutes that inevitably fail, the perverse subject makes demands, always believing that a particular object will 'do the trick'. But in our time, she argues, desire and demand have become confused: if a surfeit of things is always instantly available in response to demand, where is the place for desire in these circumstances?

Anne Worthington also investigates the shifting definition of perversion but here to explore rather the utility of Lacan's view of perversion as a structure, both as a riposte to the queer critique of psychoanalysis and as a subjective, structural response to Oedipus and castration. Through clinical cases she demonstrates how the perverse subject seeks a solution to the Oedipal dilemma, in offering him or herself as the object-cause of *jouissance* in the (m)Other, or in the use a fetish as a way of creating separation from the maternal Other. At the same time, she observes that the disavowal that structures perversion also implies something incomplete in relation to the paternal function and the law. Thus, paradoxically, transgression is often a call for more authority, a theme echoed elsewhere in the book.

Patrick Landman shifts the historical perspective to focus on changes in the direction of the treatment itself. In place of Freud's hierarchy of drive objects (oral, anal, genital) and their relation to infantile polymorphous perversion, and the early Lacanian hierarchy of desires, he finds in later Lacan a focus on freeing the drives from the clutches of desire, enabling a certain accommodation to *jouissance*. In this light, he asks whether there could be said to be an equality of *jouissances* at the end of an analysis? And, if *jouissances* are equivalent, does that mean that practices ordinarily considered perverse become newly available to the subject? Landman carefully distinguishes between this possibility and perversion as a psychic structure, situating it in the contemporary world with the changes it has wrought in the paternal function. His response to this question offers a contemporary account of the psychoanalytic 'cure'.

If Gessert and Worthington both emphasise the value of a structural approach to perversion, Gorana Bulat-Manenti, in the final contribution to this section, points to the tension between perversion as a psychic structure and the perverse traits that can also be seen in neurosis and psychosis. She examines the relation of the subject to the mother, the father, and the phallus, in two illuminating clinical case studies: in both cases, acts of perversion are seen as a psychotic defence against an excess of *jouissance* which, in the absence of access to the symbolic father function, cannot be regulated.

1.2.2 Part II: Symptom or Structure, a Dichotomy?

The tension, already seen, between perverse traits and perversion as structure pervades the book, but is interrogated most directly in Part II. Arguably, such a tension was already present in Freud's 'Three Essays' in which he radically 'deconstructs' the opposition between perversion and normality, transforming heterosexual 'normality' into a contingent psychosexual domestication of that initial perversity in the process. Yet—as Gessert and Worthington both discuss—this results in the paradoxical difficulty for Freud of how to characterise perversion as a pathology. His faltering attempts to do so range from an early emphasis on regression and fixation to the distinction he draws between perverse, unconscious neurotic fantasies and the conscious enactment of fantasies in perversion proper. It was not until later texts such as 'Fetishism' of 1927 that Freud began to focus on the mechanism of denial of maternal castration and the related 'solution' of the fetish as a substitute maternal phallus. For many—but not all—Lacanians today, the mechanism of disavowal (*Verleugnung*) that Freud identified justifies the diagnosis of a perverse structure as distinct from perverse traits and behaviours that may be observable across the psychic structures. As the chapters in this section suggest, the Lacanian field remains heir to the tensions bequeathed by Freud in this regard.

Taking Freud's 'Three Essays' as her starting point, Hélène Godefroy insists robustly that, inasmuch as the disavowal of castration—anxiety of loss—is an operation that occurs in *both* neurosis and psychosis, there is no justification for a third, separate structure. Remnants of polymorphous perversity always survive, she argues, giving rise to perverse traits in adult life, irrespective of psychic structure. And yet Godefroy acknowledges that with patriarchy fading, there has been a liberation of desire such that new forms of perversion have emerged, offering subjects hitherto unimaginable possibilities (a change of biological gender, for example). She hypothesises that such examples of contemporary perversion are to be interpreted as an appeal for a more present Father.

In engaging with Lebrun's concept of 'ordinary perversion'[15] Roland Chemama uses the distinction between polymorphous perversity and perversion as structure to ask what can be understood from the new social discourses that gave rise to the term? In today's world, he suggests, the relationship to desire and *jouissance* has changed inasmuch as contemporary society favours a denial of loss and a demand for pleasure. He notes that the adoption of the perverse patterns so available in the modern era are in part a function of our potential for perversion; they are not created ex-nihilo by modern technology. But such accessibility of the object leads to the disappearance of any feeling of transgression. If, because of this availability, behaviour that was once considered perverse is now commonplace, if transgression has become problematic, how is the contemporary subject to contest the norm when it becomes too burdensome? he asks. The clinical case he presents takes up this question, cautioning us against the temptation to consider all our contemporary behaviours as the expression of perversion.

Noting that the field of perversion has been progressively diminished in successive editions of psychiatry's *Diagnostic and Statistical Manual of Mental Disorders* (DSM) Dany Nobus is prompted to ask: "why psychoanalysts insist on preserving the notion of perversion"? He offers four reasons, that range from authorisation of the term by Freud and Lacan to the occasional use of the classification 'pervert' by psychoanalytic institutions to reject certain candidates. While he stresses that analysts have a

[15] Lebrun, J.-P. (2007). *La Perversion Ordinaire*. Paris: Denoël.

responsibility to work through their own perverse traits, he asks whether the term has outlived its usefulness?

With a focus on the post-colonial context of Mauritius, Ariana Cziffra takes up Nobus' challenge. Elaborating the distinctions between perversion as clinical structure, perverse fantasies and perverse defences, categories which are not mutually exclusive, she defends the idea that 'perverse relations do exist'; and further that a psychoanalytic understanding of perversion in all its manifestations offers a way of both reading and intervening in a post-colonial community. Like Nobus, she invites analysts to recognise and explore their own "père-versions" in order to avoid bringing these to the consulting room. But if colonial history lends a complexity to the idea of transgression, in Mauritius where incest and paedophilia have increased over the years, so also have the uses of religion on the one hand and of the fashionable diagnosis of "narcissistic pervert" on the other. How to think perversion in this complex historical/ethnic/ cultural/ linguistic context? The question about the perverse effects of post-colonialism reverts back, she argues, to the question of perversion as a structure that is always everywhere present.

Finally, and somewhat unexpectedly, C. E. Robins takes the tragic 2015 crashing of Airbus 9525 into the French Alps to make a case for the perverse psychical structure of the co-pilot, Andreas Lupitz who staged it, at the cost of his own and 149 other lives. Vividly dramatising the event, Robins uses media coverage, including that of Lupitz's history insofar as it could be reconstructed, to elucidate his motivation as fundamentally perverse. The paper makes fascinating—and disturbing—reading, but not without raising again the question of whether or not overtly perverse practices might best be read as a defence against psychotic fragmentation, as Bulat-Manenti suggests earlier in the volume?

1.2.3 Part III: The Fetish and the Feminine

Feminist histories have problematised the tendency to gendered psychopathological categories,[16] paradigmatically in hysteria with its supposed

[16] Bronfen, E. (1998). *The Knotted Subject: Hysteria and its Discontents*. Princeton: Princeton University Press.

link to the 'wandering womb', an ancient reference durable enough for male hysteria to remain a controversial diagnosis well into the second half of the 19th century.[17] It is much less often noted that related normative assumptions about gender roles may also have shaped the framing of perversion as an intrinsically male phenomenon. Once again, Freud is implicated in this assumption, for example in mapping masculinity and femininity onto active and passive positions respectively. His theory of the fetish as maternal phallus, too, seems to imply conventional gender roles. But the possible existence of female perversion has been the source of much debate and questioning within the psychoanalytic movement, as well as without.[18]

The later Lacanian notion that feminine and masculine structures do not map, necessarily, onto biological categories of male and female,[19] opens a new approach to the question of female perversion. Addressing Freud's exasperated question, 'What do women want?', Lacan outlines in Seminar XX a non-phallic *jouissance* only available on the female side of the tables of sexuation, an Other *jouissance* intimated, he suggests, in the visionary writings of female mystics. These new co-ordinates are useful in separating clinical questions about the possibility of female perversion from the burden of cultural assumptions about female sexuality.

Gerard Pommier begins the first paper in this section by exploring a rarely considered aspect of fetishism that links the fetish with the paternal taboo. The father of Totemism, Pommier argues, imposes a fetish on young women, in the form of clothes and jewellery which have the function of protecting them from other men. This fetishism on the side of the father is implicated in Lacan's term '*père-version*': when the male subject imposes the fetish on a woman, the subject is no longer the phallus for the mother. Pommier then asks whether there is a form of *père-version* specific to women? Taking the example of the Christian mystics, whose orgasm was witnessed by the Church and transcribed by painters and

[17] Micale, M. (2008). *Hysterical Men: The Hidden History of Male Nervous Illness*. Cambridge, MA: Harvard University Press.

[18] See Kaplan, L. (1993). *Female Perversions: The Temptations of Madame Bovary*. London: Penguin Books Ltd.

[19] Lacan, J. (1998). *The Seminar of Jacques Lacan, Book XX. On Feminine Sexuality, The Limits of Love and Knowledge*. B. Fink (Trans.). London: W. W. Norton & Company.

sculptors, he asks whether the *jouissance* is in the suffering itself or in its transcription? His response is that it is on the presence of the voyeur that the *jouissance* of suffering depends, and that this might characterise the sexual *jouissance* not only of mystics. Just as radically, he examines the way in which motherhood offers the possibility for female perversion through the fetishisation of the child.

While Pommier seems to assume sexual difference grounded in anatomical gender, Arlette Pellé's chapter revolves around the contemporary possibility of eradicating sexual difference. She asks whether queer practices are new forms of perversion or can they rather be considered new ways of understanding feminine *jouissance*? The "queer" transformation of the body into "hybrids composed by natural and artificial organs" in order to obtain "something mobile and fluid", lies outside phallic logic, away from the biological male-female binary, eliminating the "supposed natural" feminine position. Pellé asks whether biological reality can really be side-lined in this way? Is it necessary to retain the reference to the phallus, product as it is of heterosexual discourse, its anatomical origin only too evident? If queer theorists' response to Freud's question "What is a woman?" is a striving towards the disappearance of femininity and feminine *jouissance*, making a new norm of polymorphous perversion, Pellé asks whether there is another possibility, a different status for the feminine exception?

Estella Welldon's seminal book *Mother, Madonna, Whore*[20] made the case for female perversion almost three decades ago, but from the theoretical perspective of object relations. Her contribution draws on extensive clinical experience to argue, in contrast with Pellé, for the direct psychic impact of anatomical sexual difference. From this viewpoint, she also differentiates male and female perversion, primarily with respect to their aim: in men, she argues, the perverse act is aimed at something external, in women it is against themselves, or against objects of their own creation, their babies. Focusing on this "other side of motherhood" she argues that for some women, motherhood causes a deep sense of inadequacy, which can easily turn into hatred towards their children.

[20] Welldon, E. (2000). *Mother, Madonna, Whore: The Idealization and Denigration of Motherhood*. London: Karnac.

1.2.4 Part IV: Sublimation>Sinthome>Culture

As our opening reference to *Dottie Gets Spanked* suggested, cultural production can be a site for explorations of perversion as well as an occasion for perverse practices as such: both are evident in the penultimate section, which explores the interrelations between sublimated artistic practices, the sinthome as theorised by later Lacan, and culture generally as a treatment of the real that has subjective effects.

For Freud, sublimation involved renunciation of the drive and redirection of libido away from sexuality and towards culturally valorised practices. His reading of the young Leonardo Da Vinci[21] frames artistic practice more precisely as sublimation of a putatively perverse, homosexual drive. Lacan, in contrast, stressed less the 'civilised' side of sublimation and associated notions of 'high culture', and more its function as a treatment of the real, and thus something ultimately enigmatic, unsymbolisable.[22] In his later period, this culminated in the idea of the 'sinthome' which he elaborated in relation to the writings of James Joyce.[23] If in his most structuralist phase Lacan conceived of the symptom as an encrypted message addressed to the symbolic Other, the later sinthome was rather a kind of singular subtraction from language and the capacity for signifying chains to carry meaning. According to Lacan, Joyce used his writing as a way of knotting his singular mode of enjoyment. If this interpretation is based on the presumption of a psychotic structure in Joyce, where does this leave perversion or indeed *père-version*, as he puts it in the same seminar? Can one speak of a perverse sinthome?

Diana Kamienny and Michael Newman both approach the complex and intricate relationship between an artists' life and their (perverse) productive output. Kamienny considers the photographs of Pierre Molinier and the writing of Ryū Murakami, in both of whose work she identifies loss—real in the one case, fictional in the other—that has not been sym-

---

[21] Freud, S. (1910). *Five Lectures on Psycho-analysis, Leonardo Da Vinci and Other Works*. S.E. 11. J. Strachey (Trans.). London: Hogarth, 1957.

[22] See, in particular Lacan, J. (1997). *The seminar, Book VII: The Ethics of Psychoanalysis*. J.-A. Miller (Ed.) & Denis Porter (Trans.). London: W. W. Norton & Company.

[23] Lacan, J. (2005). *Le Séminaire de Jacques Lacan, Livre XXIII: Le Sinthome*. Paris: Éditions du Seuil.

bolised, as a source of *jouissance* for the subject around which their work revolves, and leading to perverse practices. While she acknowledges this might point in the direction of psychosis, she also writes that if the subject is not totally without the phallic law this *jouissance* can legitimately be linked to perversion.

Michael Newman turns to a precursor of Molinier, the artist Hans Bellmer, identifying three aspects of his output—image, anagram, trait—to argue that his work constitutes *a* subjective symbolic, as opposed to *the* symbolic, and thus that his perverse artistic practices are not so much sublimation as sinthome. Both Bellmer and Molinier followed contradictory impulses of irruption and reassembly in their photomontages and photographs, creating 'frozen moments', returning again and again to the same scene of fixation that came in place, as Kamienny says, of denial of the mother's castration.

Luigi Burzotta's text examines the dialectical relation between perversion and sublimation. He reads Genet's *The Balcony*, a play set in a brothel in which the clientele play the roles of archetypal societal figures, the judge, the bishop and so on; in one sense a representation of the world we inhabit. Following Lacan, he elaborates the movement between society and culture where a gap is exposed for the logical subject, a gap within which Lacan situates the function of desire. Caught in this dialectical movement subjects adopt certain identifications, which may constitute the normalising tendencies of society, but which are alienating; perversion reflects the protest against precisely this normalising tendency. In the play the characters are called on to play in society the parts they had perversely assumed in the brothel. Burzotta asks whether we can call this reversal sublimation?

Reflecting on the protagonists in the film *The Piano Teacher* by Michael Haneke, Jean-Claude Aguerre demonstrates once more, albeit from a different perspective, the view that perverse behaviours—such as those exhibited by the piano teacher herself—do not necessarily indicate a perverse structure. As suggested earlier they can point rather to a perverse turn within a psychotic structure, a defence against the *jouissance* of the Other. Aguerre points to the moment in the film when Erika proposes a sadomasochist contract with her young pupil/lover, Walter Klemmer. At first sight this might suggest a perverse scenario yet Aguerre detects embedded in it a demand for love, whereas a truly perverse contract would be pronounced rather in the name of the law. In contrast, Aguerre unexpectedly finds in the response of the young man the truly perverse heart of the story. His *jouissance* derives from confronting a woman who believes in her fetish with the void of castration that she refuses.

In the final chapter of this section, Željka Matijašević uses the notion of fetishism to explore today's 'borderland' culture. Examining death in Lacan's discourse and his exploration of the relation between mechanicism and vitalism to underscore the autonomy of the symbolic order, she posits the death drive in the liminal zone between the symbolic and the real, mediating *jouissance.* If 'borderline' is a diagnostic category in psychiatry it can also be regarded as a cultural category that implies an intensity of affects, anxiety of fragmentation, and narcissistic omnipotence. The 'inhabitant of the borderland' is, for Matijašević, short-hand for our incapacity to negotiate the relation between the mortifying machine on one hand, and life-bearing forces on the other. She reads the contemporary popularity of the new vampire genre as a cultural manifestation of this psychic struggle.

1.2.5 Part V: Social Discourse, Politics and the Law

The final section of the book takes a wide-angle lens to examine the relation between perversion and shifting legal and moral dimensions of contemporary social and political power and discourses. This relation is visible to the extent that perversion involves a *jouissance* of transgression that often tempts the pervert towards the prohibited, the scandalous, the obscene, and thus towards a kind of brinkmanship with legal authority that attempts to provoke anxiety.

A central figure here, of course, is the Marquis de Sade, whose perverse writings/writings on perversion not only led to years of imprisonment and infamy, but also lent his name to the specific perversion of 'sadism' (its oft-assumed opposite, 'masochism', has a different literary provenance in the writings of Sacher-Masoch). Both André Michels and Colin Wright orient their chapters around lessons still to be learnt from de Sade's life and works, particularly their complex reception in psychiatry and sexology, Surrealism and (Lacanian) psychoanalysis.

André Michels takes seriously the notion that perversion throws down a challenge to psychoanalysis in posing the questions: What is a man who is capable of committing such actions? What epistemic status is to be given to perversion at a time when we are witnessing unprecedented violence—pure aggression, unlimited hatred—in the world? In reply he argues that the import of the work of Sade, though thoroughly grounded in its time, tipping point of a change in the relationship between science and ethics, could only be fully appreciated retrospectively, and especially through a psychoanalytic lens. It is Lacan who allowed us to take proper account of the Sadean excesses as coextensive with Enlightenment rationalism. This viewpoint makes of Sade not a first 'prince' of perversion but possibly its first theorist. Unlike a Gilles de Rais (who murdered hundreds of children for the sake of an enjoyment it would be hard not to call 'sadistic'), Sade framed perversion within a practice of writing, a project conducted under the sign of truth, of undermining reason with the tools of reason itself. Sade's texts teach psychoanalysis about the radicality of *jouissance*, an insistent *beyond* of the pleasure principle. Sadean crime says something more 'true' about enjoyment than can dutiful obedience. He places the Law itself on trial, exposing the body of the Judge always covertly at work in legal judgements. If, in our times, law and criminology are moving toward a 'bodyless' science, rooted in genetics and neuroscience, are they becoming increasingly perverse as they do so?

Colin Wright's chapter argues for the intimate historical connection between perversion and modernity as, in part, a challenge to the Law of the Father which reverberates within the legal system itself. Drawing on Lacan's seventh seminar as well as on his écrit 'Kant with Sade', Wright outlines the relationship between law and the body in perversion. Through a discussion of the so-called 'Spanner Case' in which consensual sado-masochistic practices led to sixteen men being found guilty of 'assault occasioning bodily harm', he then isolates the central yet paradoxical status of the concepts of *consent* and *harm* in liberal law. He concludes by suggesting that contemporary perversions may yet be able to expose law's superegoic focus on a body regulated by the pleasure principle, and its related inability to legislate for what Wright calls the 'unruly body of jouissance'.

Ian Parker identifies a fundamental ambivalence in the politics of perversion: on the one hand, we seem to have a narrative of subversion of the norm in favour of libidinal freedom, but on the other, psychoanalytically, we can also see perverse resistance to the norm as a mode of the refusal of castration, something we would hope to moderate over the course of an analysis. What appears progressive can actually be entirely reactionary, and vice versa. This is vividly illustrated by Parker's discussion of an interview in the *Guardian* newspaper in 2006, in which the interviewee claims an 'identity' constructed around the signifier 'paedophile', calling for more debate about the issue in the register of rights and representation, analogous to the claims of radical feminists and black activists. Moreover, the interviewee credits his psychoanalytic treatment with curing him of his 'morally abominable desires', yet as Parker notes, the analysis failed to cure him of this imaginary identification with a psychiatric category. Parker's key point is that what is done through words in analysis, including words that circulate culturally as pathologised identity positions, cannot then re-circulate outside the analytic setting without becoming something else entirely, all-too amenable to corruption and betrayal.

In a similarly timely piece, Monique Lauret draws on co-ordinates from Freud's *Civilization and its Discontents* and *Group Psychology and the Ego* to reflect on the capacity for the libidinal bonds necessary for social cohesion to become hijacked and colonised by sectarian movements, often linked to religious convictions. In the wake of terrorist attacks claimed by Islamic fundamentalist groups, it is not difficult to see the relevance of these Freudian arguments for our own epoch. Lauret pushes these arguments further by way of Lacan's five discourses (the master, the hysteric, the university, the analytic, and the capitalist), suggesting sectarianism as a sixth discourse. She argues that isolating the underlying logic of a sectarian discourse might help to cut through much of the cultural and historical baggage that distorts the way that Islam, for example, is seen via a certain Orientalist western gaze, but that also obfuscates the rise of a Christian fundamentalism that may be subject to many of the same discursive traits.

The final chapter brings the book to its starting point, in using the notion of perversion to bring together Freud, Marx and a critique of contemporary capitalism, here specifically in the form of neoliberalism.

If neoliberalism, as a project aimed at rescuing capitalism and restoring the power of the dominant classes, has won legitimacy under the concept of freedom, it is a freedom that refers to capital not to people. Using both critical theory and psychoanalysis Izabel Szpacenkopf explores the fetishism, cynicism and self-objectification evident in today's resultant consumer culture. Drawing on the work of Axel Honneth, she suggests that self-reification and competitiveness, which belie prior self-acceptance, give rise to a sense of self as object, commodity. She argues that in this neoliberal era, in which performance is fetishised and individual differences are disavowed, narcissistic suffering is exacerbated, the subjective consequences of which are to be heard in the psychoanalyst's consulting room.

We hope that the breadth, depth and diversity of the contributions to *Perversion Now!* succeed in opening the concept of perversion—overdetermined by the discourses of psychiatry, sexology, literary and art theory, law, media and, of course, psychoanalysis itself—to renewed critical scrutiny. We also hope that in emphasising the vitality of clinical practice, the book demonstrates the rigour of the psychoanalytic engagement with the paradox that while we live in a time of apparently infinite 'right' to unlimited market-based *jouissance* which gives the appearance of perversion, this stultifyingly permissive atmosphere also gives rise to the difficulty for the 'true' pervert to attain the *jouissance* of transgression.

Of course, as many questions have been raised as answers suggested. How can we understand the media-driven moral panics around that remaining figure of the pervert-as-deviant, the paedophile? Is it helpful to approach the phenomenon of religious fundamentalism and terrorism through the lens of perversion as if, in the pursuit of the Other's anxiety, perverts have moved from the Sadean terrain of sexual transgression to the transgression of criminal violence? Are there important cultural and contextual differences around perceptions of perversion that need to be accounted for in psychoanalytic theory, in order not to repeat the colonial violence it has sometimes been accused of, namely, universalising a Eurocentric model of subjectivity? Clinically, too, we might ask if there is evidence, whether contemporary or historical, of transformative work with analysands deemed to have a perverse structure? Are there sustained and detailed case-studies, of a richness comparable to Freud's, that could indicate ways of directing the treatment with today's perverts? And how does this clinical knowledge interact with other, more dominant forms of discourse ?

These questions indicate that perversion will continue to be 'now'; we hope others will interpret our title as an imperative, a call to continue unsettling assumptions, within and without psychoanalysis, about perversion.

Part I

Clinical Reflections from Freud to Lacan

2

Pervert, the Professor?

Xavier Fourtou

When I spoke to French colleagues about the 'Perversion et Modernité/ Perversion Now' Conference and told them the Conference title in English, they immediately understood it as a summons: "Perversion, now!"

The theme for the conference seemed to suggest that contemporary society offers more space for manifestations of perversion than used to be the case, that the repression of desire has been "much diminished" and that the denial of castration has been "trivialised". But is there really more perversion around nowadays? Or is it rather that we want more of it "now"?

As explained in the introduction to this book, I was part of the cartel that met in London to explore the evolution of Freud's theorisation of perversion and that led to the conference and to this book. At one of our sessions we discussed the case of 'Little Hans'. I found the text difficult to

X. Fourtou (✉)
Psychoanalyst in private practice

D. Caine, C. Wright (eds.), *Perversion Now!*,
DOI 10.1007/978-3-319-47271-3_2

read. No doubt, it is a complex work. Freud himself writes at one point: "it is not unlikely that the extensive and detailed character of the analysis may have made it somewhat obscure".[1] But it seemed to me that my resistance was not primarily to do with the length of the text or its level of detail.

My resistance probably had to do with one of the major themes developed in the work: that of castration. Being brought face to face with the reality of castration for a hundred pages or so was unlikely to be an agreeable experience. Be that as it may, I will put forward the hypothesis that my reluctance to follow Freud in his exposition had to do with certain elements of perversion that can be discovered in the approach taken by the "Professor". I will try to unwrap and explore the feeling my reading gave me.

I will begin in the first part by commenting on the setting of the treatment, before going on, in the second part, to look at how Freud apprehends the subjectivity of Hans, who was 5-years-old at the time. Might this case of Freud's suggest that, contrary to what can be read into the title of the conference, clinical practice *now* is less infiltrated by perversion than it was a century ago?

2.1 About the Setting…

My attention was drawn to two points: the fact that the patient and the analyst were related to each other (Sect. 2.1.1) and the demonstrative nature of Freud's approach (Sect. 2.1.2).

2.1.1 The Treatment of a Relative

Freud receives "reports" from a father about his young son, Hans. "I have for many years been urging my students and my friends to collect observations of the sexual life of children",[2] Freud tells us. He says nothing else

[1] Freud, S. (1909a). *Analysis of a Phobia in a Five- year-old Boy*. S.E. 10: 5–149. London: Hogarth Press, 1953, p. 116.

[2] ibid., p. 5.

about the person who supplies these reports. Is he a student or a friend? Today we have part of the answer to this question, thanks to an article entitled "Reminiscences of Professor Sigmund Freud"[3] published in 1942 by Max Graf, the father of Hans.

> I met Freud in the same year in which he published the Interpretation of Dreams [...]. Freud had at the time been treating a lady whom I knew. This lady would tell me after her sessions with Freud of the remarkable treatment by means of questions and answers [...] These new ideas [...] aroused my interest in the new investigator. I wanted to know him personally. I was invited to visit him in his office.[4] [...] I was for several years a member of this group of friends, which met every Wednesday in Freud's house.[5] [...] A personal contact had developed between Freud and my family which made Freud's human warmth particularly valuable.[6]

So, Hans' father was both Freud's student and his friend.

Freud took an interest in the reports on Hans, and the three participants—Hans, his father and Freud—set to work. Freud states that "the treatment itself was carried out by the child's father"[7] who provided the "reports"[8] and acted as the "physician".[9] Freud "lays down the general lines of the treatment".[10] He "suggests"[11] to the father what he should say to Hans, or "arranges with"[12] the father to what extent Hans should be "enlightened".[13] So the analyst is the patient's father. And the person who plays the role more or less of supervisor to the analyst is a friend of the analyst.

---

[3] Graf, M. (1942). Reminiscences of Professor Sigmund Freud. *Psychoanalytic Quarterly*, 11(4): 465–476.

[4] ibid., p. 467.

[5] ibid., p. 470.

[6] ibid., p. 473.

[7] Freud, 1909a, op. cit., p. 4.

[8] ibid., p. 5.

[9] ibid., p. 122.

[10] ibid., p. 4.

[11] ibid., p. 27.

[12] ibid.

[13] ibid.

The Little Hans case history was published in 1909. In "Recommendations to Physicians Practising Psycho-Analysis", one of the papers on technique, Freud wrote: "As regards the treatment of [...] relatives I must confess myself utterly at a loss, and I have in general little faith in any individual treatment of them".[14] This text postdates Little Hans by three years. Are we to suppose that, when Freud wrote the case, he still had faith in the treatment of relatives? But what seems to me most fraught is not so much the plain fact that Freud endorses the cure of a child by his father, as the way in which the treatment is conducted.

2.1.2 A Demonstrative Approach

Hans is subjected, on his father's own admission, to "close questioning".[15]

'I: "When the (..) horse fell down, what colour was it? White, red, brown, grey?"
'Hans: "Black. Both horses were black."
'I: "Was it big or little?"
'Hans: "Big."
'I: "Fat or thin?"[16]

The pressing investigation by the father is designed to relieve his son of phobic symptoms. But it is also designed to meet the expectations of Freud, who, as we saw above, is on the lookout for materials regarding the sexuality of children. This, undoubtedly, is one major source of my discomfort. Hans is certainly apprehended as a subject by his father and by Freud, who listen to his unconscious productions, but the child also seems to be an object, by means of which Freud expands the field of his knowledge and verifies certain assumptions.

Freud established that the neuroses of adults are related to their sexuality during childhood. He wants to observe this sexuality and its evolution

[14] [12] Freud, S. (1912). *Recommendations to Physicians Practising Psychoanalysis*. S.E. 12: 111–120. London: Hogarth Press, 1955, p. 119.

[15] Freud, 1909a, op. cit., p. 35.

[16] ibid. p. 50.

during the first years of life. As he admits: "Even a psycho-analyst may confess to the wish for a more direct and less roundabout proof of these fundamental theorems. Surely there must be a possibility of observing in children at first hand and in all the freshness of life the sexual impulses and wishes which we dig out so laboriously in adults".[17]

In 1912, in his "Recommendations to Physicians Practising Psycho-Analysis" Freud sets out major aspects of the technique, which he has developed over a period of 20 years. He stresses the dangers of an approach that defines a domain of interest *a priori*:

> For as soon as anyone deliberately concentrates his attention to a certain degree, he begins to select from the material before him [...]. This, however, is precisely what must not be done. In making the selection, if he follows his expectations he is in danger of never finding anything but what he already knows[18]

What if the use made of Hans is that of demonstrating predetermined assumptions, the benefits of what Freud (in the same paper) called "evenly suspended attention"?

Freud states at the end of the case: "My impression is that the picture of a child's sexual life presented in this observation of little Hans agrees very well with the account I gave of it (basing my views upon psychoanalytic examinations of adults) in my *Three Essays*."[19] Where is Hans in this assertion and in this approach? Where is the unknown, the singularity of this subject? Hans is reduced to a "picture of infantile sexual life".

2.2 The Question of Subjectivity...

The subject Hans is not only erased (Sect. 2.2.1) but also, to some extent, denigrated (Sect. 2.2.2).

[17] ibid., p. 5.

[18] Freud, 1912, op. cit., p. 111.

[19] Freud, 1909a, op. cit., p. 100.

2.2.1 An Erased Subject

The signs of erasure of the subject Hans are numerous. It can be detected from the very title of the article: "Analysis of a Phobia in a 5-Year-Old Boy." What is analysed is not a subject but a pathology. The use of the word "case" to describe the work with Hans also appears to me problematic. Hans disappears behind his symptom, the phobia, or behind the general, classificatory and desubjectivising term "case".

The *Cinq psychanalyses*,[20] the classic French translation of Freud's case histories, covers five nosological categories: phobia, hysteria, obsessional neurosis, infantile neurosis and paranoia. Each of them is illustrated by work carried out with a patient. It is as if a label were stuck onto Hans, Dora, the Rat Man, Senatspräsident Schreber and the Wolf Man. A label that refers not to the identity of these subjects but to the predominant type of their mental construction.

Hans did not ask to be inserted in a catalogue, wedged between hysteria and psychosis. As one case among many, he is placed on a level with Senatspräsident Schreber, who presents a relatively extreme case of suffering and madness.

Moving on from the title, Freud announces at the beginning of the article that his theme will be "the course of the illness and recovery of a very youthful patient".[21] Again, we must not expect to discover a person through acquaintance with a part of his life and his meeting with an analyst: what is to follow is the account of an illness.

For Freud the end seems to justify the means. He intends, contrary to the fundamental principle of confidentiality, to publish the intimate material of a subject, moreover of a child. The content of his dreams and fantasies, the details of his sexual practices, one of his drawings. Certainly, Hans' graphic production is limited. His opus consists of two contiguous lines drawn under the body of a giraffe sketched in rough outline by his father. But the fact remains that this work—portraying a *widdler*—is highly personal.

---

[20] Freud, S. (1954). *Cinq Psychanalyses*. Paris: Presses Universitaires de France.

[21] Freud, 1909a, op. cit., p. 4.

Maybe this is what bothered me most in Freud's approach. The publication, without justification, of the drawing by a child, of a line drawn by a child. Particularly since it gives rise to an interpretation by Freud, even though he was not physically present when Hans produced this drawing.

2.2.2 A Denigrated Subject

The article's subtitle might also raise questions about respect for the subjectivity of the child. "Little Hans". Why should Hans be branded with the adjective "little"? Can we hear a certain denigration here? Hans is associated, for eternity, with a concept of littleness. Certainly, Hans is only five-years old, but the complexity and richness of the material he brings are anything but little, sparse, inadequate or limited.

The boy's first name appears, if not in the title, then at least in the subtitle of the article, but "Hans" is in brackets (I refer to the French edition of 1928, translated by Marie Bonaparte, published in the *Revue française de psychanalyse* under "the auspices of Professor Sigmund Freud").[22] It would be fair to say that Hans is in brackets throughout the study. The point is not to listen to him but to allow him to prove the pertinence of Freudian constructions.

Not only is the child's name in brackets, but it is also written, at least in the French edition, in small letters. "Analyse d'une phobie chez un petit garçon de cinq ans" ("Analysis of a Phobia in a Five-Year-Old Boy") appears in a large font size, while "Le Petit Hans" ("Little Hans") is in a smaller font. The analysis of a phobia is of major importance, Little Hans is incidental.

Having made him into a case, put him in brackets and lumbered him with the adjective "little", Freud slights the child's intelligence. "I arranged with Hans's father that he should tell the boy that all this business about horses was a piece of nonsense and nothing more",[23] Freud writes. But the unconscious construction, which Hans' symptom represents, is far

---

[22] Freud, S. (1928). *Analyse d'une Phobie Chez un Petit Garçon de Cinq Ans (Le Petit Hans).* M. Bonaparte (Trans.). *Revue Française de Psychanalyse*, 2(3): 411–540.

[23] Freud, 1909a, op. cit., p. 27.

from nonsense. Quite the contrary. It is a work of art, intensely personal, constructed with artistry, complex, disabling but also protective.

Having learnt that Hans had kissed a cousin of his own age and said "I *am* so fond of you", Freud comments: "This is the first trace of homosexuality that we have come across in him, but it will not be the last. Little Hans seems to be a positive paragon of all the vices (*perversités*)."[24] Why vices and not perversion? In the *Three Essays on the Theory of Sexuality* Freud presents homosexuality as a deviation of the sexual drive from the object deemed to be "normal" (of the opposite sex) and therefore qualifies this sexual practice as perverse. This adjective is, for Freud, supposedly detached from any value judgment. "No healthy person, it appears, can fail to make some addition that might be called perverse to the normal sexual aim; and the universality of this finding is in itself enough to show how inappropriate it is to use the word perversion as a term of reproach."[25]

But reproach is not lacking in the term Freud uses in respect of the child's homosexuality. *Perversité*, as defined by the Larousse dictionary, is a "tendency to do evil consciously out of pleasure in causing harm". The German term used by Freud is "Schlechtigkeiten"—"vices". What grounds are there to suppose that kissing his cousin and telling him "I *am* so fond of you" originate in Hans from any such source? On whose side is the perversity here? The Professor's motivation may not be conscious, but it certainly has an aggressive dimension.

Freud wrote in his paper "The Future Prospects of Psycho-Analytic Therapy": "We have become aware of the 'counter-transference', which arises in him [the psychoanalyst] as a result of the patient's influence on his unconscious feelings"[26] I find it regrettable that, in the study of Hans, Freud tells us so little about the influence that the young patient and his father must have had on his own unconscious. Recognising the counter-transferential elements would have been another means of highlighting

[24] ibid., p. 14.

[25] Freud, 1905, op. cit., p. 159.

[26] Freud, S. (1910). *The Future Prospects of Psycho-Analytic Therapy.* S.E. 11: 139–152. London: Hogarth Press, 1955, p. 143.

Hans' subjectivity. Is a patient's existence not also a matter of the unconscious effects which he or she evokes?

2.3 Conclusion

I tried to gain a clearer understanding of a feeling of discomfort and even recoil, experienced when reading Little Hans. If the term "perversion" occurred to me in respect of the Professor, it is probably because his approach illustrated, for me, the well-known phrase of Octave Mannoni, "I know perfectly well … but all the same…"[27]

The treatment of Little Hans seems, on many points, to go against the rules and recommendations that Freud develops in his articles on psychoanalytic technique. Hans' analysis is conducted by his father. Where does that leave the neutrality between patient and analyst, the evenly-suspended attention of the analyst, the issue of payment for the treatment and the need for a fixed time frame?

The Professor "knows perfectly well" about these technical and theoretical aspects, but "all the same", he feels justified in describing the work as analytic treatment, seizing upon Hans as a specimen, transforming him from a subject into an object of research.

"An unrestricted satisfaction of every need presents itself as the most enticing method of conducting one's life, but it means putting enjoyment (*jouissance*) before caution",[28] says Freud in *Civilization and its Discontents.*

One might argue that the progress of analytical science is a cause that could justify overriding or bending some prudential rules. But Freud's position on this issue is very clear. He writes in 1913 in his paper "On Beginning the Treatment": "Certain patients want their treatment to be kept secret, often because they have kept their neurosis secret; and I put no obstacle in their way. That in consequence the world hears nothing of

[27] Mannoni. (1969). This article, which discusses disavowal of castration in perversion, is translated at: http://ideiaeideologia.com/wp-content/uploads/2013/05/Mannoni-I-know-very-well.pdf.

[28] Freud, S. (1930). *Civilisation and its Discontents*. S.E. 21: 64–148. London: Hogarth Press, 1961, p. 76.

some of the most successful cures is, of course, a consideration that cannot be taken into account."[29]

The work carried out with Little Hans continues to make its impact on the contemporary world, but has sufficient attention been given to the question of respect for confidentiality and for the child's subjectivity? In February 2011, on the occasion of a conference entitled "Herbert Graf as Producer", the psychoanalyst François Dachet wondered where and when Graf—better known as Little Hans—"learned that, for there to be life, there must first be sounds, music, the grain of the voice, lights, movements, gestures, clothing, touch, etcetera, and not just a text and the story it tells, the letters and notes that write it and the theories that make use of it."[30]

According to Dachet's hypothesis, the fact that Herbert Graf became an opera producer at the age of 22 years was specifically and "essentially" due to his "early meeting with (…) the invention of psychoanalysis". Psychoanalysis that was not based on the study of weekly reports, but on a meeting between persons. Little Hans and Sigmund Freud met only once in the course of the analysis, but we may well think that this session had foundational significance for the child.

I think that the text of Little Hans has special importance today, when we are faced with new temptations and threats that imperil the interpersonal encounter between analyst and analysand. The ever more frequent use of Skype in clinical practice seems to me particularly illustrative. Skype certainly opens up new modes of contact, but it does not allow the same sensitivity to the grain of the voice, movements or their absence, musicality, gestures, the aspiration to or avoidance of touch.

So should the use of Skype in the clinic be a matter for particular concern? Is it not the analyst's duty to be always attentive to establishing and maintaining—freely and creatively—the best possible set up for the emergence and deployment of life?

[29] Freud, 1912, op. cit., p. 135.

[30] Dachet, F. (2008). *L'innocence violée?: le petit Hans Herbert Graf: devenir metteur en scène d'opéra.* Paris: Unebévue.

3

Exploring Transgression from a Lacanian Perspective

Astrid Gessert

Two of the questions raised in the preliminary notes to the conference 'Perversion et Modernité/Perversion Now' were: "What constitutes transgression today?" and "Are people really more inclined to transgress now than formerly?" These questions imply that transgression is a relevant concept in connection with perversion and it is this idea with which I want to engage.

Perversion is indeed commonly associated with transgression, especially in the realm of sexuality, with what is considered abnormal, devious sexual behaviour. The word 'transgression' implies 'stepping over'. For something to be transgressed there must be a line, a division. It also often has a negative connotation, with the idea that this stepping over a line is illegitimate, that there is a homebase where one should rightfully be and another realm that is out of bounds.

A. Gessert (✉)
Centre for Freudian Analysis and Research, and College of Psychoanalysts UK

D. Caine, C. Wright (eds.), *Perversion Now!*,
DOI 10.1007/978-3-319-47271-3_3

Historically, the homebase with regard to sexuality has been defined in various ways, with reference to religious, moral, social and legal norms defining acceptable and unacceptable forms of behaviour; stepping outside these norms has meant entering the realm of sin, of what is amoral, antisocial or unlawful.

Today, attitudes towards sexual behaviour have changed and have become quite permissive. The norm is no longer a set of behaviours, rather it has become a question of 'informed consent between adults'. The consent may involve setting limits that are not to be transgressed, like in children's games: You may tickle me, but only until I say "enough", but these limits are not pre-given norms, they are negotiated between the participants.

These shifts are reflected in the latest edition of the Diagnostic and Statistical Manual of Mental Disorders (DSM-5).[1] The term perversion has disappeared altogether from the DSM-5, to be replaced with 'paraphilic disorders'. Paraphilia is a term which was introduced in the 1920s by Wilhelm Stekel, a patient and colleague of Freud, who used it in his work on sexual aberrations. 'Paraphilia', coming from Greek, means literally something like 'love of the beyond' [para = near/beyond; philos = friend/love] and it has been contrasted with 'normophilia', a term introduced by the American sexologist John Money (1988), referring to "a condition of being erotosexually in conformity with the standard as dictated by customary, religious, or legal authority".[2] 'Paraphilia' therefore means standing besides, outside this standard. The idea remains that in cases of paraphilic disorders some standard or norm is being transgressed.

However, for the purpose of diagnosis the emphasis is no longer on atypical behaviour or atypical sexual interests as such. This alone is not considered to constitute a mental disorder. A disorder is only diagnosed if this atypical behaviour or interest causes distress to either the persons themselves, or to others. While the idea persists that there is something like atypical behaviour or interests, this is no longer the criterion for diagnosing a disorder. Thus it is possible now for a person "to engage in consensual atypical sexual behaviour [e.g. masochistic behaviour, fetish-

[1] American Psychiatric Association (APA). (2013). *Diagnostic and Statistical Manual of Mental Disorders,* fifth edition (DSM-V). Washington, DC and London: American Psychiatric Publishing.

[2] Money, J. (1988). *Gay, Straight and In-between: The Sexology of Erotic Orientation.* New York: Oxford University Press, p. 214.

ism] without inappropriately being labelled with a mental disorder", as noted by the American Psychiatric Association.[3]

Another interesting, more subtle feature with regard to the DSM-5 is that the emphasis is not only on behaviour, but also on desire. The American Psychiatric Association explains: "To be diagnosed with a paraphilic disorder, DSM-5 requires that people with these interests [i.e. atypical sexual interests]… have a sexual desire or behaviour that involves another person's psychological distress, injury, or death, or a desire for sexual behaviour involving unwilling persons or persons unable to give legal consent."[4] The way in which the presence of desire is acknowledged in the diagnosis and treatment is another matter. What is interesting first of all is that a concept that belongs to the realm of psychoanalysis, the concept of desire, has slipped into the psychiatric diagnosis. From a psychoanalytical point of view, the form of psychopathology a person develops cannot be understood precisely without engaging with the question of how they manage their desire.

This is quite different from the question of transgressing a norm, which is not a psychoanalytic concern. Of course, using the term psychopathology seems to imply that there is something like a healthy norm from which the pathology deviates. But Freud developed the entire theory of psychoanalysis on the basis of observing pathology and concluding from these observations what the normal state would be, emphasising always that it is a question of degree, that in pathology we only see an exaggeration of what is normal. According to Freud, then, we are dealing with a continuum, not with two different realms divided by a line. As he says in the *Three Essays on Sexuality*: "an unbroken chain bridges the gap between the neuroses and all their manifestations and normality".[5]

This is particularly notable in the case of perversions which, Freud continues, are so widespread that the disposition to perversions "must form a part of what passes as the normal constitution".[6] And yet Freud called the first chapter of his *Three Essays on Sexuality* 'The sexual aberrations'

[3] APA, op. cit.

[4] ibid.

[5] Freud, S. (1905d). *Three Essays on the Theory of Sexuality.* S.E. 7. London: Hogarth, 1953, p. 171.

[6] ibid.

which seems to imply that there is a sexual norm from which we can deviate. However, it becomes clear from reading just the first couple of pages of these essays that Freud considered this supposed norm to be the common but highly problematic view of what are normal sexual objects and sexual aims. He proceeded then to explore the many ways in which large numbers of people deviate from these supposed norms, a point later supported by the Kinsey report.[7]

3.1 Freud's View

With regard to perversion, the essential point that Freud is making in the 'Three Essays' is that in the case of young children we find an assembly of partial drives that do not privilege a specific part of the body or a particular sexual practice as being more satisfactory or appropriate than another. Only in the course of the child's psychosexual development and the tackling of the Oedipus Complex are these partial drives subsumed under the primacy of genitality that represented the medically approved norm in Freud's day. But even if such 'streamlining' of the drives is achieved, the partial drives do not completely disappear but continue to form components of genital sexuality in a subordinate way.

Already in this early understanding of infantile sexuality two things become clear:

1. The homebase that is left behind is not what is commonly thought of as 'normality', but is rather a polymorphous perverse position. As many psychoanalysts have recognised, there is a move from perversion to 'normality', not the other way round. Perversion, then, is itself normal, it is universal in children, it is in Freud's understanding "*internal* to normality".[8]
2. Even in what then becomes regarded as 'normal', i.e. heterosexual genital intercourse, so called perverse traits persist, supporting and

[7] Kinsey, A. (1948). *Sexual Behavior in the Human Male.* Bloomington: Indiana University Press, 1998.

[8] Dean, T. (2006). "Lacan Meets Queer Theory", in D. Nobus and L. Downing (Eds), *Perversion: Psychoanalytic Perspectives.* London: Karnac, p. 277.

enhancing sexual arousal and satisfaction. Hence, there is no line to be transgressed; rather there is a move along a continuum where different components carry different weight at different phases.

This account highlights a problem in Freud's formulation: If there is a continuum along which the partial drives and their objects circulate, how can a distinction between normality and perversion be sustained? Freud acknowledged this problem by pointing out that 'for the time being' in the field of sexuality there exists an insoluble difficulty in drawing a sharp line between mere variations of sexual aims and pathological symptoms. The somewhat awkward solution he nevertheless suggested was to distinguish between normal and pathological perversion, defining pathological perversion as the state in which perversion has replaced normal sexual aims and objects exclusively, and has become fixated.[9]

This understanding leads to the conundrum that an exclusive fixation on heterosexual genital intercourse should then also be considered as perverse.[10] In fact, one can argue that according to this way of thinking "*the process of normalization itself is what's pathological,* since normalization 'fixes' desire and generates the exclusiveness of sexual orientation [whether homosexual or heterosexual] as its symptom".[11] In this process the mobility, or metonymy, of desire becomes "increasingly limited ... first towards persons, then towards persons of the opposite sex, then towards specific sexual acts with persons of the opposite sex, and often towards specific acts with a specific person of the opposite sex", as Dean aptly observed.[12]

3.2 Lacan's View

It was already clear from Freud's observations that sexuality resists normalisation. Following from this, Lacan engaged with the question of normality in a more radical way than Freud, transcending the dilemma

[9] Freud, 1905d, op. cit., pp. 160ff.

[10] Dean, 2006, op. cit., p. 278.

[11] ibid.

[12] ibid., pp. 278ff.

of how to distinguish perversion from normality.[13] In Lacan's structural approach there is no category of normality. To become human and part of human society every living being has to give up something and the way s/he manages this loss will determine whether they will turn into a neurotic, psychotic or perverse subject; there is no 'normal' way of dealing with this loss—what is considered 'normal' are merely socially and culturally approved ideals. Perversion is, like neurosis and psychosis, an attempt to find an answer, a solution to this fundamental loss with which every human subject is confronted.

While the concepts of loss, of lack, and of desire arising from it, are often seen as concepts distinctive to Lacan's theory, all psychoanalytic schools agree that human life starts with loss: loss of homeostasis for Freud, birth as traumatic loss, the loss of the breast, etc. Loss is a necessary condition for emergence from the symbiotic relationship with the mother as a separate human being and for beginning an active engagement with the world.

What is specific about Lacan's understanding is that he regards perversion—as well as neurosis and psychosis—as a specific configuration between the child as emerging subject; a significant Other from whom the child has to separate, usually the mother; and, as a third factor, the lack that both will suffer as a result of this separation. Where Freud spoke of perverse partial drive components, Lacan speaks of a perverse triangular relationship or structure that involves three components: child—Other—lack.

3.3 How Does a Perverse Structure Come About?

Initially, there is a symbiotic relationship between mother and child that provides for both of them a particular enjoyment in the sense of feeling complete. This is disrupted, first at birth and subsequently with the introduction of language, which signifies separation with the terms: 'you', 'me', 'mother', 'father', 'child'. What the child loses then, is not

[13] ibid., p. 276.

so much the mother, but this pleasure in the feeling of oneness and the object that would guarantee it. This loss has been conceptualised by Lacan as the loss of an object which at the moment of separation is both created and lost. From then on, this object functions as the cause of desire.

This is how desire is born; the child will now strive to restore the original unity. The mother too will yearn for the immense satisfaction of being united with her child, and desires to regain it. However, the original loss is irrevocable and the object is irretrievable. This is not entirely unwelcome to either mother or child, because, while yearning for ultimate union they also dread being devoured or engulfed by the Other, as has often been depicted by psychoanalytic theories; it would be too much to be good.

To help the child, and also the mother, to deal with this dilemma the father, understood as a symbolic agency, must intervene, basically to show to the child that it cannot return to the union with the mother, and thereby satisfy both its own and her desire. Through his intervention the child has to understand that there are things the mother desires which are beyond the child's capacity and reach. Although frustrating to the child it is also thereby rescued from its abortive attempts to be the object that would satisfy the mother, and is enabled to become a subject with a desire of its own, seeking substitutes for what it has lost.

This process relies on the introduction of signifiers, of words, that articulate the lack. Only when supported by signifiers can desire start to move beyond the early fixation to an imaginary object, and lead from one signifier to another. Instead of the insistent "imaginary demand to be supplied with the object of its satisfaction once and for all, desire which is mediated by the signifier is in its essence a movement … producing new reverberations of meaning in each step of its unfolding… this emergence of desire via the signifier effects a certain deconstruction of the imaginary object …" and allows substitutions, while desire itself has no object that can satisfy.[14]

[14] Boothby, R. (1991). *Death and Desire*. New York and London: Routledge, pp. 164ff; see also Fink, B. (1995). *The Lacanian Subject*. Princeton and Chichester: Princeton University Press, pp. 90ff.

This happens in neurotic development, where loss has been accepted, symbolised and repressed, and the person makes do with substitutes in a more or less successful way, while always complaining that nothing is ever the right thing, nothing can fill the original lack. Neurotics will always struggle with their desire and the desire of the Other. The problem for the perverse subject, on the other hand, is that they think there is an object that can satisfy. There is, as Freud said, fixation instead of desire; desire is "diametrically opposed to fixation".[15] The perverse subject does not desire but demands, and demand is directed at an object.

What fails in perversion is precisely the separation of the child from the *demand* of the mother to restore the original symbiosis and the enjoyment related to this. Here, the child does become separated from the mother, there is a 'you' and 'me', the child is no longer part of the Other, it has a place in relation to the Other. But the child fails to separate from the mother's lack, which it perceives in terms of a demand for *jouissance* and the missing object *a*, rather than in terms of desire. Having suffered a first loss, a symbolic castration by having submitted to an order that is alien to it and that breaks up the original unity, the perverse child will strive to restore it, and so may the mother. At that level castration has not been effected. The child assumes that the mother demands nothing but it, that it is the object of the Other that could provide her with *jouissance*. In not being discouraged in its attempts to restore unity, the child remains trapped in incarnating the object that the mother is missing, denying that both she (the mother) and it (the child) are missing anything—what Freud called the disavowal of the mother's castration.

What Lacan adds to Freud's understanding, then, is that the child disavows the mOther's castration by identifying unconsciously with the lacking object of the mOther's fulfilment. Thus the child becomes, and sees itself as, an instrument of the mOther's enjoyment. As both the mother's and the child's desire remain unarticulated, the child has not encountered the phallus as signifier, as something that symbolises a lack, as opposed to an object as such that is lacking. It believes that something, an object, can fill the mOther's lack and that it can itself be this object. The mOther's lack is not perceived in terms of desire, but in terms of an object that can

[15] Fink, 1995, op. cit., p. 90.

bring ultimate enjoyment.[16] The traumatic moment for the child is not so much the discovery that the mother has no penis, as Freud understood it, but that there is no signifier for this lack that would stand in for the hole in the mOther and thus protect the child from falling into it. The lack of the signifier leaves open the possibility for the child to try to be the object that will complete the mOther, unable to acknowledge without such a signifier that the mOther will always be lacking and desiring.[17]

Instead of desire which, by definition, can never be completely satisfied, there is overwhelming unmediated enjoyment involving not words, but the body. What concrete form this enjoyment takes will depend on how the child interprets what the mother wants and enjoys. Initially, many of the mother's messages to the child will focus on basic bodily functions that correspond to the partial drives that Freud identified. She may devote herself to elaborate feeding practises or she may pay meticulous attention to the child's toilet training, she may use her gaze and her voice to enchant her child. In this way the partial drives are reinforced in the relationship between mother and child, each coming with its own separate object and erogenous zone on which the child may become fixated.

It follows that in cases of perversion the aim is not to rein in desire. On the contrary, desire has to be created where before there was identification, demand and the idea that lack can be filled. To find a different solution to lack, the perverse subject has to want something outside the exclusive relationship between him/her and the mOther, they have to create something in the space that cannot be filled. In perversion such creation is missing.[18]

3.4 Consequences of This Understanding

To reconnect this view with the concept of desire that has found its way into the commentary of the diagnosis of paraphilic disorders according to DSM-5, when "people… have a sexual desire or behaviour that involves

[16] Swales, S. (2012). *Perversion. A Lacanian Psychoanalytic Approach to the Subject.* New York and Hove: Routledge, p. 42.

[17] André, S. (2006). "The Structure of Perversion: A Lacanian Perspective", in D. Nobus and L. Downing (Eds), *Perversion: Psychoanalytic Perspectives*. London: Karnac, p. 112.

[18] Verhaeghe, P. (2001a). Perversion I: Perverse Traits. *The Letter,* 22: 74.

another person's … distress …", we could say that from a Lacanian perspective the problem is that subjects with a perverse psychic structure do **not have** a desire, they have had no chance to articulate the initial loss in the form of desire. What they have instead is an identification with an object that compels them to enact desire rather than articulate it, thereby eradicating it. We could also wonder if, instead of desire they articulate a demand which, unlike desire, is repetitive, always asks for the same, and in relation to which there is a fixation to a specific object.[19]

If, in perversion, desire and demand have become confused, it may also be a feature of our time that there is a more general shift from desire to demand. Amongst the various factors contributing to this shift two phenomena seem to be quite clear: first, the law giving father does not function any longer in the way he did even in Lacan's days, 50 years ago[20] and second, the fact that many commodities are on offer and instantly available now, stifles desire and rather serves demand. Lack does not have to be articulated anymore as lack, because in many cases we do not even have to demand, objects are thrown at us 'three for the price of two', ensuring that we get not only what we want but more than enough.

The questions 'What constitutes transgression today?' and 'Whether people are today more or less inclined to transgress?', should, I suggest, give way to the question of what has become of desire in a 'perverse' world in which acknowledging the inevitability of limitations and articulating what cannot be, has given way to expectations that everything should be possible and to an imperative to enjoy. The sky is no longer the limit, infinite opportunities are offered continuously to satisfy demand, at the cost of the articulation of desire and the ability to bear it.

[19] Fink, B. (1997). *A Clinical Introduction to Lacanian Psychoanalysis*. Cambridge and London: Harvard University Press, p. 26.

[20] Verhaeghe, P. (2015). *Contemporary Madness Does Not Make Sense*. Unpubl. lecture delivered at Centre for Freudian Analysis and Research, 3.5.2015.

4

Perversion Now

Anne Worthington

The title of the conference—Perversion Now—captured something of the contemporary contestation of its meaning, resonating with the chant of activists on marches and demonstrations, by which a demand is made: 'What do We Want? PERVERSION', accompanied by a time-scale: 'When do we want it? NOW!' While Freud's conceptualisation of perversion was relatively free of disapprobation, in a climate of increasingly liberal attitudes to fetishism, sado-masochism, homosexuality and other sexual practices that used generally to be considered perversions, there is a manifest articulation of a demand for an end to the discrimination, and the silence, that surround such practices. This demand is accompanied by suspicion of situating perversion as a clinical category, both from those with an interest in the creative and dissident potential of transgression, and from those who position certain sexual practices as perversion in a juridical context or indeed a moral one.

A. Worthington (✉)
Middlesex University, London

D. Caine, C. Wright (eds.), *Perversion Now!*,
DOI 10.1007/978-3-319-47271-3_4

4.1 Freud

Freud, too, seemed to have some reticence about the term. He wrote that:

> Perversions are sexual activities which either (a) extend, in an anatomical sense, beyond the regions of the body that are designed for sexual union, or (b) linger over the intermediate relations to the sexual object which should *normally* be traversed rapidly on the path towards the final sexual aim.[1] (*My emphasis*)

It is curious that Freud offers a definition of the perversions in a series of essays in which he seeks to undermine the prevalent notion that the primary aim of human sexuality is reproduction and to divorce sexuality from its too close connection with the genitals. Indeed, later in the *Three Essays* he argues that we all have an innate disposition to polymorphous perversity.[2] His contention, gleaned from his clinical experience, that 'the sexual instinct and the sexual object are merely soldered together'[3] means that for Freud, human sexuality is precarious.

If the sexual drive, as the *Essays* elaborate, is made up of components with a multiplicity of erotogenic zones and aims and there is no natural, 'automatic' object then perversion loses its status as a pathological category. If there is no qualitative distinction between abnormality and normality, and if innate factors cannot account for the situation, is not the concept of perversion displaced?

At the same time, Freud seems reluctant to abandon the notion of perversion altogether. In the quotation from the *Three Essays* above, Freud defines perversion with reference to 'extending' and 'lingering' but I would like to put the emphasis rather on '*normally*'. Freud seems to refuse the logic of his own argument that human sexuality is fundamentally perverse when he qualifies his statements with words such as 'usually' and 'generally' and with the notion of the 'appropriated'. Perhaps it is Freud's

---

[1] Freud, S. (1905). *Three Essays on the Theory of Sexuality* S.E. 7: 123–243. J. Strachey (Trans.). London: Hogarth Press, 1953, p. 150.

[2] ibid., p. 191.

[3] ibid., p. 147.

reluctance to embrace his own conclusions that has contributed to the controversies surrounding the concept of perversion within psychoanalysis, and that results in perversion being such a bone of contention for both psychoanalysts and their critics.

4.2 Queer

Queer critics found perversion to be a useful locus for engagement with psychoanalysis. In the same way that definitions of the psychoanalytic project are numerous, reflecting the different schools of psychoanalysis and giving particular weight to preferred theoretical constructions, so too are those of queer theory. Indeed, it is frequently said that queer theory resists and undermines the very notion of definition; nevertheless, its project could perhaps be said to be to challenge the validity and consistency of hetero-normative discourse and of normality as such. As Halperin defines it: "Queer is by definition whatever is at odds with the normal, the legitimate, the dominant. There is nothing in particular to which it necessarily refers. It is an identity without an essence. 'Queer', then, demarcates not a positivity but a positionality vis-à-vis the normative."[4] Queer theorists have engaged with the concept of perversion through analyses of sexual practices, to pursue an opposition to the hetero-normative and to situate sex as a site of subversion. As Dollimore, for example, claims: "perversion is a refusal or attempted subversion of those organizing principles of culture which are secured psychosexually, principles which include sexual difference, the law of the father and heterosexuality."[5]

There is, of course, a difficulty. Not all sexual practices can be categorised as either progressively transgressive or 'healthily' normal. Nor can perversion be a category reserved for those who break the law, when the law is so frequently revised and subject to cultural and political

[4] Halperin, D. (1995). *Saint Foucault: Towards a Gay Hagiography.* Oxford: Oxford University Press, p. 62.

[5] Dollimore, J. (1991). *Sexual Dissidence: Augustine to Wilde, Freud to Foucault.* Oxford: Clarendon Press, p. 198.

revision. The sexual practices investigated by queer theorists are those which take place between "consenting adults" and in a political and cultural climate in which the increasing tolerance of what was once deemed transgressive, which is not to say that all sexual practices are exempt from disapprobation, even within liberal cultures—as illustrated by the concerns about child sexual abuse—whether "historical" or not. Freud seemingly attempts to re-constitute the category of perversions with his example of 'licking excrement or of intercourse with dead bodies' as 'pathological'.[6] But this definition relies on the fact that those who enjoy such practices 'successfully overriding the resistances of shame, disgust, horror or pain'[7]... those 'mental forces which act as resistances ... of which shame and disgust are the most prominent'.[8] And for Freud—taking as an example the idea that we might feel disgust at the thought of using someone else's toothbrush—disgust is 'often purely conventional'.[9] Thus the classification of perversion, both for queer writers and for Freud, is contingent on a transgression of mores specific to context.

4.3 Lacan

Lacan's formulation of perversion, that it is not contingent on notions of transgression and normality, arguably resolves these issues. He asks:

> What is perversion? It is not simply an aberration in relation to social criteria, an anomaly contrary to good morals, although this register is not absent, nor is it an atypicality according to natural criteria, namely that it more or less derogates from the reproductive finality of the sexual union. It is something else in its very structure.[10]

---

[6] Freud, 1905, op. cit., p. 161.

[7] ibid.

[8] ibid., p. 162.

[9] ibid, pp. 151–2.

[10] Lacan, J. (1991)[1953–4]. *The Seminar of Jacques Lacan Book I: Freud's Papers on Technique.* J.-A. Miller (Ed.) & J. Forrester (Trans.). New York: W. W. Norton & Company, p. 221.

So from a Lacanian standpoint, it is possible to rule out sexual practice as the denominator of perversion. Perversion is not a deviation of reproductive sex, nor dependent on 'good morals' and social acceptability: 'it is something else in its very structure'.[11] Every human being faces the same dilemmas in becoming a human subject. What differentiates the categories of neurosis, psychosis and perversion is that each is but one way to resolve the problems of having a body, of becoming a man or a woman; to solve the difficulties of making sense of the world, and of finding our place in relation to others.

It is by means of passage through the Oedipus complex that we take up a position as either a man or a woman, choose our sexual object and that determines how we understand the limit to desire and to *jouissance* and how to situate ourselves in relation to the Other, prototypically the mother. The mother is the first Other and the prematurely born infant is at her mercy. The question of her desire, or what will make her happy, is critical for our survival. We begin to be freed from subjection to the mother's desire at the time of Oedipus, when we perceive the castration of the mother, The law/father puts paid to her desire, Lacan's imaginary phallus, deprives her of what she wants, preventing the child from imagining that it can satisfy her desire. In psychosis and perversion, however, there is 'something essentially incomplete in the Oedipus complex'.[12]

How does someone with a perverse structure deal with the dilemma of human subjectivity? In what ways is the perverse solution incomplete? I will attempt to answer this question with some published clinical material.

The pervert's solution is disavowal: they perceive that they are deprived, that they lack and thus desire, but disavow the fact at the same time. "The whole problem of the perversions consists in conceiving how the child, in relation to his mother … identifies himself with the imaginary object of this desire in so far as the mother symbolizes it in the phallus."[13] With the desire of the other disavowed, the pervert concerns themselves with

---

[11] ibid.

[12] Lacan, J. (1977)[1955–6]. On a Question Preliminary to Any Possible Treatment of Psychosis in *Ecrits: A selection.* A. Sheridan (Trans.). London: Routledge, p. 201.

[13] ibid., pp. 197–8.

their pleasure and 'the subject here makes himself the instrument of the Other's *jouissance*'.[14]

Jacques-Alain Miller[15] suggests that perversion is not often seen in the psychoanalytic clinic because perverts are quite happy with their way of life and their sexual practices and/or they fear that the analyst will force them to give up their enjoyment. Nevertheless, there are published accounts in the psychoanalytic literature that illustrate the perverse solution to the question of subjectivity.

4.4 The Clinic

Stein's account of her analysis of Alice, while not written from a Lacanian perspective, describes her patient's commitment to offering herself as the object-cause of *jouissance.*[16] Stein's aim in the work was for the 'the resumption of split-off and projected parts of the personality, and the birth/growth of a 'true self''.[17] Alice's mother is described as domineering, over-stimulating and intrusive, the father, in contrast, as 'humble and virtuous'.[18] This parental constellation might be interpreted as one in which the father function—the privation of the mother—has been incomplete. Alice's strategy, positioning herself as cause of enjoyment, can be illustrated by her dream : '*I am in a cab; I'm lying in the rear seat. I take off my clothes. I get up and ask the driver if my breasts are pretty. The driver, a religious Chassidic Jew, sees me and becomes mad with lust.*'[19] This position is repeated in her relationship with her boyfriend who 'she would arouse … to masturbate himself while talking to him through the door of men's restrooms'.[20] Stein's account of her response to the material confirms this.

---

[14] ibid., p. 323.

[15] Miller, J.-A. (1996). On Perversion, in *Reading Seminars I and II: Lacan's Return to Freud.* R. Feldstein, B. Fink, M. Jaanus (Eds). Albany: State University of New York Press.

[16] Stein, R. (2005). Why Perversion? 'False Love' and the Perverse Pact. *International Journal of Psychoanalysis*, 86: 775–99.

[17] ibid., p. 783.

[18] ibid., p. 786.

[19] ibid., p. 783.

[20] ibid., p. 784.

Stein argues that, in analysis, perverts attempt to establish a 'perverse pact' with the analyst.[21] Stein 'had the feeling of being prey to a cunning predator, a sense of exquisite vulnerability to her, feelings of excitement and the disturbing realisation of how compelling I found her'[22] acknowledging that, in this creation of the perverse pact Alice was, as "Lacanians call it, 'being the mother's phallus'".[23]

There is another solution by which someone can separate from the mother, from the problematic of the impossibility of the satisfaction of the mother's desire. Here, a fetish object takes the place of the mother's missing phallus, becoming the representation of the mother's desire.

In Fink's report of his analysis of W, a boot fetishist, the boot functioned as a replacement of himself as the object of his mother's desire.[24] It is a rich case history, elaborating multiple significations of the fetish object and its relation to the patient's speech and history. W was disturbed both by his homosexuality and his fetishism, and had sought treatment for depression. He had no signifier for sexual difference and the boot came to function as a marker of 'sexual difference and non-difference … boots had both masculine and feminine attributes to his mind'.[25] The analysis uncovered the associations to the black shiny boot, ' which had an opening, making it vagina-like, but it also has a shaft … making, it penis-like … the fetish can be understood as creating a space for both lack … and its possible filling … thereby eliminating W's anxiety.[26] Fink quotes W: 'The boot is the eye of the needle through which I pass to the male side'; 'the boots stand for me'.[27] In response to an absence of a name for female genitalia, for what his mother lacked and thus desired, W put in place the fetish object, the boot, to stand in for his penis, which was seemingly demanded by his mother.

---

[21] ibid., p. 792.

[22] ibid.

[23] ibid., p. 794.

[24] Fink, B. (2003). The Use of Lacanian Psychoanalysis in a Case of Fetishism. *Clinical Case Studies,* 2(1): 50–69.

[25] ibid., pp. 53–4.

[26] ibid., p. 67.

[27] ibid., p. 56.

There is something singularly incomplete in the Oedipus complex that results in the perverse structure. Stereotypically in Oedipus, the father—or Name-of-the-Father, as Lacan refers to it—functions as the name for that something that the mother desires beyond the child. While this destroys the illusion of the exclusive and mutually satisfying relation between the child and the mother, it also rescues the child from being nothing other than the mother's only love object, making a space for a desire that is beyond the mother/child dyad. W understood from his mother that his father was not of interest to her, but boots were associated with her own father, 'a real man'[28] and with other 'real men, unlike her husband'[29] of W's childhood story book about pirates, that was known in the family as the 'boot book'.[30] W's father, too, liked black boots and had a large collection of boots; the word 'boot' also had a connection to the father's name.[31] As Fink conceptualises the fetish: 'The boot could be understood as an attempt to assert a father substitute between himself and his mother'.[32] The boot, the fetish object in this case, can be seen as *a* Name-of-the-Father, supporting the operation of separation. The fetishist's response to castration anxiety and the lack of the mother can be seen as creative. Here, W created a space that enabled him to reclaim his body from the mother.[33]

The prohibition central to the Oedipus complex, imposed by the father while maintaining the subject at a safe distance from the desire of the mother, also results in the installation of the super-ego which, from a Freudian perspective, functions as a moral agency, regulating desire. The "father function", the law-giving Other, is incomplete in perversion; a transgressive act can paradoxically serve to prop up this function, thereby solving the problem of limiting enjoyment. Swales' case history of Chris illustrates this point. 'Chris, a man in his fifties reported that he had committed thousands of acts of indecent exposure', although convicted for

---

[28] ibid., p. 66.

[29] ibid., p. 53.

[30] ibid.

[31] ibid., p. 66.

[32] ibid.

[33] ibid., p. 57.

less than ten.[34] In this case, the limit came about when Chris imagined the presence of a police officer. If the woman to whom he was exposing himself screamed or reached for her phone, Chris would leave the scene.[35] Chris' actual father is described as a 'monstrous figure who threw "temper tantrums"',[36] who left all child-rearing duties to his wife. Swales' analysis is that while this father adequately fulfilled the function of the Name-of-the Father insofar as the prohibition of incest was concerned, his childishness and inconsistencies resulted in something incomplete in the role of the law-giving Other.[37] Chris had other strategies to invoke the law-giver. Swales' diagnosis of perversion is not totally dependent on his sexually-offending behaviour. She interprets Chris's decision to enlist in the military, an organisation representative of the law, as a further attempt to support the paternal function. His habitual writing of letters of complaint are also interpreted as a creative and law-abiding way to prop up the paternal function'.[38] Whether the letter complained about his psychiatric treatment, his conditions of employment or service in a restaurant, Chris appealed to an authority figure to recognise that 'a moral law had been broken' and who 'would enforce the rules more strictly'.[39]

4.5 Treatment

I cite these cases in an attempt to demonstrate that, from a Lacanian perspective, a diagnosis of perversion does not rely on the presence of sexual transgression; rather that subjectivity is always sexed and that having a body is a universal dilemma to which perversion is but one response. The clinical illustrations also suggest a direction for treatment. If perversion

[34] Swales, S. (2012). *Perversion: A Lacanian Psychoanalytic Approach To the Subject.* New York: Routledge, p. 124.

[35] ibid., p. 125.

[36] ibid., p. 138.

[37] ibid.

[38] ibid., p. 140.

[39] ibid.

is an attempt at completing something 'essentially incomplete',[40] how might the analyst support those attempts?

Alice, while not resolving her inhibition of writing, went on to become 'a most gifted and sought-after teacher and lecturer. Talking about topics that touch people's core, she won great recognition and fame'.[41] One might wonder here about sublimation. She also experienced 'her first loving/affectionate sexual encounter with a man'[42] although somewhat poignantly Stein reports that the man did not stay with Alice. Stein understands that the success of this analysis was the result of 'working through the removal and transformation of perverse structures that had been built upon such defences as means-ends reversals, faked innocence and sado-masochistic uses of the effects and impacts one has on the other'.[43] But perhaps it was also the fact that Stein 'understood her frequent complaint that *she did not satisfy me*' and that Stein determinedly 'remained unsatisfied' that had significant effect.[44]

Fink itemises ten changes that took place during the course of W's analysis. He sees the success of the treatment as being due to a number of factors. Firstly, Finks' own 'agreement' to 'occupy the place of the unconscious for him, that (often aggressive) part of himself that he considered unacceptable'.[45] Furthermore, it was of importance that Fink expressed his desire for the work to continue in the face of the analysand's reluctance.[46] Fink also came to take the place of the boot, becoming an object placed between W and his mother[47] whose job as W put it was 'to "cut out" the mother in him, or to "splice" her out'.[48] And Fink poses the question: 'Is psychoanalysis, then, a new Name-of-the-Father?'[49]

---

[40] Lacan, 1955–6, op. cit., p. 201.

[41] Stein, op. cit., p. 793.

[42] ibid.

[43] ibid., p. 783.

[44] ibid., p. 794.

[45] Fink, op. cit., p. 63.

[46] ibid.

[47] ibid., p. 67.

[48] ibid.

[49] ibid.

Chris was imprisoned and his wife divorced him. On release, he 'went beyond the stipulation of his parole and participated in once weekly individual and group psychotherapy sessions'.[50] While Swales does not report the treatment strategy in Chris's case, her discussion of the dominance of the scopic drive in exhibitionism suggests that the group may have served as substitutes for the women to whom he showed his penis, whose function was to alert the law-giving Other. The group could not understand the depth of his distress about poor service (whether in restaurants or from psychiatry) and perhaps disapproved or were horrified by his complaints? They certainly reminded him about how his threatening letter of complaint had, on one occasion, led to his re-imprisonment.[51] In group psychotherapy, it seems that Chris was able to get someone else 'to bolster the lawgiving Other through … gazes of protest that substitute for enunciations of the moral law itself'.[52]

4.6 Conclusion

This small selection of published case histories demonstrates the creativity and inventiveness of the perverse subject in their attempts to complete that essentially incomplete something of the Oedipus complex. Sometimes, they seek help with the task of strengthening the law-giving Other. When they do, the analyst's job is to assist in bolstering the paternal function.

[50] Swales, op. cit., p. 124.

[51] ibid., pp. 140–1.

[52] ibid., p. 126.

5

From a Hierarchy of Desires to an Equivalence of Jouissances

Patrick Landman

5.1 Is There a Hierarchy of Desires?

In the context of psychoanalysis, we could understand the idea of a hierarchy of desires from either a clinical or a theoretical point of view. The same is true about the equivalence of *jouissances.*

Firstly, following Freud and especially Karl Abraham, we can establish a kind of hierarchy of objects that are aimed at a desire for satisfaction. In this view, oral and anal objects, for example, are less elaborated, more primary, than the genital object, as is suggested by the notion of stages—the oral, the anal and the genital. This developmental schema, with its outcome of the election of the genital object as the object of genital love, often creates confusion between the object of desire and the object of love. Although it is schematic, this perspective is not incorrect. What we must add to it, however, is the hierarchy between the partial and

P. Landman (✉)
Espace Analytique

D. Caine, C. Wright (eds.), *Perversion Now!*,
DOI 10.1007/978-3-319-47271-3_5

the total object. Partial objects are connected to infantile polymorphous perversion and therefore are seen as regressive by nature. These different objects are not properly speaking objects of desire, but objects of the drives. However, in the course of psychical development the drives are ruled by desire because they are driven by a desire for satisfaction.

In Lacan we also find a hierarchy of desires, with the desire of the analyst at the top. The desire of the analyst is what drives the treatment and struggles against resistances—it is a kind of pure desire resembling a function or a limit rather than an ideal. This desire makes it possible for the treatment to unfold because we can never count on the desire of the analysand, who is often lacking, lost, trapped in his own demands, fixated on various objects and especially influenced by the discourse of the Other, i.e. essentially the signifiers of the parents who had thus sealed his fate.

Based on this conception of the analyst's desire, Lacan transforms Freud's theory of unconscious desire. Unconscious desire is indeterminate and has no "natural" object, as opposed to the demand, which is determined and affixed to a specific object. Fulfilling a determined desire, such as becoming involved in a love relationship or choosing a career, can be completely at odds with the subject's indeterminate desire and sooner or later he realises that the path he had chosen has nothing to do with his desire, and instead leads to an impasse. This feeling of being stuck has an explanation: no determined desire can be dissociated from either a fantasy that pushes towards its realisation or a demand that strives towards satisfaction; yet the analyst's desire should be exempt from both. Unconscious desire is not searching for an object yet a particular object can be the cause of a desire: Lacan called this the *object a*, a new notion in psychoanalytic terms, which nonetheless has certain links to Klein's partial object and Winnicott's transitional object. Because desire stems from lack rather than satisfaction the subject paradoxically needs to maintain this lack at all costs: hence the notorious unsatisfied desire of the hysteric, and the impossible desire of the obsessional. As Lacan teaches us, it is the disappearance of this lack that produces anxiety.

How do we approach unconscious desire in the analytic treatment? Essentially through dreams. By satisfying an unconscious desire in a dream, the dreamer is able to maintain its structure of lack—what Freud calls the navel of the dream—while, as we also know, a dream is never a reality. In addition to narrative elements, the dream contains unconscious signifiers that have to do with unconscious desire, mixed together with the help of the fantasy.

Dream interpretation should not be exhaustive in terms of meaning and signification; instead it should fuel the enigma of desire by displacing it; it can play this crucial role of maintaining the lack by remaining equivocal, but also by sticking to what the dreamer says rather than what he would like to say because what counts are the literal associations made by the patient on the basis of the dream's signifiers, as Freud shows with his Rat Man case. His patient moves from *ratten* (rats) to *raten* (a dividend, an instalment) and *spielratte* (players, gamblers), associations made via the letter rather than meaning.[1]

How are we able to speak about a hierarchy of desires? The explanation lies in the fact that desire is related to the Other, that it is the desire of the Other, which it needs in order to construct itself. The work of the treatment does not consist in fulfilling one's desire, but in the oh-so-difficult and vulnerable effort of detaching oneself from the Other and his discourse, generally constituted by the subject's history, his interactions with the parents, but also the possible traumas that have determined his destiny.

In the Lacanian model, at the beginning of analysis the analyst is in the place of the Other; in the patient's mind the analyst's desire is conflated with the desire of the Other supposed to know. This stage is necessary for the establishment of transference and in order to set the analysand's desire in motion. Starting from the 1960s and especially 1964, however, Lacan's practice led him to realise that desire was no longer the revolutionary element driving the cure; that desire and its pursuit lead to an impasse, for two essential reasons. Firstly, desire is metonymical, it is constantly displaced in order to preserve the lack and therefore has no possible endpoint; secondly, desire is consubstantial with the Law. It cannot quite detach itself from the Law and therefore from the Other because it upholds the Law, so as to either submit to it or oppose it.

In order to illustrate the impasse inherent to desire, I am going to use a small clinical vignette. As a child, this patient was constantly tossed

[1] Freud, S. (1909b). *Notes upon a Case of Obsessional Neurosis*. S.E. 10: 151–318. London: Hogarth Press, 1953.

between his parents, who separated shortly his birth and for the next ten years continued to argue about custody rights. He had no place, no position that would be guaranteed for him by the Other. After several years of analysis things had improved, his phobic symptoms disappeared and he was able to become involved in professional and personal projects that he found satisfying. He thought that at last he had found his place. He decided to stop his analysis and I agreed. He told me: "I feel much better, but there is something I've never understood—the transference. I don't really have any particular feelings towards you, or they are just very banal. I am leaving my analysis with this question." In order to explain this vignette, it is necessary to recall that my family name is *Landman*. I didn't tell this patient anything about transference. The following session he arrived, lay down on the couch and said: "Just imagine, I had the most incredible dream. I was lost in an unknown place and all of a sudden I saw a sign telling me I was in a '*no man's land*.' And that I must have taken the wrong turn." The patient's dream shows that separation from the Other was still very precarious. He was afraid of moving from the '*no landman*', a signifier of the transference, to the '*no man's land*' of his traumatic childhood. It also shows that his desire to stop his analysis, although clinically quite justified, was yet another demand addressed to the Other. Above all, he was worried about suddenly becoming disoriented.

Although the subject is always subjected to the law of the Other, we should not look at the outcome of an analysis as a kind of emancipation of desire that would take the form of a decided, determined or rectified desire, or a desire that one does not give up on. This "cleansing" of the subject's desire from the desire of the Other does of course bring a certain relief, but there is always the famous limit of the "bedrock of castration." Faced with this clinical observation, Lacan turned to a different subject, that of *jouissance*.

5.2 An Equivalence of Jouissances?

The impasse of desire can be contrasted with the drives, the Freudian id, which are never in an impasse—they are untameable and have no relationship to the law. On the other hand, desire can act as an obstacle to the drive, which is striving towards satisfaction, towards *jouissance*. Having moved through desire, the subject finds a part of his lost *jouissance* in fantasy. In Lacan's new understanding of the treatment, the emphasis now is on satisfaction and the modalities of *jouissance*; the focus is no longer the subject's relation to the Other's desire, but his relationship to the different partial objects, the different *objects a* that provide satisfaction.

This subject is still more distant from the traditional philosophical or psychological notions of subjectivity; it is a headless, acephalic subject, with no tangible link to signifiers and the Symbolic. Schematically speaking, we could say that the drives originating from the id are initially related to the Other's demand, with the subject's demand responding to the demand of the Other and vice versa; later their path towards satisfaction is obstructed by the Other's desire and their tie to the law. Finally, they are correlated to the "object a" through the satisfaction for which they are striving. This is the course followed by analysis. Drives remain inscribed in language, in the symbolic register, as passive or active, but they play their part irrespective of the Other, their demand or desire. These three stages correspond to the three registers of the Symbolic, the Imaginary and the Real. It might seem that the aim of analysis is to free the drives from the clutches of desire, in order to become a kind of 'non-stop pleasure-seeking" being, or that *jouissance* becomes mandatory due to the effect of the superego. But the point is rather simply for *jouissance* to become allowed or possible, to let the drives strive for their partial objects freely. In this sense, there is indeed a certain equality of *jouissances* at the end of analysis: on the face of it, the subject's situation thus approximates a perverse position.

How should the treatment be directed, what technique should be used so that the subject is led to question his relationship to *jouissance*? First of all, when the analyst, who was previously in the place of the Other, comes to occupy the position of the *object a*, when the desire of the analyst becomes identified with an *objet a*, the analysand is able to mobilise, in the context of transference, all his drives and shed light on their relationship to partial objects. The effects of *jouissance,* that the subject ignores because they are obstructed by desire, can also be emphasised and pinpointed through punctuations and scansions which, if they are pertinent, function without a need for interpretation. When *jouissance* is recognised, it can be emptied out, or at least the subject can take responsibility for it and possibly avoid repetition—the "subject's choice" can, so to say, be made anew.

However, the essential thing is what Lacan calls *traversing the fantasy*. The unconscious fantasy has in fact many different functions: in what we are interested in here, it acts as a filter against the recognition of the effects of the subject's *jouissance*; it fixates this *jouissance* in a narrative, a scenario characterised by a certain misrecognition. As the subject slowly opens himself up to knowledge about his *jouissance*, the fantasy loses its importance—it is traversed, as Lacan says. When Lacan speaks about traversing the fantasy, he is of course referring to the fundamental fantasy, the one that sets the tone for all other fantasies. It is this movement through the fantasy that gives the subject, at the end of analysis, access to the recognition of his mode of *jouissance*—without letting him fall into perversion.

Perversion in fact requires the staging of fantasmatic scenarios that try and establish the limits of *jouissance* by addressing the Other as the embodiment of the law. The perverse scenario is a staging of the Other; one of its aims is to make the Other exist and to search for the limits of *jouissance*. So in regards to the analytic treatment, there is no perverse solution at the end of analysis, except for those that choose it. Instead, the fantasy is drained of the *jouissance* that saturates it and the subject can arrive at a recognition of his own singular modalities of *jouissance*, which the cure has managed to modify. In relation to the analyst's desire, Jean Clavreul has spoken about *an ethics without morals;* perhaps we could apply this term to the subject's relationship to *jouissance* at the end of analysis. In any case, we are far from a perverse construction.

5.3 Is There an Expansion of Perverse Modalities in the Functioning of Today's Society?

It is sometimes argued that there is an expansion of perverse modalities in the contemporary world, using sociological and anthropological studies to support the claim. It has been argued that the conditions of equality on which democracy is founded have expanded into the field of *jouissance*. All types of *jouissance*—with some notable exceptions such as paedophilia, homicide or incest—have become not only equivalent, but equally legitimate. People have a degree of liberty in choosing the modalities of *jouissance* they wish to practice. The explanation that is generally given is based on the idea of a "decline of the paternal function". However, this pays no heed to the fact that it is precisely a call to the father that characterises perversion or, as Lacan puns in French, the "version of the father" or *père-version*. Others have spoken about the growing use of gadgets, which serve as *objets a*, providing a partial and endlessly repeated *jouissance* and breaking down educational and social barriers through the addiction their *jouissance* sustains.

In reality, it seems to me that clinically, we see that the traditional or classical "figures" of the "Name of the Father" have disappeared: they are no longer a given, they are no longer legitimate, primarily because they rely on values that are becoming increasingly unacceptable, such as masculine hegemony or certain types of the discourse of the master. Instead, it is up to each of us to look for figures that could play this role, to find our own substitutes and *suppléances* (replacements). These are very complex changes and—even if those who confuse the Lacanian Symbolic with patriarchy might not like it—they are also irreversible. The speed at which our symbolic frameworks have evolved has especially given rise to concerns. Some are afraid of a kind of drifting, one that would open the way for all kinds of excesses, especially the perverse ones; however, this view often precipitates a moralistic criticism that certain communities, certain minorities rightly see as reactionary and segregating, as reliant on concepts that are sometimes borrowed from psychiatry's troubled legacy of segregation, discrimination, racisms and colonialism.

In thinking of the term perversion, for example, its use may imply that there is a norm of *jouissance* that is universal and that those who do not submit to it should be labelled perverse. Likewise, if we understand the term perversion as designating a particular psychic structure, there is a risk of implying a kind of hierarchy of structures in which each structure is a function of a developmental arrest corresponding to an evolutionary stage: alienation for psychosis, separation for perversion, the bedrock of castration for neurosis. But an explanatory model such as this cannot be taken for scientific truth and, as Freud tells us, there is 'madness' and 'normality' in each of us. Every psychic structure is based on incompleteness, and different types of psychic organisation are sometimes woven together to respond to the impossibility of the human condition and to the trauma of being confronted with the Real. In reality, things are much more nuanced and more open than theoretical and ideological debates would suggest.

In my clinical practice, I have for example noticed that in the case of hyperactive children who are labelled with Attention Deficit Hyperactivity Disorder and who are subject to the law of the maternal fantasy—often with a good post-modern father, trendy or conformist, who advocates equality and the rejection of authority, obviously quite inadequate ideas in this case—what often functions as a separator between the child and the mother's discourse is the prescription of medication. The medication castrates the maternal *jouissance*, removing the child from its ambit. When the drug has an effect on behavioural symptoms, it works as a separator and acts as the paternal function. In some cases, though not always, the separation effected by medication can be used to help transform the child's psychic dynamics, its interaction with the parents, its place in the family, and to carry out analytical work that brings to light the family's speech and history, in other words other issues than the medico-biological and particularly behavioural factors. This is a development of clinical practice to which we should adapt. As Paul Valéry, the great French novelist, put it: "We do not have to love the age we are living in, but we must try to understand it."

6

Perversion and Perversity in Contemporary Love

Gorana Bulat-Manenti

While for Freud, "a tendency to perversions is one of the characteristics of a psychoneurotic constitution",[1] Lacan always maintained that there is no such thing as pure desire. In 1963 in his seminar on the transference Lacan noted:

> If society brings about, by its censoring effect, a form of disintegration which is called neurosis, it is in a contrary sense of development, of construction, of sublimation – let us say the word – that perversion can be conceived when it is produced by culture. And if you wish, the circle closes in on itself: perversion bringing elements that torment society, neurosis promoting the creation of new elements of culture.[2]

[1] Freud, S. (1905). *Three Essays on the Theory of Sexuality.* S.E. 7. London: Hogarth, 1953, p. 171.

[2] Lacan, J. (2001)[1960–1]. *Le Séminaire, Livre VIII: Le transfert,* 23.11.60 (2ème édition). J.-A. Miller (Ed.). Paris: Seuil.

G. Bulat-Manenti (✉)
Fondation Européenne pour la Psychanalyse

D. Caine, C. Wright (eds.), *Perversion Now!*,
DOI 10.1007/978-3-319-47271-3_6

Neurotic perversity attests to the imbrication of the two: the unconscious fantasy of the neurotic is the exact opposite of the perverse act in reality. But does the act of the fantasy in the pervert, in its turn, do nothing more than approach a psychotic structure where the *passage à l'acte* would be the fulfilment of a delusion? Freud seems to say something about this when, in *Civilisation and its Discontents*, he speaks of the crowd ready to follow and to identify itself with the delusion of a paranoid leader in its need to have a father who will act in its place, a father who would hold the truth, in sum, a father incarnating the father of myth in *Totem and Taboo*, a place of speech, of imaginary *jouissance*.

At the same time, the relation to sexuality and to the problematic of castration differs in the different psychic structures. The paternal function, the paternal complex, is not articulated in the same way for a hysterical or obsessional subject as for a psychotic or perverse subject. Central to this difference is the relation to loss which, for both Lacan and Freud, is constitutive of the formation of the subject. For both, the subject's relation to the lost object determines their psychic structure. The function of "a" as object, destined to keep the subject on the edge of the hole of castration, is "the function of a transferable object, separable and carrying somewhat primitively something of the identity of the body, antecedent to the body itself, as regards the constitution of the subject … ".[3] The possibility of acceptance of the loss is linked to the place given to the paternal function.

In "Formations of the Unconscious" Lacan notes, for example, the importance of examining, in the cure, "how the subject has taken up, in a certain way at a given moment in his childhood, a position on the role that the father plays in the fact that the mother does not have a phallus." He adds that this moment is never elided. "Do not doubt, you can verify and confirm it each time you get a chance to see it", Lacan emphasises,

> experience shows that, to the extent that the child does not surmount this nodal point, that is to say does not accept the mother's privation of the phallus effected by the father, one observes that as a rule and I underline this 'as a rule' because here, it does not simply have an importance as an

[3] Lacan, J. (1962–3). *Seminar X: L'angoisse*, 26.06.63.

> ordinary correlation – the correlation is based on the structure – a certain form of identification to the object of the mother, this object that I have represented to you from the start as a 'rival' object, as one might say, and that, whether it be a question of phobia, neurosis or perversion, this is a reference point – there is perhaps no better word – around which you can group the elements of observation by asking this question in each particular case: what is the specific configuration of the relation to the mother, to the father and to the phallus, which makes the child not accept that the mother is deprived by the father of the object of her desire? To what extent is it necessary in a particular case to point out that correlatively with this relation, the child maintains his identification with the phallus?[4]

It is widely held that postmodernity is particularly vulnerable to perversion because of the fall of patriarchy and the absence of God the Father, in heaven as on earth, as agent of the law. (Although, if liberal capitalism and the fetishisation of money has opened the door to the depreciation of the values of civilisation, one can also ask whether the liberation of women and their new status has not inhibited the tendency to the exploitation of the other? It should not be forgotten that in patriarchal societies, just a few decades ago, women were submissive and objectified, fetishised, having no right to their own subjectivity!).

The direction given by Lacan to "do without" the name of the Father "provided you use it" is sometimes understood as the possibility of being able to make do without a father at all. This can be understood as grounds for the curious hope of putting an end to the father, always so troublesome, so embarrassing! To deny the father is the—hardly credible—aim of such a position. But those who hold the opposite position, defenders of the threatened father, are no further forward in designating themselves guardians of the patriarchal order. They feel obliged to embody God on earth: to be in the place of the exception, the father of the Totem, the mythical father, the place of the call of the drives—the place of address. Here is a perversion that protects from the abyss when the symbolic father is not put in place.

---

[4] Lacan, J. (1998)[1957–8]. *Le Séminaire, Livre V: Les formations de l'inconscient*, 22.01.58. J.-A. Miller (Ed.). Paris: Seuil.

6.1 "What Is a Woman?"/"What Is a Father?"

The question, dear to Lacan, "What is a woman?" finds itself thus reformulated in our times in correlation with that of "What is a father?" with new data, as disturbing as it is promising. It is precisely the problematic of the tension between these two points, "What is a woman?" unfolding into that of "What is a father?", the answers to which determine psychic structure, which will help us to shed light on the issue—so thoroughly contemporary, if only in its intensity and extent—of what is referred to today as belonging to perversion.

We have first a place which localises the father, the agent of maternal 'castration'. If this place is incarnated by a father, we have the father of the name, the totemic father. But to enter into the symbolic, it is necessary to kill this father and to identify with him, to take his place. There is therefore first of all a father who permits the phallus to be taken as one of his traits, while the genital remains unknown. To emerge from the shelter of the father who protects from the act, it is necessary for the subject to make a dialectic jump, to commit the act on his own account and to sign in his own name, to be able to transmit it. Subjects for whom the symbolic fails must try to cobble a father together from the pieces, a violent father if necessary, since a father who beats would be better than no father at all.

Let us try then to differentiate perversion as it manifests itself in the different psychic structures. Perversion can appear as a defence in the neuroses, because of its very particular relationship to lack, to privation that for the child appears in the form of maternal castration, obviously imaginary. Here, while it is the father who will be identified as responsible for this damage, this maternal injury, paradoxically it is also the father who will offer hope of regaining the lost *jouissance* through the phallus, instrument of *jouissance*. Hatred of the father will be repressed; instead he will be loved as a saviour before the threat of the maternal demand, of identification with her demand. In psychosis things happen differently: here, hatred of the father cannot be transformed into love, he cannot be idealised. He does not open the way to the stabilisation of the ideal ego, as the case of Schreber observed by Freud shows, because he is not recognised in the desire of the mother on the one hand, and because he is mired in blatant hostility towards the son on the other.

Although perverse traits, in the widest sense, may pervade erotic life irrespective of structure, Freud also situates perversion, alongside neurosis and psychosis, as one of three psychic structures. As a structure, perversion represents an extension into adulthood of the polymorphous perversion of the child. It reflects the impossibility for the subject of confronting the feminine, a certain inability to accept the lack of a penis in the mother. Fetishism is at the centre of this Freudian discovery where an object (a shoe or a piece of cloth, for example), would stop the fall into "nothing" in the place of the "something" that would not be there in a woman. When it comes to perversion as structure, sexual satisfaction in adulthood will be obtained by means of the fetish, in a violent objectification of the other. The subject is reduced to the thing, desubjectivised, offered to the *jouissance* of the Other. Thus perversion aims to support the jouissance of the Other, in a transgenerational denial of the feminine: the child *is* the phallus, the tip of the flesh belonging to the maternal *jouissance*. It is the disavowal that blocks the confrontation with "castration" that inclined Freud to define perversion as a clinical structure, with its principal characteristic the primordial place accorded to the fetish, dead thing.

6.2 Two Clinical Vignettes

Here are some contemporary clinical sequences which illustrate a tension between perverse traits and psychic structure.

6.2.1 The Lover

In the first, a young man having met with many psychoanalysts, all men, since adolescence, came to see me for suicidal thoughts, apathy, inability to act, to work, or to love, that arose, he said, following the breakup of a relationship. With time, and thanks also to his diligence in therapy, he gradually emerged from his black hole. Although he did not bring any dreams, some associations from slips of the tongue produced material for analytical work and through strength and subjectivation, things changed; life improved for him with new strength supporting the transference, one function of which was to invest the subject where before he did not exist. For example, when he first came to see me, he signed his electronic creations by an "xy – Anonymous." A year later, in one of the sessions he told me that the signature had become the figures of his date of birth.

All seemed to be going as well as could be hoped. He found a job and met a girl who was to his liking and the question of marriage approached. He reduced the frequency of his sessions. Yet, despite this happiness almost attained, one day, shortly before the wedding date, he came to tell me a "horrible" thing that threw him into panic and filled him with anxiety. For some time, going to work, on the subway, he would cling to women in order to obtain a sexual satisfaction that he had not found with his fiancée, who was so prudish that she was a virgin when they met. "A respectable girl," he told me. Two days before the wedding ceremony he had a dream in which his brother committed suicide during the celebration of the event. He was upset, crying during the session, invaded by a new despair.

It was in this context that something vital, hidden until that point, was finally revealed: his brother, seven years his senior, had initiated him in homosexual practices from the time he was six years old! They had continued this activity until the recent departure of his brother from their home: they had done it frequently, at the same time as leading romantic lives with women. This practice, experienced by the patient as consenting and brotherly on his own part, nevertheless remained secret, and happened only in the family home.

The split between woman as "mother" and as "whore" is evident: a "pure" young girl, the bride-to-be is excessively idealised, opening to the debasement of another young woman, a "whore" because dressed provocatively, according to him. The latter, the "whore", in fact takes the place that he had held for the brother who had sadistically used him as an object, to safeguard, at the moment of his adolescence, the idea that the mother had the penis, since he is in that place. He was unable to pass into adulthood, to reduce the polymorphous perversion of the child by acknowledging the genitalia, the free and living feminine. Does the split not come here in place of the possibility of subjectivation? The young man who here reproduced an objectification of the other "had nothing to do with it" since "it" happened in spite of himself….

Hence a perverse practice, exploiting somebody anonymous—a stranger in the subway—for his *jouissance*, occurred as an attempt to overturn the situation to which the patient had long been subjected: he fetishised the other that he sacrificed to castration and to the objectifying, alienating, mortifying maternal *jouissance*. As a result, the mother does not have the phallus, for to have it through this process of denial where the other is objectified is offered to him as a thing enjoyed by force.

The work on what this young patient had suffered and his complicity in the abusive behaviour of his brother began to change the image of their innocent childhood. He fell ill, he was very distressed by what had gone on. I learned that his wife, held as "holy", controlled him by not letting him decide anything, to such an extent that she chose meals for him at a restaurant, as well as making decisions about the other "menus" of his life: his timetable for coming home, the timing of his departure for work, his daily schedule.

One day he exposed himself in front of a neighbour. What was happening there? Marriage, the evocation of the primal scene, produced an excitement and an anxiety before the impossibility of symbolising the father. An identification with a violent, castrating father instead of repression of polymorphous perversion and emerging acceptance of the maternal flaw, left him only an impersonal place, an exchange of places in fact, for hatred of the father was never successfully transformed into love. The moment of the perverse act presents a moment of patricide: the father is there, but only as a rapist whose place he took. He put an other, by force, in the place where he himself had been abused.

The annihilation of the other holds *jouissance* in place, depersonalised. Is it a question of a passage for the young man facing a particularly strong anxiety at the moment the idea of becoming a father himself begins to be established? We can bet on this hypothesis because guilt and a certain shame are there, as well as a violent anxiety, which characterise psychotic decompensation.

6.2.2 The Lure of Suicide

A second case concerns a young researcher who, in moments where his hierarchical superior bullies him or does not recognise his work, however exceptionally brilliant it is, is at risk of committing suicide. He wants to jump into the void, he spends nights beside people who protect him from this *passage à l'acte* and at the same time he submits to sadomasochistic practices which involve violence towards himself, the indelible traces of which he bears on his body. His manager is in the place of an omnipotent father; it is on his patronage that the young man's security depends!

When "God on earth" rejects him, the young man has a strong impulse to jump from the window. To restrain himself at the edge of the abyss, as he says, he mutilates himself or permits others to mutilate him. The pain makes him feel alive! This patient is very close to his mother. He tells me at one session: 'I am my mother's hand', where there is some faltering confusion in his pronunciation of *'la main'* (the hand) and *'l'amant'* (the lover). He takes care of his mother, he is 'at her service' as he says. The authority of this mother is so incontestable that the idea of disobeying her never arises. If the mother does not have the phallus, he risks falling into the abyss. His father, hated by the mother, has been deprived of his paternity since the patient's birth. Quite simply, he does not exist. Gérard Pommier, in No. 16 of the *Revue la Clinique Lacanienne* put forward a hypothesis which is demonstrated here: for the pervert, the father cannot be killed since the mother has already accomplished the murder in his place.[5]

The young man plays cards with his mother almost every evening. 'Obscene remarks about my sexuality gush out', he tells me, 'especially allusions to the size of my penis'. This man has, in his infancy, been victim to being interfered with by, and subjected to the exhibitionist demonstrations on the part of, an uncle who was a sex maniac, such that the appearance of an erect penis continued to fascinate him, as puzzling as it was traumatising. Today, in his sexual practices with other men, he seeks situations where exhibitionism is a primary feature.

---

[5] Pommier, G. (2009). Des Perversion polymorphes de l'enfant à la perversion proprement dite. *Revue La Clinique Lacanienne*, 16: 245.

In the course of his analysis this man has passed from the desire to lose himself in the shadows of a Parisian park, from men who sodomise him, to virtual meetings which pacify him very much. Other elements of this treatment show that for this patient too it would be a question rather of a psychotic than of a perverse structure, that here perverse defences are organised as a stop at the edge of the castrative hole. The object 'a' which as cause of desire should permit deployment of the fantasy gives way, the fantasy is too fragile, the Name-of-the-Father can neither be captured, nor taken, nor used as his own. One version of the father of the horde is imposed, in its brutality, the father supposed to possess knowledge of the truth, an absolute truth that forecloses the subject.

6.3 Conclusion

The patients of whom I have written here both make the other endure what they themselves have been subjected to. Is their perversion not an attempt to master an excitation which has carried them away by its excessive force at a precocious moment in their lives, and which no other excitation would be able to equal from then on? It is in this way that they try to master what has failed to divide them, what has been too big, too 'grand' (in a sort of 'confusion of tongues'), as violence, to be assimilated. If the goal of the drive is to identify the human body with the maternal phallus, a response to the desire of the mother, as can be seen in these two cases, the pervert instead fetishises the body of the other, objectifies it to avoid maternal castration. The other, reduced to the status of object, is offered to the "Mother" to be protected from the idea of her castration. The pervert does not fantasise the crime, he commits it.

Part II

Symptom or Structure: A Dichotomy?

7

Perversion Since Freud?

Hélène Godefroy

The conference, '*Perversion et Modernité*/Perversion Now' initiated a debate about a crucial question: Today, when we speak about the concept of perversion, is it something other than that which Freud had succeeded in theorising in the first of his *Three Essays on the Theory of Sexuality*?

First of all, I propose by way of a hypothesis that perversion does not amount to a third structure, which would be distinct from neurosis and psychosis. If we start out from the nodal point that the Oedipus complex represents, we can only identify two major structural orientations. Either the child succeeds in grasping the existence of a more or less operational paternal function beyond the maternal space, foreshadowing an organisation, after the event, of a neurotic type; or the search for this father, supposed to be bearer of the phallus and so the mediator of desire, remains indefinitely foreclosed, in which case the development of the structure tends towards psychosis.

H. Godefroy (✉)
Fondation Européenne pour la Psychanalyse

D. Caine, C. Wright (eds.), *Perversion Now!*,
DOI 10.1007/978-3-319-47271-3_7

In my opinion, the possibility of a "localised foreclosure" cannot be entertained. At least, it is unimaginable as a disavowal of castration, which would define perversion as a major structure. The disavowal of castration cannot be a "localised" mark of foreclosure, because it is a question of a mode of defence which always has to do with *the anxiety of imagining that castration is real*. From this perspective, disavowal is an aspect of the early development of all children, whether female or male. At certain points during their psychosexual trajectory, every child is confronted with the anxiety of loss. In fact, the necessity of putting into play the disavowal of castration[1] during psychosexual development, inevitably concerns every structure. This inescapable fact prevents us from thinking of disavowal as being exclusive to a third structure.

Moreover, since perversion is always considered as being dependent upon its corollary, the disavowal of castration, it seems logical that all of the structures, in themselves, necessarily have their own perverse trait.

From this perspective, my position is no different from that described by Freud, or indeed that upheld by Lacan in his seminar *RSI*. Perversion can only, in fact, be considered in the direct relation that it maintains with the disavowal of castration. Every partial drive which does not pass through the renunciation that symbolic castration imposes (the latter belonging to the function of the father in psychical terms), remains in force in its infantile form during adulthood. A *plus de jouir* continues. A surplus jouissance remains "fixed" to one of the stages, dating from the time of the child's *polymorphous perversity*. An overflow of excitation that could not be successfully repressed. From that point on, everything relating to perversion in the arrangement of the structure has to do with whatever of the drive manages to penetrate the psychic barrier of repression; a part of drive satisfaction which would continue to substitute itself for the imaginary full *jouissance* of the One father (said to be the *exception*). In that regard, this excess of the drive cannot form a structure as such, but rather perverse *sequences* in any structure whatsoever.

Perversion is equivalent, in short, to the *pleasure principle* itself. Is it not the case that the neurotic—who by virtue of his structure remains

[1] Freud expresses this very clearly in his 1923 text "The Infantile Genital Organisation", a text subsequently added to the second of his *Three Essays* (Freud, 1905).

perpetually unsatisfied—may only satisfy himself through his perverse traits? This operation of the drive and the relation to its aim are still present in our contemporary clinic.

So why is it that our discourse about perversion seems to have changed, as if today everything had become possible (that is, possible to transgress)? This question opens the way to my second hypothesis.

I do not think that, in any case, the structure of the subject itself can be modified (in phylogenic terms). Rather, it is our collective discourse on the question of the father which has been somewhat transformed. The decline of the *Patriarchat* has brought with it the decline of his moralising and inhibitory discourse; a repression that was nothing other than a pathological addition to ordinary repression. In other words, patriarchal repression represented one layer too many, a re-entrenchment of repression. This decline of belief in patriarchy (and in all its prejudices) liberated desire and, in its wake, thought; and above all subjective thought which, supported by the voices of a few liberatory thinkers, had an immediate collective impact.[2] This liberation created new social phenomena that had never been seen before!

Nevertheless, looking at it more closely, we can see that these social phenomena merely transgress the *censuring* limits of patriarchal orthodoxy. For example, women who have begun to prioritise their *jouissance*, delaying maternity until later. However, this liberation of desire is not without consequences. From the perspective of the clinic, we can see very clearly that the transgression of prejudices separated from social discourse is curiously distressing, and consequently creates symptoms.

To account for the appearance of these new behaviours, the idea has passed around that the father might have lost all authority, that he might not be up to the task of fulfilling his role as educator anymore; that he might even slip away from it, fleeing his paternity. In other words, from a structural perspective, a decline of his function would have to be considered, the signifier of the Name-of-the-Father would have to be gradually emptied of its meaning.

[2] These were the participants of the May '68 revolution, and a few intellectuals who followed in their footsteps, such as Foucault, Derrida, etc.

Of course, as patriarchal morality has been diluted, the perverse effects of *jouissance* seem to have become disinhibited, and thus intensified, giving rise to the idea of an everyday perversion. We would no longer be neurotics, but subjects stuck to the *innocent* side of the *polymorphous perversity of the child*. In short, the new generations would have launched an assault on repression … Sometimes, I hear it said that young people no longer have any other ambition than transgression, that everything has become possible for them.

And at the same time, in certain quarters of the psychoanalytic world, a new clinic is thought to be emerging, based on the conviction that our symbolic reference points have been weakened, and that prohibition is in disarray. Yet with respect to prohibitions, I observe that the father of the child (the *daddy*) is still today the one who puts in place the incest prohibition! I have never heard it said that incest has become commonplace within families. As "kind" as he may be, his place as a "third" is sufficient, in itself, to ensure that the father is still the one who, in the imaginary of the child, places limits on *jouissance*.

Moreover, even in families where there is no *daddy*, the phallic function can still be discerned in a substitutive figure. Every limit that the child encounters in the maternal sphere puts in place the Oedipal triangulation. Whilst the father remains the "gold standard" of this third position, a father-in-law, an older brother, an uncle, a lover of the mother, a stranger, even another woman, can be sufficient to assume this separating role for the child. Each of these substitutive "thirds" may be imaginarily marked by the child as being *the* possessor of the phallus, in so far as the latter mobilises in one way or another the desire of the mother. The Oedipus complex thus remains a modern myth which, in my opinion, will persist as a structural constant.

Therefore, in declaring that the father no longer exists, is society not rather continuing to fantasise about his murder?

There is no increase in perversion and it has not become commonplace. It seems that the difficulty is not situated on the side of the prohibitions of the *symbolic*, but rather on the side of the *imaginary*. Everything depends on what the *concept* of the father represents within social discourse. A great deal of confusion has been introduced into the cultural imaginary, and more precisely, into the place of the "images" given to the father by certain trends within civilisation. The image of the patriarchal father is nothing other than a cultural construct; the ideological creation of a discriminatory system convinced of the supremacy of the male organ over the female organ, which therefore imposed masculine domination over the feminine. This representation of the father was nothing more than a pure belief, since it has been, in the end, defeated by a powerful feminist parricide. Women detached themselves from the idea, which they had shared with men, of being arbitrarily submitted to their domination.

In fact, this sexist image of the patriarch was only a collective symptomatic representation of an Other-*father*, one who is himself without a face because he is *purely psychical*. Freud gave this psychical father another image, perhaps the most metaphorical; that of the *Totemic* father. That is, a ghost of the father who might return at any moment. The eternally living father must always be murdered in order to be made to exist—to be made to exist for both sexes![3]

---

[3] For all subjects (men and women) there is always (and still in our modern world) this need to have always and incessantly "killed" the father. Freud explains this through the myth of *Totem and Taboo*. It is a perpetual murder … When the subject renounces his Oedipal desire, he simultaneously fantasises about the murder of the father (the one who makes the law in the sense of the *child being beaten*—see Freud, 1919). It is in this way that the subject fully assumes his subjective desire and gives up the desire of the Other (which objectifies him). This first (psychical) murder of the totemic father, immediately repressed, opens up a place for his symbol: the signifier of the Name-of-the-Father, as the *product* of symbolic castration.

Throughout the subject's life, he encounters events which disturb his subjectivity (this could be a romantic encounter, a problem of rivalry, the birth of a child, etc.). These events can recall once more the infantile fantasies, which put the subject back in the position, prior to Oedipal repression, of the child beaten by the father. This unconscious fantasy resurfaces, coming out from under its repression. The subject is once again caught in the desire of the Other, which is embodied in the emergence of a new symptom or of a persecutory situation which is only the substitute for this archaic Other, the support of his infantile fantasy.

From that point on, the fantasy of parricide is reactivated until the subject (either woman or man) once again finds a way to renounce his infantile drives. That is, to once more give up the position of passive submission, in the position of object, to the Other's persecution, by confronting it actively. It is through this reorganisation of the drive that the subject re-enacts his fantasy of parricide. In this way, he again achieves the repression of his infantile fantasy. And this follows each disturbance of his subjectivity. That is why we cannot claim that the father of the law has disappeared; because he is "structural". Psychically, he always threatens to come out from his repression. And in fact, in each disturbance encountered over the course of his life, the subject finds himself perpetually confronted with having to carry out once again the psychical murder of this totemic representation, in order to salvage the signifier of the Name-of-the-Father, and thus his own subjective desire.

In short, the *psychical* father is always both dead and alive. He is always the agent of a "dual" role in the psyche.

To be precise, this *Totemic* father differs from the patriarchal father, because he places man and woman in an egalitarian relationship vis-à-vis the phallus.[4] It seems that it is the unveiling of the psychical father—who had himself remained hidden behind the patriarchal invention—which, in restoring a place for women in the phallic domain, has caused an overturning of ideals, and with this the illusion that "everything is possible".

This father (solely psychical) continues to function without our knowledge. For example, he is, for the two sexes, the archaic monster of our nightmares; he sometimes appears as the fear of speaking in public, or the traumatic part of desire during a romantic encounter, or even the resistance of the subject to analytic work … This father, who is not cultural (but who has more to do with the real), is "structural"; a kind of entity or apprehension, imbued with a terrifying and fearsome affect, the only one, in every case, who generates *the anxiety of imagining that castration is real.*

If there is a disavowal of castration, it is because there is anxiety; and if there is anxiety, it is because the father is always behind this anxiety, psychically alive. It counts as a symptom! Alain Vanier has even argued that it is "a symptom of psychoanalysis".

In light of this argument, I propose a third hypothesis: is what prevailing discourse formulates as the "banalisation" of perversion not rather the external clothing of the symptom (itself intrinsically structural), which tends to change its form according to current scientific, ideological, and societal inventions? When we consider this question of the symptom, what exactly are we considering? It always has to do with the same compromise: a piece of *jouissance*, an infantile fixation which defies the law of the father, but which also appeals to it at the same time. From one age to another, the psychical economy of this compromise remains identical. However, its exterior form changes according to the reigning cultural signifiers.[5] And this psychical father—who makes a symptom within discourse—over the course of time, also takes on multiple forms. The more we seek to deny it, the more it insists and reappears in new and updated forms.

---

[4] For the two sexes, the phallus remains a *signifier* divided within the fantasy between the one who gives and the one who receives.

[5] Lacan, J. (2006). "Beyond the Pleasure Principle" in *Écrits: The First Complete Edition in English*. B. Fink (Trans.). London: W. W. Norton & Company.

So we discover it everywhere in the new phenomena of society; phenomena which are at once strategies for bypassing the law (thus causing anxiety), and at the same time involve an unavoidable appeal to the law. The subject is always incited to enjoy [*jouir*], since the drive always continues to function.[6] But he is also eager to ensure that his *jouissance* always runs up against a phallic limit.

Thus 'the father' today is that which society challenges (which was not the case during the patriachal era); that which it challenges while paradoxically, and now more than ever, appealing to his *function*. For example, the masters of science, in offering the possibility of changing the sex of one's body at will, are they not seeking to take for themselves the exceptional place of the father, challenging his law about the difference between the sexes? And to be precise, are they not trying to push back the limits of what is possible, and so moreover to commit parricide?

In another field, the homosexual community in France has appealed to the legislature in the hope of gaining "the right to marriage for all".[7] Is this not a question of an appeal made to the father, even while challenging his law, pointing to the discriminatory consequences of its symbolic function in the cultural register?

Moreover, the question of *gender*, and its multiple forms, seems to be at the heart of this challenge to castration. Yet, even if the concept has been invented by feminists, the notion of gender is in itself nothing new. Throughout his work, Freud himself theorised *psychical bisexuality*. But his concept, which reflects an element of psychical economy, is generally ignored. Yet it is directly related to the law of the father, because it is that which feminises! When it comes to symbolising "castration", it is above all a question of a *feminisation* by the father, in the sense that the girl, like the boy, renounces a part of the drive. A phallic act which gives rise in the young subject to a multitude of economico-psychical possibilities between the masculine and the feminine.

---

[6] Freud, S. (1915). *Instincts and their Vicissitudes*. S.E. 14: 109–40. J. Strachey (Trans.). London: Hogarth, 1957.

[7] A wish that came true in 2014. But it is also interesting to note that, in respect of this law, other countries like the UK have met with little opposition, unlike France. What might explain this difference in cultural opinion?

Remember that bisexuality was also subjected to this irreducible repression, from the time when overly masculinised men were believed to have to dominate women. Nevertheless, this bipolarity of the drive came out from this repressive constraint when the phallic field was found to be shared by the two sexes. As a result, this bringing to light of the different degrees of transgenderism in a subject do not make him a pervert today, any more than yesterday.

Has everything really become possible in terms of transgression and of limits? Despite the possibility of changing the sex of one's body, has this body itself lost its sexual identity? Even if families fall apart and get back together, have the bonds of parenthood truly renounced their Oedipal representations? Isn't there always somewhere a mother and a father for a child, whoever they might be? Has a baby conceived in a test-tube really escaped from the primal scene? With the fading of the conservative ideology of which the patriarch made himself the absolute master, we imagine an overturning of the phallic limits which, from this point forward, evacuate the capacity of the psychical economy to produce the fantasy. However, the theories of infantile sexuality realised in the laboratory, the fantasy of parricide, the continuation of the complaint of the *beaten child* that we hear every day on the couch, are these not the product of all of these unprecedented phenomena belonging to our postmodern world?

So structure has not changed! We are not more transgressive. If the portrayal of the father has been modified in his imaginary representation, his law persists without equivocation. The agony of our contemporary civilisation, leading us to imagine a resurgence of perversion, in fact turns around this question of the father and parricidal desire. Only, the lifting of the inhibiting repression of the drive – blunting a little the effects of guilt in the younger generation – leads new patients to come into analysis, seeking, less frequently than before, an unlocking of their desire. Rather, they seek to identify with it, so as to grasp its singularity. Before, they came because of an "excess of castration"; now, they are anxious because they do not feel its effects strongly enough.

It is true that in the early sessions we often hear the anxiety of a drive which overflows, giving the appearance of a failure of castration, which could leads us to think of an "everyday" perversion. They say that they encounter few obstacles in their lives. However, just like in the Lacanian cures, when they were at their most popular and highly sought after, we always hear today the same *dissatisfaction*. This dissatisfaction still reveals a stable Freudian metapsychology, in its structural mechanisms, but one that is, it is true, enveloped within the ever-moving prevailing discourse. Because this persistent dissatisfaction has changed its shape, we are now more likely to see a desire saturated by an oversupply (the father today commands us to "enjoy [*jouir*]!"). The subject, under the demands of an environment buzzing with media, technology, culture, etc., has become more sensitive to the excesses of the drive (contributing to the formation of perverse traits within his structure). He comes to seek, by way of a cure, lack and repression instead. In short, he is now in search of subjective breathing space, supported by a demand just like that which, twenty years ago, pushed a future analysand to cross the threshold, for the first time, of her psychoanalyst's consulting room.

8

A Few Questions About the Idea of Ordinary Perversion

Roland Chemama

Given my title, many of you must have assumed that it contained a clear reference to Jean-Pierre Lebrun's book on the same subject.[1] However, although I would indeed like to take his work as my starting point, it is not in order to mine it for reassuring truths, but rather to look for a possibility of discussing what I see as essential questions linked to the contemporary clinic.

What does Jean-Pierre Lebrun argue in his book *Ordinary Perversion,* published in 2007? It is not, as some might believe, that the contemporary subject in general is a perverse one, nor that he or she strictly speaking falls under what we would describe, with Freud and Lacan, as the 'perverse structure'. Lebrun simply thinks that in today's world the subject's relationship to *jouissance* and desire has changed, not in the sense

[1] Lebrun, J.-P. (2007). *La perversion ordinaire*. Paris: Denoël.

R. Chemama (✉)
Fondation Européenne pour la Psychanalyse

D. Caine, C. Wright (eds.), *Perversion Now!*,
DOI 10.1007/978-3-319-47271-3_8

that individuals have become more perverse, but that social discourses have encouraged the choice of modes of *jouissance* that bring the perverse structure to mind, to say the least. However, to take this discussion further, we must first add a few clarifications.

Firstly, because I am going to try and speak about what an 'ordinary perversion' might be, I must say right away that 'perversion' can have different meanings, not all of which can be reduced to the pathological structure that would be part of the traditional clinical picture, alongside neurosis and psychosis. I tend to agree with Gérard Pommier, who argued during a recent conference in Madrid[2] that we can come across perversion in all structures, in the sense that sexual desire is fundamentally erratic, that nothing binds it to what we might call a natural object. In this way we could argue—and it would not really be an oxymoron—that the child is a 'normal' pervert: in other words, that it is normal for sexuality in the early periods of life to move through all the different possibilities, in the same way that the range of the phonemes used by the child is larger than what he will retain later.

And yet, Freud distinguishes the child's polymorphous perversion from perversion properly speaking. This is because the so-called perverse adult is not engaged in an exploration prompted by an especially mobile desire. In fact, as Freud points out, he quite often selects one partial object, which from then on comes to represent all that he can legitimately have as a source of *jouissance*. Based on this we can in fact try and distinguish what constitutes perversion as a structure. The latter consists in securing a *jouissance* we could define as full, intact and always accessible. As for desire, it is reduced to the practical search for this *jouissance*. Lacan puts this in a different way. Calling the object that causes our desire, but is itself fundamentally lost, the *object a*, he says that perversion means reinserting the object in the place from which it is missing, let us say in social exchange, which is always also an exchange of speech, and which can therefore realise the dimension of the Other. This is the case of, for example, the exhibitionist, who reintroduces the gaze precisely where it is usually (socially) excluded.

[2] I am referring to Gérard Pommier's paper, 'Pourquoi la perversion angoisse-t-elle?', given at the colloquium of the *Fondation Européen Pour La Psychanalyse*, 'Angustia y Perversiones/Angoisse et Perversions', Madrid, 16th May 2015.

Based on this summary, we can now return to a number of elements in Jean-Pierre Lebrun's analysis, which is itself a continuation of his conversations with Charles Melman in *L'homme sans gravité*.[3] The problem today is that social discourses encourage a certain denial of loss, a denial of our obligation to give up on at least some of our *jouissance* (with the specific exception of paedophilia). I know that this is all a matter of debate. However, it seems to me that in the social field today there is a kind of ideal of claiming, if we could put it that way, one's *right* to pleasure and *jouissance*, a claim that is in itself also relatively superegoic. This leads to two things: firstly, a kind of discontent for those who do not voluntarily fit this picture, but also and especially, a kind of perverse style among those who are caught up in it, a style that, for example, reduces the other to an object of consumption.

I myself showed in Madrid how modern technology facilitates what I have called the 'neo-perversions': these concern subjects who slide towards certain types of behaviour that are not, so to say, part of their structure. I will not go back to the case I discussed there, which concerned a man who was a real computer whizz, a talent that allowed him to secretly enter various virtual situations and spy on naked women. On the internet today, the most ordinary voyeurism is simply watching pornographic videos.

And perhaps in connection to this some would argue that fundamentally the fact of using a new technology (such as the internet) adds nothing new, nothing that would make the modern subject's relationship to *jouissance* any more specific. Surely there have always been spaces of pleasure where the visitor was not just able to meet prostitutes, but also access all kinds of spectacles? And yet, I do believe that there are significant differences.

I will not spend time on trying to list the different scenes that can be found on these sites, which are often classed by category so as to make things more practical, and which range from the most banal things to those that are, for example, most degrading to the female characters. It is enough to say that there is apparently no limit between what can be shown and what is forbidden. This can lead to a feeling that all objects of

[3] Melman, C. (2005). *L'homme sans gravité*. Paris: Denoël.

jouissance are equivalent or, if you wish, to a feeling of omnipresence, of a kind of ubiquity of a gaze which is reintegrated into the field of the Other and possibly becomes persecutory.

I will also not enumerate the different ways in which the subjects – who are very different from one another and who consume pornography or sometimes let themselves be consumed by it – position themselves vis-à-vis this vast field of *jouissance*. I will simply say that the accessibility of the object, which is available only at the cost of a simple internet subscription, leads to a general disappearance of any feeling of transgression. And yet this transgression could, after all, constitute the value of yesterday's perversion (let us say in the 19th century). Even transitory perverse behaviour allowed the subject to contest the norm, when it became too burdensome. Nothing of that kind happens here, which is also one of the reasons why we can no longer speak about perversion in the former sense of the term.

Having said that, I will return to the multiple meanings of the word 'perversion', as it can help us understand what facilitates the contemporary ordinary perversion. I have mentioned 'normal' perversion: the one linked to desire that has no natural object or aim. I also spoke about the child's polymorphous perversion. We should not let go of the latter—today, there is a strong tendency to restore the image of the child as pure and desexualised, unless he is corrupted by an adult. But that is not all. We should also not let go of the fact that unconscious fantasies, those that structure everyone's desire, are perverse. Now, there is certainly no gender equality in this matter. When Lacan says that sexuality is perverse, he is speaking about men. It is perverse in the sense of a kind of ordinary fetishism, which, as he argues, ties the possibility of *jouissance* to the specific and required characteristics of the object.

However, what I would like to say, and what I am more concerned with today, is that these different forms of perversion as a human potentiality no doubt encourage the adoption of the perverse patterns that are made so available to us by the modern era. If voyeurism was not an ordinary component of human sexuality, it could not, it would seem, be created ex-nihilo by modern technology. On the other hand, if the latter did not exist, not so many individuals would be obsessed by it. There are after all many young people today who over the course of many years replace any attempts at a real encounter with watching, as an everyday pastime, hours and hours of Internet porn.

Before concluding, I would nevertheless like to say that it would obviously be a simplification to understand all of our contemporaries' behaviour as simply the expression of a perversion, no matter how ordinary. Of course things are more complex than that, and I will illustrate this with a case that has been presented and discussed on other occasions, although I can only do so very briefly here.

This case concerned a female patient who confided in her analyst that she had recently met a man whom she liked and that, for the first time in her life, she felt she could start a life with someone. But before she did so, she wanted to 'make a deal'. The idea was that they would agree, in advance, that if she ever met someone else, she could go ahead with this new adventure, while also maintaining the relationship with her partner. The colleague who was presenting the case obviously did not consider adultery a perversion. However, she felt that the idea of making this 'everything is still possible' clause part of a private agreement had to do with the ordinary perversion of today's era.

This gives me the opportunity to explain that, in my opinion, although the notion I have been discussing seems to me helpful in accounting for many different aspects of modern subjectivities, I disagree with what seems to be, on this occasion, its unwarranted extension. Why can we not instead say that this patient, who is conscious of the uncontrollable nature of her desire, is trying to live with it by linking it to something that now functions as a norm or a law, even if it is by means of a private contract? Although we know the importance of contracts in masochism, not all contracts are necessarily perverse. It seems to me that in this case, which I could only touch on briefly, it is more likely evidence of a certain split – between the ideal of 'sexual freedom' and a need for norms.

And this notion of the split is where I would like to end. The modern subject can of course become caught up in a perverse discourse that commands it to enjoy at all costs. However, if at the same time the individual is not perverse in his personal structure, he is fundamentally *split*. This Freudian concept, as I have come to believe over recent years, is one of the most illuminating in trying to explain modern pathologies.

9

Perversion in the 21st Century: A Psychoanalytic Conundrum

Dany Nobus

"Modern society is perverse, not in spite of its puritanism or as if from a backlash provoked by its hypocrisy; it is in actual fact, and directly, perverse."[1] Thus spake Michel Foucault back in 1976, in the first volume of his critically acclaimed *History of Sexuality*. Rather than a trenchant reflection upon the social impact of regulatory power structures in Western civilisation during the 1970s, this provocative declaration was Foucault's idiosyncratic interpretation of the way in which the diversity of human sexual expressions had started to proliferate as distinct perversions, both at a symbolic taxonomical level and as real, embodied sub-

[1] Foucault, M. (1978). *The History of Sexuality. Volume 1: An Introduction*. R. Hurley (Trans.). New York: Random House, p. 47.

D. Nobus (✉)
Brunel University London

D. Caine, C. Wright (eds.), *Perversion Now!*,
DOI 10.1007/978-3-319-47271-3_9

jectivities, with the advent of sexological science in Europe during the second half of the nineteenth century.[2]

To most of us, although none of us would have had any direct experience of it, it would seem that the world has changed dramatically since the emergence of our *scientia sexualis* during the late Victorian era. To most of us, it would seem that the world has also changed dramatically since Foucault wrote the first volume of his *History of Sexuality*. Since Freud published his famous *Three Essays on the Theory of Sexuality*, over a century ago, restrictive moral and legal standards regulating human sexuality have been challenged successfully by sexual activists and political pressure groups, at least in the Western world.[3] The classic example, here, is the gradual de-criminalisation and de-pathologisation of homosexuality during the second half of the twentieth century, on both sides of the Atlantic.[4] At the same time, our knowledge about the genetic,

---

[2] For general historical surveys of how the term 'perversion' entered European sexological discourses and the Western cultural imagination during the second half of the nineteenth century see, for example, Lanteri-Laura, G. (1979). *Lecture des perversions. Histoire de leur appropriation médicale.* Paris: Masson; Rosario, V.A. (1997). *The Erotic Imagination: French Histories of Perversity.* New York and Oxford: Oxford University Press; Roudinesco, É. (2009). *Our Dark Side: A History of Perversion.* Cambridge: Polity; Schaffner, A.K. (2011). *Modernism and Perversion: Sexual Deviance in Sexology and Literature 1850–1930.* Basingstoke: Palgrave Macmillan; Chaperon, S. (2012). *Les origines de la sexologie (1850–1900).* Paris: Payot; Mazaleige-Labaste, J. (2014). *Les déséquilibres de l'amour. La genèse du concept de perversion sexuelle, de la Révolution française à Freud.* Paris: Ithaque.

[3] Freud, S. (1905d). *Three Essays on the Theory of Sexuality.* S.E. 7: 123–242. J. Strachey (Trans.). London: Hogarth, 1953.

[4] See American Psychiatric Association. (1987). *DSM-III-R.* Washington, DC: American Psychiatric Press. Following widespread social protest and extensive discussion, the term 'homosexuality' was removed from the 7th edition of the *DSM-II* in 1974, and replaced with 'sexual orientation disturbance (homosexuality)', to be restricted to "individuals whose sexual interests are directed primarily toward people of the same sex and who are either disturbed by, in conflict with, or wish to change their sexual orientation." The *DSM-III* (1980) continued to refer to 'ego-dystonic homosexuality' (category 302.00), yet this term was removed in the *DSM-III-R*. In the *DSM-IV-TR* (2000) category 302.9 ('sexual disorder not otherwise specified'), had as an example "persistent and marked distress about sexual orientation", which could refer equally to heterosexuality as to other sexual orientations, although it is no doubt less likely to be applied to the former case, because a predominantly straight culture is less likely to instill anxiety, shame and anger in those who identify as heterosexual than in those who do not. The latest on-line update of the 10th edition of the *International Classification of Diseases* [(*ICD-10*), 2015] still refers to 'ego-dystonic sexual orientation' in its category F66-1. It should also be noted that the psychoanalytic community has been much slower than its psychiatric counterpart in adopting a non-discriminatory policy against homosexual candidates for training—the American Psychoanalytic Association (APA) in 1991, and the International Psychoanalytical Association in 2002. See World Health Organisation. (1992). *The ICD 10 Classification of Mental and Behavioural Disorders: Clinical Descriptions and Diagnostic*

physiological and evolutionary biology of human sexuality has increased substantially, although the findings are undoubtedly less robust than its proponents would want to believe. In addition, the last fifty years have seen a veritable cornucopia of historical, sociological and philosophical research projects, often conducted in opposition to the (socio-) biological approach, on the way in which the various components of human sexuality operate in a culturally and historically contingent fashion. These projects often rely upon what Foucault described as a 'discursive formation' of truth, that is to say a "general enunciative system that governs a group of verbal performances", which exercises its power through the simultaneous construction and organisation of objects, subjective positions, concepts and strategic choices.[5] The traditional, 'natural' binaries of male and female, masculine and feminine, have accordingly been destabilised and exposed in their discursive quality of manufactured, fluid semantic performances, with no 'inner truth' other than that assigned by a "decidedly public and social discourse", which regulates, politicises and disciplines all sexual enactments.[6] Following a number of groundbreaking anthropological studies, we now also know that our Western dimorphic categories of human sexuality do not have universal applicability, insofar as quite a few non-Western cultures recognise 'alternative' sexual roles, identities and behaviours that would be considered perverse, i.e. as clear instances of sexual (psycho-)pathology, were they to occur within a Western context. Of course, apart from our moral standards, our general knowledge and our awareness of cultural differences, something else has changed about the way in which human sexuality is conceptualised, practiced and experienced. Today's sexuality is not Krafft-Ebing's, Freud's and even Foucault's sexuality anymore, because much like every other

---

Guidelines. Geneva: World Health Organisation. On the homophobic policies of the psychoanalytic establishment, see Roughton, R.E. (1995). Overcoming Antihomosexual Bias: A Progress Report. *The American Psychoanalyst,* 29 (4): 15–6; Roughton, R.E. (2002). The International Psychoanalytical Association and Homosexuality. *Journal of Gay and Lesbian Psychotherapy*, 7 (1/2): 189–96; Isay, R.A. (2009). *Becoming Gay: The Journey to Self-Acceptance*, revised and updated edition. New York: Vintage Books, pp. 147–67.

[5] Foucault, M. (1989). *Archaeology of Knowledge*. A.M. Sheridan Smith (Trans.). London: Routledge, pp. 130–1.

[6] Butler, J. (1990). *Gender Trouble: Feminism and the Subversion of Identity*. London and New York: Routledge, p. 136.

aspect of the human condition sexuality has been revolutionised as a result of the invention and domestication of the wonder that is the 'computer'. Virtual environments play a crucial part in how twenty-first century human beings live, perform and develop their sexuality, so much so that one may feel tempted to argue that a large swathe of contemporary human sexual experiences should be recognised as 'E-sexuality' or iSex. Had Lacan lived long enough to witness the current overwhelming presence of computer-mediated interactions, he may have considered adding the fourth register of E to his famous triad of the Real, the Symbolic and the Imaginary. Partly as a result of the impact of computer-mediated communication on our lives, partly owing to broader transformations in the gender and identity politics of Western culture, the language of sexuality has also changed (and expanded) dramatically over the past twenty years or so, with new notions being introduced on an almost daily basis.

In light of all this, I wonder what Foucault would have said had he written the first volume of his *History of Sexuality* in 2015 rather than 1975. If we are to take Foucault's statement as indicative of the ubiquity and ongoing multiplication of perversion under conditions of rational modernity—as a purportedly scientific category of sexual (psycho) pathology, a reifying label of sexual deviance, an insidious tool of social control and exclusion, and a type of real, embodied and subjectified sexuality, which is how he would want us to read it—then it can only come across as no longer valid, open to revision and in need of a certain *aggiornamento*. Although the term 'perversion' was never included as such in the *Diagnostic and Statistical Manual of Mental Disorders (DSM)*, the allegedly more scientific and less pejorative term 'paraphilia', which was substituted for 'sexual deviation' in the *DSM-III* and placed within the broader category of 'psychosexual disorders', has now also been removed from the *DSM-5*, and replaced with 'paraphilic disorder'.[7] What

[7] American Psychiatric Association. (1980). *Diagnostic and Statistical Manual of Mental Disorders (DSM), third edition* (*DSM-III*). Washington, DC: American Psychiatric Press, pp. 266–7. A critical analysis of the changing psychiatric terminology for sexual disorders, and the decision-making processes underpinning the changes, would require a book-length study. At the risk of providing the reader with a simplified 'wikipediatic' survey, the changes can be summarised as follows. In the first edition of the *DSM* (1952), 'sexual deviation' (category 320.6) was included as a type of 'sociopathic personality disturbance' (alongside 'antisocial reaction', 'dyssocial reaction' and 'addiction') and defined as "deviant sexuality which is not symptomatic of more extensive syndromes, such as

distinguishes a 'paraphilia' from a 'paraphilic disorder' is that the latter is "causing distress or impairment to the individual", or involves a paraphilia "whose satisfaction has entailed personal harm, or risk of harm, to others".[8]

In sum, judging by the world's most prominent diagnostic manual of mental disorders, which Foucault would definitely have regarded as one of the most powerful instruments of social control, perversion (under the heading of 'sexual deviation' and subsequently 'paraphilia') has shrunk to the point where only a handful of disordered individuals remain—those who suffer from their paraphilia (a clear minority), and those whose paraphilia constitutes a crime within a given judicial system of social regulation. Echoing Tim Dean, in a thought-provoking paper which has implicitly served as the intellectual background to my exposition until now, one is therefore prompted to raise the vexed question: "Where have all the perverts gone?".[9]

---

schizophrenia and obsessional reactions … [and which] includes most of the cases formerly classed as 'psychopathic personality with pathologic sexuality'. The diagnosis will specify the type of the pathologic [*sic*] behavior, such as homosexuality, transvestism, pedophilia, fetishism and sexual sadism (including rape, sexual assault, mutilation)", pp. 38–9. In the *DSM-II* (1968), section 302 (sexual deviations) was completely revised to include eight examples: homosexuality, fetishism, pedophilia, transvestitism, exhibitionism, voyeurism, sadism and masochism. It specified that the category of sexual deviation should be reserved for individuals whose sexual preference is "directed primarily toward objects other than people of the opposite sex, toward sexual acts not usually associated with coitus, or toward coitus performed under bizarre circumstances, as in necrophilia, pedophilia, sexual sadism, and fetishism", p. 44. When the *DSM-III* (1980) was published, 'sexual deviation' was replaced with 'paraphilia', under the broader category of 'psychosexual disorders', whereas the term 'ego-dystonic homosexuality' (category 302.00) was substituted for 'sexual orientation disturbance'. In the *DSM-III-R* (1987) 'psychosexual disorders' were replaced with 'sexual disorders', including the sub-set of the 'paraphilias', and 'atypical paraphilia' became the 'paraphilia not otherwise specified'. In the *DSM-IV* (1994) and *DSM-IV-TR* (2000), paraphilias were defined as "recurrent, intense sexually arousing fantasies, sexual urges or behaviors generally involving (i) nonhuman objects, (ii) the suffering or humiliation of oneself or one's partner, or (iii) children or other nonconsenting persons that occur over a period of 6 months [Criterion A], which cause clinically significant distress or impairment in social, occupational, or other important areas of functioning [Criterion B]." In *DSM-V* (2013), category 302.9 has been renamed as 'unspecified paraphilic disorder', which no longer includes any reference to sexual orientation. See APA. (1980). *Diagnostic and Statistical Manual of Mental Disorders (DSM), third edition (DSM-III)*. Washington, DC: American Psychiatric Press; APA. (2000). *Diagnostic and Statistical Manual of Mental Disorders, fourth edition, text revision (DSM-IV-TR)*. Washington, DC: American Psychiatric Press; APA. (2013). *Diagnostic and Statistical Manual of Mental Disorders, fifth edition (DSM-5)*. Washington, DC-London: American Psychiatric Publishing.

[8] APA, 2013, op. cit., pp. 685–6.

[9] Dean, T. (2008). The Frozen Countenance of the Perversions. *Parallax*, 14 (2): 93.

The question is by no means rhetorical, nor is it meant to insinuate that the perverts have disappeared from the socio-political and clinical radar altogether, that they have once again manoeuvred themselves below the surface, or that they have managed to cunningly change their sexual guise so that they can go unrecognised in our pervasively perverse twenty-first century society. Answering his own question, Dean is as clear as he is bold:

> If today one wishes to see creatures such as the buffalo that were amazingly populous during the nineteenth century, he must repair to the zoo; likewise if one wishes to observe perverts in the twenty-first century, she must turn to where they have been corralled, in the pages of the [very Lacanian] *Ecole de la Cause Freudienne*.[10]

Before I unpack this statement further, I must insist that, much like buffalos do not *only* continue to exist in the zoo—although they might be easier to observe there than in those rather inhospitable habitats where they continue to roam freely—perverts are not *only* to be found in the *Ecole de la Cause Freudienne*, in its pages, that is, and this is presumably not what Dean had in mind in the first place. Restricting myself to the Anglophone world, although I have no reason to think that things would be different in Francophone or Hispanophone countries, perverts continue to exist in the world of glamorous make-up products, as well as in common parlance, that is to say in the language of the street-corner, where they have even been turned into a verb: "He was definitely perving it to her last night!". Furthermore, they regularly feature on the cover of tabloid newspapers, where the word 'pervert' has become almost synonymous with such other sensationalist terms as 'sex monster' and 'sexual predator', and where it is invariably utilised to characterise rapists, paedophiles and other callous perpetrators of heinous sex crimes. And if it is true that perverts live on in the *Ecole de la Cause freudienne*—in the pages of its books, papers and conference reports, we must assume—it should also be acknowledged that they continue to operate in other psychoanalytic schools of the Lacanian orientation, and in many psy-

[10] ibid., p. 96.

choanalytic organisations outside the Lacanian stream, for example in the International Psycho-Analytic Association, and its various neo-Freudian, Annafreudian, Kleinian and independent traditions, in their books, papers and conference reports, that is.[11] And so Dean's original question—'Where have all the perverts gone?'—should really be replaced with a different one, which is much more difficult to answer: 'Why do perverts continue to exist within psychoanalytic circles, at a time when even the American Psychiatric Association, the quintessential representative of a pathologising power system, has definitively abandoned the category of paraphilia as a mental disorder which *de facto* necessitates medical and/or legal intervention?'

Of all the controversies that psychoanalysis has elicited over the years, of all the mystifications that it has reportedly sustained, this may very well be the biggest conundrum of all. What is the point of perversion? Within the space of this chapter, I can only provide a rudimentary outline of a possible answer to this question, and for didactic reasons, I shall briefly develop it along four different axes, which may also serve as motives and explanations for the continued psychoanalytic existence of the pervert: (i) the authority argument; (ii) distinct, objective clinical realities; (iii) the anxiety of the analyst; (iv) the institutional framework governing psychoanalytic training, with its inclusion and exclusion criteria. The first two motives are readily acknowledged by psychoanalysts themselves, although it is questionable whether they can be upheld as solid reasons for maintaining the category of perversion. The other two motives are far less likely to be recognised by the psychoanalytic community, yet they may very well constitute the more important, albeit more insidious reasons as to why the category of perversion is maintained. I shall concentrate on the first two motives, restrict myself to some brief remarks about the third motive, and leave the fourth one largely unexplored, as a hypothesis for further investigation.

[11] The psychoanalytic literature on perversion remains vast, and although some authors recognise the problematic status of the concept, it continues to inform psychoanalytic theory and practice across institutional and intellectual boundaries. For recent non-Lacanian psychoanalytic views, see for example, André, J., Catherine, C . and Guyomard, P. (Eds). (2015). *La perversion, encore.* Paris: Presses Universitaires de France. For a Klein-inspired approach, see Wood, H. (2014) Working with Problems of Perversion. *British Journal of Psychotherapy*, 30 (4): 422–37.

The first motive crucially relies on the theoretical contributions of the founders (architects, engineers and recognised keepers) of psychoanalysis in the realm of perversion in order to secure its survival as a clinical category or structure. Following Dean in the aforementioned paper, it is interesting to see, in this respect, how one of Lacan's definitions of perversion, namely that it consists of a *père-version*—a turning towards, or an appeal to the father (the paternal law, the phallic function, and everything it entails)—can also be applied to how psychoanalysts continue to endorse the notion of perversion with reference to, and because of its allegedly consistent and coherent conceptual status in the works of, say, Freud and Lacan.[12]

In Freud's works, two central paradigms of perversion can be identified, that of the drive and that of fetishism. In the first paradigm, the drive is defined as an intrinsically perverse, bio-psychological force, which alternates between activity (sadism) and passivity (masochism), and which under normal, i.e. neurotic circumstances, is curtailed into and channeled towards some form of genital hetero-sexuality, under the influence of shame, guilt and so-called 'civilised' sexual morality. The first implication of this view is that the classic question as to how someone ends up being a pervert shifts towards an alternative puzzle, notably how the child with its polymorphously perverse disposition ever succeeds in becoming sexually 'normal'. The conventional Freudian solution would evidently be 'through the dissolution of the Oedipus complex', were it not for the fact that Freud never believed that anyone is ever able to completely resolve the Oedipal conflict. For Freud, the successful resolution of the Oedipus complex is but an ideal scenario, which does not accord with any actual, lived sexual experience.[13] The second, more wide-ranging implication is that, from a Freudian point of view, the traditional medico-sexological category of perversion, as one of four possible alterations of the natural sexual instinct (alongside augmentation, diminution and abolition), no longer makes sense, because the sexual instinct, once

[12] For perversion as *père-version*, see for example, Lacan, J. (1975–6). *Le Séminaire. R.S.I.*, *Ornicar?* 5, leçon du 8 avril 1975, pp. 37–46; Lacan, J. (1995). "Spring Awakening." S. Rodríguez (Trans.). *Analysis,* 6, p. 34.

[13] Freud, S. (1916–17). *Introductory Lectures on Psycho-Analysis.* S.E. 16. J. Strachey (Trans.). London: Hogarth, 1963, p. 337.

re-defined as a (partial) drive, is inherently perverse, i.e. excessive, disorganised, versatile, uncontrollable and endlessly varied in its permutations and combinations of its four constitutive components (source, urge, goal and object).[14] In the second paradigm, that of fetishism, perversion is the outcome of the male child's reacting to sexual difference, more specifically to his observation that the mother does not have a penis, with something called disavowal (*Verleugnung*), through the installation of a fetish-object, which then serves the purpose of maintaining the belief that the mother has not been castrated.[15] As Freud had already claimed early on in his career, the fetish is a substitute for the "painfully missed, prehistorically postulated penis of the woman" (*schmerzlich vermißten, prähistorisch postulierten, Penis der Weiber*).[16] Apart from the fact that Freud would subsequently be forced to concede that he did not know why some boys react to this observation, and the associated castration anxiety, with disavowal, whereas others (the majority of children, we must assume) manage to overcome it in a more streamlined, or at least less complicated way, the implication is also that girls are exempt from disavowal and that women cannot grow up to be fetishists, because they cannot experience castration anxiety.

Until this day, the Freudian mechanism of disavowal tends to be employed by psychoanalysts in order to account for the mental economy of the pervert, despite the fact that Freud himself initially reserved it for just one particular type of 'sexual proclivity', before eventually extrapolating the mechanism to a wider range of psychic constellations, and reducing its power to that of a 'half-measure'. Indeed, in Freud's posthumously published "An Outline of Psycho-Analysis", disavowal no longer represents the distinctive aetiological mechanism of fetishism (and, by extension, of perversion), but denotes a much more general type of withdrawal from (sexual) reality: "Disavowals of this kind occur very often and not

[14] Freud, S. (1915c). *Instincts and their Vicissitudes*. S.E. 14: 109–40. J. Strachey (Trans.). London: Hogarth, 1957.

[15] Freud, S. (1927). *Fetishism*. S.E. 21: 147–157. J. Strachey (Trans.). London: Hogarth, 1961.

[16] Falzeder, E. (Ed.) (2002). *The Complete Correspondence of Sigmund Freud and Karl Abraham 1907–1925*. C. Schwarzacher (Trans.). London and New York: Karnac, p. 106. See also Rose, L. (1988). Freud and Fetishism: Previously Unpublished Minutes of the Vienna Psychoanalytic Society. *The Psychoanalytic Quarterly*, 57: pp. 147–66.

only with fetishists; and whenever we are in a position to study them they turn out to be half-measures, incomplete attempts at detachment from reality."[17] Hence, in Freud's works, there is no such thing as a specific nosological category of (sexual) perversion, for three reasons. Firstly, the intrinsic perversity of the drive, which can never be conclusively cancelled out, makes every human being into a residual pervert, so that perversion is but a measure of the success with which a human being has managed to control this polymorphous perversity of the drive.[18] Secondly, starting from the assumption that the drive is intrinsically perverse, the traditional category of perversion is no longer valid or, more fundamentally, if it is to be used as a synonym for a specific alteration of the sexual drive, then fixated sexual normality (reproductive, hetero-sexual genital normativity, or normophilia) would paradoxically become the most perverse expression of the human sexual spectrum. Thirdly, with the theoretical extension and 'normalisation' of disavowal, fetishism loses its value as the distinct, paradigmatic sexual economy of perversion or, alternatively, one might say that all human beings have fetishistic tendencies, or that perversion is but a function of the balance between various types of withdrawal from traumatic (sexual) realities.

At this point, one may feel inclined to argue that Freud was confused, or did not care all that much about perversion, much as he did not have all that much to say about psychosis, and that the category of perversion only came into its own with Lacan, in whose works it emerged as the third of the three great mental structures, alongside neurosis and psychosis, and where it was coherently theorised as conditioned by the psychic mechanism of disavowal (*désaveu, déni*). And in effect, Lacan is much more effusive than Freud when it comes to perversion, both in his elaborations on the generic term, and in his discussion of its variations, especially the Freudian triad of sadism, masochism and fetishism, so much so that a detailed critical analysis of Lacan's comments on perversion would

[17] Freud, S. (1940a)[1938]. *An Outline of Pychoanalysis.* S.E. 23: 139–207. J. Strachey (Trans.). London: Hogarth, 1953, p. 204.

[18] On perversion as a historical (and contemporary) diagnosis of sexual self-control, see the fascinating recent study by Mazaleigue-Labaste, J. (2014). *Les déséquilibres de l'amour. La genèse du concept de perversion sexuelle, de la Révolution française à Freud.* Paris: Ithaque.

require a volume the size of a scholarly monograph.[19] Nonetheless, whatever Lacanians may have said about the distinctiveness of perversion, and the specificity of the 'perverse structure' in Lacan's writings and seminars, this is more representative of their own desire to organise and standardise Lacan's work, in an act that is not dissimilar to what Otto Fenichel and David Rapaport did with Freud's ideas after World War II, than it is of what Lacan himself effectively contributed to the question of perversion. Unlike neurosis and psychosis, perversion never received the 'structural treatment' from Lacan. Nowhere, neither in his voluminous writings, nor in his equally elaborate seminars, did Lacan single out disavowal as the key aetiological mechanism in perversion, separate from repression and foreclosure. On those very rare occasions when he did refer to perversion or one of its 'subsidiaries' in properly structural terms, i.e. as a relationship between subject, object and Other, one feels extremely hard-pressed to recognise in these developments evidence of perversion as a distinct psychic structure and a separate mental economy. When he launched his theory of the four discourses during the late 1960s and early 1970s, he designated one of them as the 'discourse of the hysteric', and proclaimed that psychosis resides 'outside discourse', but to the best of my knowledge he never said anything about where perversion is to be situated in these discursive arrangements, and never contemplated the possibility of a 'discourse of perversion'.[20] Whenever Lacan examined the eroto-sexual dynamics of fetishism, sadism and masochism, he did not hesitate to do this under the banner of perversion, yet this in itself does not warrant the identification of a separate structure of perversion in Lacan's theory. If anything, Lacan argued in favour of a continuity between perversion and neurosis, as is crystal clear from the following passage from *Seminar*

[19] The closest we have in English to this type of work is the recent book by Stephanie Swales, which remains hugely instructive, despite the fact that it tends to interpret Lacan's remarks on perversion from a streamlined (post) Lacanian perspective, rather than problematising the text. See Swales, S. (2012). *Perversion. A Lacanian Psychoanalytic Approach to the Subject.* New York and London: Routledge. The most succinct post-Lacanian synthesis of Lacan's take on perversion can be found in Fink, B. (1997). *A Clinical Introduction to Lacanian Psychoanalysis: Theory and Technique.* Cambridge, MA and London: Harvard University Press, pp. 165–202. Lacan's scattered comments on perversion have also been discussed extensively in Fondation du Champ freudien. (1990). *Traits de perversion dans les structures cliniques.* Paris: Navarin.

[20] Lacan, J. (2007)[1969–70]. *The Seminar, Book XVII: The Other Side of Psychoanalysis.* R. Grigg (Trans.). New York: W. W. Norton & Company.

V, where he also expressed his disagreement with Freud: "Perversion does not appear as the pure and simple manifestation of a drive, but it seems to be attached to a dialectical context which is as subtle, as composite, as rich in compromise, and as ambiguous, as a neurosis."[21] Later in the seminar, he was even more explicit about the neurotic 'quality' of perversion: "[P]erversion … also presents itself as a symptom, and not as the pure and simple manifestation of an unconscious desire … [T]here is as much *Verdrängung* [repression] in a perversion as there is in a symptom.".[22]

If a 'turning towards the father' does not yield the hoped-for results, and should force us to reconsider the value of the term perversion as a clinical category *cum* structure, the second reason for maintaining the notion appeals to 'objective clinical realities'. Over the years, many psychoanalysts, including quite a few eminent Lacanians, have argued in favour of the preservation of perversion because the notion allegedly captures a clinical picture that is radically different from neurosis and psychosis. Persuasive as this argument may be, it is contradictory at best and disingenuous at worst, because many psychoanalysts, especially those working within the Lacanian tradition, simultaneously confess that they rarely get to see, much less work with this separate clinical reality, which invariably drives them to study perversion in the literary pages of Sade, Mishima, Gide, Genet or Klossowski.[23] One may object to this point that just because a clinical reality does not come to the attention of the psychoanalyst it should not be concluded that it does not exist. This may be true, but if it is true that perverts do not tend to find their way to the psychoanalytic consultation room, it should not be concluded either that they *do* exist—elsewhere, in their happy satisfied sexual environments, underground or behind bars … Of course, it goes without saying that psychoanalysts do come across instances of fetishism, masochism, sadism, exhibitionism, transvestitism, and other 'perverse' or paraphilic

[21] Lacan, J. (1998)[1957–8]. *Le Séminaire, Livre V : Les formations de l'inconscient.* J.-A. Miller (Ed.). Paris: Seuil, pp. 230–1. My translation.

[22] ibid., p. 336. My translation.

[23] See, for example, Castanet, H. (1992). *Regard et perversion. A partir des* Lois de l'Hospitalité *de Pierre Klossowski.* Nice: Z'éditions; Millot, C. (1996). *Gide Genet Mishima. Intelligence de la perversion* Paris: Gallimard; Jadin, J.-M. (1997). *André Gide et sa perversion.* Paris: Arcanes; Castanet, H. (1999). *La perversion* Paris: Anthropos, pp. 113–85; Uvsløkk, G. (2011). *Jean Genet. Une écriture des perversions.* Amsterdam and New York: Rodopi.

urges, fantasies and acts—'atypical' sexual interests which may be intense and persistent, and which may cause distress or impairment to the subject in question and/or entail harm, or the risk of harm to others. In some cases, these interests may in themselves be associated with anxiety, in other cases the anxiety may stem from the fear of being found out or being apprehended by law enforcers, especially when the sexual interest constitutes a criminal act. This clinical reality in itself, however, does not warrant the usage of the diagnostic category of perversion, even when it is clear that the subject does not suffer from his or her condition, because psychoanalysts should know better than to infer structure from symptom, category from trait, condition from sign, personality from cluster.[24]

Aside from these two motives, which would be readily admitted but which may not stand up to detailed scrutiny, there may be two more important reasons as to why psychoanalysts insist on preserving the notion of perversion. These motives would not be openly admitted, but may be more operative, in a surreptitious fashion, than the others. I will call the first motive the anxiety of the analyst, and the second one the desire of the psychoanalytic institution, and will restrict myself to some brief reflections on each.

One does not need extensive clinical experience as a mental health care professional—psychiatrist, psychotherapist, or psychoanalyst—to ascertain that some patients are more 'cooperative' than others, that some clients are more compliant with the rules of the game than others, that some patients are particularly easy-going whereas others are intensely challenging. Whereas Freud averred that most patients find it relatively easy to talk about their symptom(s) and only succeed in disclosing their (sexual) fantasy with great shame and embarrassment, some patients do put their (sexual) fantasy and erotic practices on the psychoanalytic table

[24] It is not uncommon for Lacanian psychoanalysts to refer to 'perverse traits', by which they mean non-normative, atypical sexual features in a patient's clinical picture, yet these are generally reserved for neurotic and psychotic patients whose sexual interests fall outside the mainstream .. Indeed, for a Lacanian, the 'perverse trait' almost by definition, and quite paradoxically, indicates that the patient is not perverse, which raises the question as to how the sexual interests of someone who is considered to be perverse, in a structural sense, ought to be understood. Not as a symptom, surely, because this would render the underlying structure neurotic again. For a more detailed discussion of this problematic, see Nobus, D. (2009). Perversion as Symptom: On Defining the Sexuality of the Other. *Analysis*, 15: 21–30.

from the very beginning of the treatment, and sometimes even at the start of the first session.[25] And whereas Lacan claimed that the transference is governed by the analysand's attribution of the function of the 'supposed-subject-of-knowing' (*sujet-supposé-savoir*), there are patients who do not invest the psychoanalyst with any knowledge at all, insofar as they are simply looking for a quick practical solution or for a professional validation of their condition.[26] Whether these 'alternative' clinical situations are testament to a clinical reality that is separate from neurosis and psychosis remains to be seen, yet in many of the aforementioned instances psychoanalysts may be led to diagnose perversion merely because they are confronted with their own anxiety. In other words, perversion then becomes a counter-transference diagnosis which serves the purpose of alleviating the anxiety of the analyst, when the analysand is seen (or heard) to infract the standard rules and regulations of the analytic space, when he or she brings irregularity to the treatment or for some reason elicits stress and discomfort in the analyst. More radically put, perversion may be no more no less than a name given by the analyst to the perceived *jouissance* of the Other, when it consciously or unconsciously triggers anxiety and threatens to destabilise his or her professional comfort.

Finally, and by way of hypothesis, I would not be surprised if the term perversion also serves the purpose of keeping psychoanalytic institutions in a state of desire, as opposed to a state of *jouissance*, or a state where desire and *jouissance* can be negotiated as two conflicting sides of the institutional economy. In preserving perversion as a clinical structure, a larger number of candidates can be excluded from psychoanalytic training, and the institution of psychoanalysis does not run the risk of descending into an organisation where the law of the master is not fully recognised, or where institutional hierarchies are not respected. Non-conformist and innovator that he was, Lacan's candidacy for psychoanalytic training could have been easily rejected by the *Société Psychanalytique de Paris* on the grounds that he was a pervert, and indeed his experimentation with

[25] On the problematic issue of the fantasy as something that needs to be 'confessed to', see Freud, S. (1919e). *'A Child is Being Beaten': A Contribution to the Study of the Origin of Sexual Perversions.* S.E. 17: 175–205. J. Strachey (Trans.). London: Hogarth, 1955.

[26] On the notion of *sujet-supposé-savoir*, see Lacan, J. (1994). *The Four Fundamental Concepts of Psycho-Analysis.* A. Sheridan (Trans.). Harmondsworth: Penguin, pp. 230–43.

the variable-length session, his trenchant critique of ego-psychology as behavioural engineering, and his visceral aversion to institutional formalisms, may very well have convinced some people in the International Psycho-Analytic Association that he was undoubtedly a pervert who should never have been allowed to become a psychoanalyst, much less a training-analyst. Perverts allow psychoanalytic institutions to function without those troublesome people who do not particularly like authority, regulatory frameworks, and endlessly regurgitated knowledge, especially when it comes from the mouth of a designated master.

As a parting shot, I would like all those who still employ the notion of perversion to think about their reasons for doing so, although I would be happy to excuse the tabloid journalists and those hanging around street-corners from the exercise. Partly because the world has changed since Krafft-Ebing, since Freud, since Lacan and since Foucault, partly because even the *DSM* no longer takes paraphiliacs very seriously, partly because perversion has always been one of the most conceptually unstable and diffuse psychoanalytic notions, partly because psychoanalysts have a duty and responsibility to work through their own anxieties—in their clinical practice as well as within their institutions—I would like to see whether a proper rationale for maintaining the non-concept of perversion can be generated. If or when the thought-process takes place, it may result in the question 'Perversion Now?' finally being resolved with the answer 'Perversion No!'

10

Wor(l)ds Apart: Perverse Effects in Postcolonial Times, or a Question of Structure?

Ariana Cziffra

Freud's paper 'A child is being beaten'[1] still provides an account of the ways in which neurotics elaborate a fantasy based on a certain idea, or belief, that was born from the repression of previous versions leading to this new idea. Another point Freud makes in this paper is that underlying fantasies always imply a perverse dimension, and that neurotics repress this dimension while perverts act it out. Neurosis can thus be approached as the 'negative' of perversion, a negative in the photographic sense.

However, if perversion is envisaged by Freud as the 'positive' of neurosis, it is precisely not so much as a flip side, as in a Moebius strip type of continuum, but rather as a different cut altogether, if we think about the positive in terms of etching, for instance. We would therefore have to deal with a neurotic structure that occasionally flips into a perverse-like

[1] Freud, S. (1919b). *'A Child is Being Beaten': A Contribution to the Study of the Origins of Sexual Perversions.* S.E. 17: 175–205. J. Strachey (Trans.). London: Hogarth, 1955.

A. Cziffra (✉)
C.F.A.R. Affiliate

D. Caine, C. Wright (eds.), *Perversion Now!*,
DOI 10.1007/978-3-319-47271-3_10

mode on the one hand, and a perverse structure that, on the other hand, remains distinctly separate.

The cultural shift operated by an id-driven world goes along with the perversity of a modern version of the capitalist discourse, one that sells the idea that nearly everything can be obtained very quickly just by pressing a button. The 21st century may have brought about a "new psychic economy",[2] one that tends to collapse the difference between the logical times of the unconscious into a succession of instants that threaten to foreclose the subjective dimension of desire by forever introducing real objects in the place of lack. Yet is this enough to conclude that the perversity of such a system produces more perversion in the structural sense? I do not think so. If today's unlimited demand for more and more *jouissance* gets in the way, for a considerable number of people, of seeking analysis to try to situate themselves differently, it may also serve to test our analyst's desire in challenging times.

It is said, in Europe at least, that this era is marked by 'a crisis of meaning'. Yet from a psychoanalytic standpoint, we can hear the extent to which human subjects are under constant threat of turning into little objects, and how many young people growing up without the equivocal dimension of language find themselves stuck in a 'sole meaning' that can be soul destroying. If the modern 'system' has perverse effects, it is perhaps insofar as these can be maddening for subjects whose psychic structures are particularly shaky in the first place.

While questioning the relations and differences between madness, perversion, and indeed neurosis in their contemporary manifestations, I will, in this paper, begin by differentiating between perversion as a clinical structure, fantasies as perverse for everyone, and perverse scenarios or defences as avatars within which people come more or less close to the *object (a)*. This will lead me to question what I have been encountering in Mauritius, in and out of the consulting room, and which has often sounded like ambivalent fascination with fantasised versions of the 'baddy'.

---

[2] This phrase was coined by Charles Melman at the very start of his exchanges with Jean-Pierre Lebrun in *L'homme sans gravité* (2002) before being developed further in a book entitled *La nouvelle économie psychique* (2010).

From a Lacanian point of view, there is not a good or a bad fantasy, but a fundamental fantasy that motivates singular ways of seeking *jouissance*. It is what we write $ ◊ a for neurotics, and as perversion is supposed, according to Freud, to constitute the 'positive' of neurosis, it is not surprising that the perverse fantasy writes itself in reverse: a ◊ $, the pervert putting themselves in the place of the object that will cause anxiety in a divided subject that they will further split. Does this distinction between two versions or two different logics not suffice to differentiate between perversion as a structure, and those pseudo-perversions that are actually perverse traits in neurotics, or perverse defences in psychotics? Lacan tells us that the pervert turns himself into the tool of the Other's jouissance. Taking this into consideration, there remains the question of the difference between the perversions that do not transgress human rights, and those that do. Although this question remains open, it also brings back something along the lines of what is fantasised as good or bad.

A dozen years ago, Dany Nobus suggested that perversion was too often considered as 'bad' and counterproductive, and that it was worth envisaging its potential creative side.[3] He is now (see chapter 9, this volume) claiming that perversion is but a name given by anxious psychoanalysts to anybody who threatens to destabilise their comfort zone. As much as I find this new question useful and thought provoking, I want to say quite clearly that I do not think we can or should do away so easily with the undeniable fact that perverse relations do exist, even if, just as it takes two to produce madness, so it also takes at least two people for a perverse logic to take place.

In other words, the pervert needs an object-relation, and a certain relation to the Other, in order to derive satisfaction. In that sense, the new trendy expression 'narcissistic pervert' is a contradiction in terms if narcissism is meant as the impossibility of sustaining an object-relation. Real perverts are, it seems to me, very good at establishing certain types of relationships and even at sustaining them. And if the proof of this statement is not to be found in psychoanalytic textbooks, it is because it's in the pudding.

[3] This idea was put forward by Dany Nobus in 2004 during a seminar given at Brunel University, Uxbridge, UK, as part of his teachings on the M.A. "Psychoanalysis and Contemporary Society".

Depending on someone's psychic structure *and* their way of positioning themselves at different points in time, they are likely to collude or not, or more or less, with somebody who offers them an alluring transgressive perspective on a plate. The confusion I feel Dany Nobus's argument now sustains (see Chap. 9, this volume) is a misrecognition of what radically differentiates transgression from subversion. It is that crucial difference that, if I hear properly, Ian Parker (see Chap. 22, this volume) has been trying to bring to light in his 'intervention'.

In my view, perversion is at once that which characterises everyone's sexual and aggressive drives, and also, on another register, that which fixates certain individuals in constant disavowal of anything that has to do with sexual difference. Acknowledging the existence of perversion as a particular way of finding enjoyment in 'splitting' has nothing to do with implying that perverts are intrinsically 'bad' people, or at least that is not the way psychoanalysts use the term in our Freudo-Lacanian orientation. Yet by demonising a fantasised figure of the pervert, the contemporary social discourse indulges in a collective *jouissance* that threatens to be more harmful than that of actual perverts by turning the average neurotic or psychotic into the accomplice of a perverse social discourse, i.e. a discourse that outcasts certain people on dubious grounds.

When a psychoanalyst thinks that someone may be a pervert, they only think so, and they can never be sure, because diagnosis is always a bet and being mistaken is always a possibility. Ultimately the proof is in the pudding, i.e. psychic structure, be it perverse, neurotic or psychotic, can only be properly revealed when the logic of a fundamental fantasy comes to be unveiled, which usually take years if not decades. Not every analysand is prepared to go that far though.

One major difference between the way in which we, as analysts, make use of diagnostic categories, and the way other people draw upon commonplace and erroneous ideas about perversion, is that psychoanalysts do not 'call' people perverts. We may however feel like 'treating' perversion by hearing it differently, rather than rushing to participate in the *jouissance* it calls for. Except that those who tend to come to the consulting room are more likely to be those who have had something to do with a pervert rather than being perverts themselves, even though some analysts testify of their clinical work with actual perverts. This does not prevent us from wondering, no matter the signifiers used by the analysand, whether they actually are or have been entangled with a pervert. I will even go further and affirm that the analysis of the one who suffers a perverse relationship can ultimately have effects on the posture of their potentially perverse partner, even if the latter never comes to address a psychoanalyst. But I suppose each one's structure will remain the same even if a new knotting takes place.

If perversion is a name indeed, it is not a label but a just word, i.e. a way for someone to find a bearing and invent a way of putting a question to work. This is very different to calling someone a selfish bastard, which is what the new appellation 'narcissistic pervert' seems to mean in what has now become common parlance.

I am therefore in favour of keeping the term perversion in order to think about clinical work, especially since the ambiguous resonance it carries, in its Lacanian translation as "*père-version*" in French, still enables me to work through it as a question. Using this signifier in such a subversive way, i.e. not only as a 'term' reserved to designate those who are mostly busy disavowing castration, could also apply to psychosis and even extend to neurosis, just as the *sinthome* is not exclusively reserved to psychotics. And just as neurotics, perverts and psychotics do not weave a sinthome in the same way, we would still be able to consider the possible difference(s) between a neurotic *père-version*, a psychotic *père-version*, and a properly perverse *père-version*, bearing in mind that every human being is bound to struggle with phallic issues and that the resolution of the Oedipus complex is an ideal, i.e. impossible to fully achieve. Taking that on board implies that we, as analysts, have to recognise our own (little or big) *père-versions* in order not to risk bringing these to the consulting room.

Somebody once said about Freud—was it Serge André?—that he had de-moralised perversion. What is undeniable is that perversion as a structure, and indeed anything that looks or sounds like it, usually poses a moral problem to those who have to deal with its effects in real life, and to the few psychoanalysts who have had to wonder how to handle the particular transference it sets up.

About the odd cohabitation between diagnosis and insult that has driven psychiatric terminology to carefully get rid of designations like 'madness' etc., Lucien Israël says this about perversion:

> It is more than an insult to tell someone that he is a pervert. But is it really injurious? Were he to feel injured, he would demonstrate that he was not a pervert in the first place. If the term 'perverse' is not used as an insult, other terms can do. Before going any further, let us imagine what would happen if A called B a pervert. In today's context, B would be quite satisfied or at least rather flattered and in this reaction we would be able to read what offers itself as the most recent discoveries about perversion. The fact that B is flattered to be called a pervert signifies something for him whose recognition he gets to read in that which A told him. What he reads is a sort of slightly worried admiration concerning a certain knowledge. We call a pervert somebody who knows a lot. Who knows a lot about what? About "how to do it"? How to do it, of course, in order to find sexual partners, and it is usually to a man that this compliment-insult is addressed. The pervert knows how to seduce women. It would not be without interest to study who is tempted to call someone a pervert in this way.

The date was 1974, the Seminar was entitled *La jouissance de l'hystérique*.[4]

Since then, some psychoanalysts have come across female versions of "the pervert", or so they say. Could perversion be conjugated in the feminine form then? Besides perverse mothers, is it structurally possible for women to be perverse?

In *L'imposture perverse*,[5] Serge André gives a clinical account of his experience with a number of supposedly confirmed 'perverts' by constructing cases that aim to show exactly how each pervert subject expresses their particular way of disavowing 'castration'. Far from being judgemental about these analysands, he explains how this denial or disavowal was put in place, why it became the only available solution for the subject, and what each of them was able to shift, or not, in their analysis with him. I was particularly interested in his readiness to consider female perversion as a possible diagnosis, unlike Freud or Lacan who seem to reserve this diagnosis only to men and mothers.

---

[4] Israël, L. (1996). *La jouissance de l'hystérique, Séminaire 1974*. Paris: Les Cahiers d'Arcanes. (My translation).

[5] André, S. (1993). *L'imposture perverse*. Paris: Seuil, 1993.

If we follow Parveen Adams' argument in chapter 3 of *The Emptiness of the Image*,[6] not all women who flirt with perversion are bound to be hysteric, obsessional or psychotic. She argues that lesbian sadomasochism as a new sexuality presents both similarities and differences with traditionally male masochistic perversions. She sums this up in this way:

> The similarities lie in the scenarios which involve fetishes, whipping, bondage, all that goes with the factor of fantasy and suspense; the differences are that lesbian sadomasochism appears not to be compulsive, can just as easily be genital or not, and is an affair of women. What is similar is what flows from disavowal and leads to a degenitalisation of sexuality, and yet the lesbian sadomasochist has the capacity for genital pleasure. [...] Technically, when disavowal leads to fetishism and beyond that to sadomasochism, we *have* to speak of perversion.[7]

In this paper entitled 'Of female bondage', Parveen Adams thus draws an unequivocal diagnostic conclusion. Yet does it suffice to have a perverse sexual scenario set up in order to be able to say *who* in this scenario is a pervert, or not? The actual pervert would be, I suppose, the one who stages and manages the costumes, the roles and the timing, even when he or she appears to be submissive.

Although Freud and Lacan did not consider perversion as a possible structure for women, we cannot deny that perverse *behaviour* now overtly takes place among subjects that are anatomically female. The question of whether these supposedly female subjects inscribe themselves on the feminine side of the structure or not is quite another matter. In her paper on 'Ravage and the Desire of the Analyst,'[8] Marie-Hélène Brousse says there is no contradiction between different aspects of the unlimited translating into ravage and/or ravishment, since ravage is related to *penisneid*, and one possible way of desiring the penis is to "ravish it from men", says Lacan in *Le savoir du psychanalyste*. Is that to say that the lesbian

[6] Adams, P. (1996). *The Emptiness of the Image. Psychoanalysis and Sexual Differences*. London: Routledge.

[7] ibid., p. 47.

[8] Brousse, M.-H. (2002). 'Ravage and the Desire of the Analyst'. *Almanac of Psychoanalysis III, The Logical Time of Ravishment*, GIEP, pp. 67–73.

sadomasochist is but a neurotic masquerading as a fetishist? Or are feminine *jouissance* and perversion not exclusive of one another?

Once again, we should not be too quick in judging what is structurally perverse for particular subjects, and what is a mere effect of social and global changes effected by the capitalist discourse combined with the advent of modern technology that, in Mauritius at least, seem to have just been roughly collaged onto an otherwise traditional culture belonging to another time.

If the new fashionable "narcissistic pervert" diagnostic category—now readily accessible to account for the difficulties some women encounter with the sexual non-rapport—has reached the Mauritian shores, it did not fail to bring along ravaging effects.

While reported cases of incest and paedophilia have officially increased, some people with particular *(a)versions* of the sexual real, which is, to some extent, always traumatic, often make a dubious use of the legal framework to defend against the possibility of knowing something about their (unconscious) fantasy. It does of course make quite a difference whether the one who denounces and sues a supposed abuser is subject to paranoid delusions, whether they're a neurotic projecting their repressed conflicting desires onto a good enough scapegoat for it, or whether they have accidentally found themselves being subjected to a form of "actual" abuse. And while this statement could apply anywhere in the world, the post-colonial real introduces another complexity with regard to transgression and subversion.

Could the stabilising function of fixed religious identifications in Mauritius be related to an anxiety about colonial History repeating itself? The fact that nearly everyone has and practices a religion, and the fact that both white and mixed race "creole"[9] people now share the Christian faith, seems to have worked as a useful sinthome or père-version to keep collective violence at bay, but at a certain cost. The social Superego seems to demand that everyone remains in their place, in their class, in their caste. This is beginning to slightly shift now, so that new cultural symptoms are surfacing.

An issue of the French magazine *L'Express* dating from 2014 uses *Dans la tête des narcissistic pervert* [Inside the minds of narcissistic perverts] as

[9] I am referring here to people whose ancestors were both masters and slaves.

its main headline.[10] However limited the readership, readers talk (or gossip) and various "professional psychologists" end up giving their opinion publicly. A number of charities concerned with the protection of all kinds of "victims" then recuperate the new diagnostic category and include it in their vocabulary. An article in a Mauritian newspaper was published last year on the so-called "narcissistic perverts" that follows a DSM logic, i.e. if someone presents this and that type of behaviour, then they are likely to be narcissistic perverts.

Most people tend to believe this, as it is presented as a quasi-scientific fact, and thanks to the duplication characteristic of hysterical identifications, a bunch of people—mostly but not only women—will spread the new word that will be adhered to like a religious truth. Not without perverse effects, of course. That is also how a certain way of hysteria—misidentifying its participation in victimisation by failing to recognise the underlying fantasies of those who incarnate both the victim and the one who produces a victim—becomes the accomplice of a perverse discourse by falling into the moralising trend that privileges a push towards denunciation over the analytic possibility of enunciation.

If the analytic discourse is the only one whose ethics involve the subject's discovery of underlying truths about themselves that are not equal to the analyst's supposed knowledge, I am still wondering what place psychoanalysis can have in a culture that privileges shared beliefs over subjective truths. What is it that makes the situation there really differ from the European situation?

I could construct an argument based on the idea that it is an underlying racism promoting endogamy as the desirable norm that perverts Mauritian society by privileging a quasi-incestuous narcissistic love for "the same or the similar", or, as Freud would put it, a narcissism of the petty difference. But saying something like that in Mauritius may also serve to reinforce the perverse effects already generated by the current discourse around paedophilia and incest that keeps confusing registers. What I note, though, is that the running discourse suggesting that "every child is at risk of being abused at any point in time" only became formalised and contagious once it was publicly said that white men could

[10] *L'Express*, N°3268 19th–25th February 2014.

also be abusers, and that they could also potentially abuse their own kind. Of course, real perverts come in all shapes and sizes, so why would they have a particular skin tone?

Since people always draw upon a context in order to construct subjective symptoms, my question about the perverse effects of post-colonialism reverts back to the question of perversion as a structure that I think has, does and will always exist in any society at any point in time. After all, whether it is veiled, foreclosed or disavowed, sexual difference is the very difference that everybody has to do with anywhere in the world, and nobody knows *already* how to do with that…except for the sexual pervert, ironically. Everybody else is worlds apart from one another, hence the social bond that words, signifiers and signs enable us to establish. In an era that promotes quick fixes and other *jouissance*-filled options, the psychoanalytic offer feels more subversive than ever in helping to reconcile the perversity of drives with creative surges of desire.

11

Staging the Crucifiction of the Father: Flight 9525's Game for the Gaze

C.E. Robins

The middle of the night in a quiet exclusive neighborhood in the western German city of Düsseldorf: inside a dark apartment bedroom, a young man and woman are in bed together. The young woman is sleeping soundly, her back to her partner who is sleeping on his back. Still asleep, he begins to move his legs slowly, and then starts to moan. He makes frail attempts to kick his legs, then his head turns side to side, now violently. "Ahhh!" he screams, and violently kicks his legs.

"We're going down! We're going down!" the young man screams, "I tell you we're going down!" Horrified, he sits bolt upright in bed with rapid, shallow breaths, his eyes wide.

His girlfriend, a local primary school teacher, offering her name to the German press as "Maria W.," will soon separate from him precisely because she became too traumatised by the stark nightmares of this scary man. Press reports that she was pregnant by him, even after she had told

C.E. Robins (✉)
Psychoanalyst in private practice

D. Caine, C. Wright (eds.), *Perversion Now!*,
DOI 10.1007/978-3-319-47271-3_11

her class that she was "going to be a Mum," were quickly denied by her. And Andreas last-ditch gift to keep her, a flashy new Audi days before the crash, was immediately given back to him.[1]

This man is 27 year-old Andreas Lubitz, the co-pilot who steered his Airbus A280 down into the French Alps on March 24th, killing himself and 149 others.

After the crash German reporters interviewed "Maria W.". She explained this to them: "It is now clear, everything he told me that I did not understand then, I understand it now." According to her, he spoke these very words: "One day I will do something that will change the system and then everyone will know my name and remember me".[2]

"One day I will do something that will *change the system* and then *everyOne will know my name and remember me*." What could he have imagined by "change the system"? Make sure a flight attendant is present in the cockpit at all times when the pilot or co-pilot has to use the bathroom? Or change the *entire* system of life—of the "Law of the Father" by which we live our limited mortal lives? To abolish the limits, to abolish, in the psychoanalytic sense, the effects of castration? To disavow (*verleugnen,* Freud's verb), to make a mockery of, to laugh at, the limits within which we all must live and die? But it is the latter part of his comment to Maria that stands out: "then *everyOne* will know my name and remember me." He is afraid of not being remembered. Good luck to the rest of us—poor players in this *Comedia* of our lives! Do Lubitz's words—adolescent?—not summon up for us Hitler's narcissistic-perverse disavowal that he too was not one of the "little people" for whom The Law applied? Especially not the one who should be slaughtered Outside the Law. Lubitz's demand—and Hitler's?—was only that he always be remembered. And that he be remembered by *everyOne*: does he intend that this *EveryOne* is the Supreme Subject Supposed To Know, the Big Other, God? "The subject supposed to know is God, full stop. Nothing

---

[1] "Germanwings co-pilot killer 'bought two Audis—one for him and one for his girlfriend weeks ago.' www.daukt nauk.cinm (26 December 2015); Read more at http://www.dailymail.co.uk/news/article-3014920/Germanwings-pilot-killer-bought-two-Audis-one-one-girlfriend-weeks-ago.html#ixzz3vRqnUpYu.

[2] Daniel Politi, "Pilot of Downed Airliner: "One Day Everyone Will Know My Name," http://www.slate.com/blogs/the_slatest/2015/03/28/germanwings (accessed 28 March 2015).

else."[3] Is Lubitz staging this suffering as a sacrifice precisely, as Lacan insists, to vex this Big Other, whose gaze beholds us from above?

Before the fateful flight we are informed that Lubitz consulted at least 41 doctors for his condition, reportedly for depression, a groundless phobia that he was losing his eyesight, and suicidal tendencies. Besides the 41 doctors' consultations, he also visited University Hospital Düsseldorf three times between February and March 10th, 2014 (he crashed the plane on March 24th, 2014).[4] What stands out for me in all his medical consultations is that he took his mother and girlfriend with him. Consider the following variants of the triangulation Lacan insists on in the dynamics of perversion: during his appointments, was his mother taking the "passive onlooker role",[5] or was Lubitz still the "phallic completion" of his mOther, guffawing at the helpless father-figure doctor who could do nothing with this "perfect son and mother"? Who had the power? Being that he consulted 41 different doctors, I think Lubitz had the power to make the doctors feel incompetent and anxious.[6] As we see in the clinic of perversion daily, it is not the perverse patient who comes to be relieved of suffering: the doctor will suffer in the treatment. The pervert is intent only on "escaping the passive position of the past"[7] on affecting a "reversal" of the past relation with the Other.[8]

One member of our weekly clinical case conference in New York is also an airline flight attendant. She told us that usually the pilot is in full command of the controls. In this case, the pilot was Patrick Sonderheimer, who had recently switched from Lufthansa to GermanWings, so that he "could be with his family more."[9] Be more of a father. Sonderheimer was in total charge of the early morning flight from Düsseldorf down

---

[3] Lacan, J. (2006). *Le Seminaire Livre XVI, D'un Autre à l'Autre*. Paris: Seuil, p. 280.

[4] Germanwings co-pilot Andreas Lubitz saw 41 doctors in five years; crash inquiry to consider possible manslaughter charges, prosecutor says," http://www.abc.net.au/news/2015-06-12/germanwings-co-pilot-saw-41-doctors-in-five-years-prosecutor/6540334. (accessed 11 June 2015).

[5] Verhaeghe, P. (2004). *On Being Normal and Other Disorders*. New York: Other Press.

[6] ibid., p. 413.

[7] ibid., p. 416.

[8] ibid., p. 412.

[9] Amy Stockwell, "Captain Patrick Sondheimer. That's the pilot's name you want to remember," http://www.mamamia.com.au/patrick-sondheimer/#hyWekP4ugZZ6Pthl.99 (accessed 29 March 2015).

to Barcelona, then landing, then taxiing to the passenger hub, letting the Barcelona passengers depart, and waiting until the Düsseldorf-bound passengers had entered and been seated. Then, he would have had to taxi the aircraft back out onto the runway, staying in line according to the orders of the traffic controller, and then finally, taking off up north to Düsseldorf. Once in the air, and once at the altitude where he can "level off" the plane (usually about 35,000 feet), Sonderheimer, under pressure to pee, now turns to Lubitz and requests that Lubitz take over until he, the captain, returns from the toilet which is located in the cabin just outside the cockpit.

It was at this point that something unusual happened. The cockpit black box recorded Sonderheimer asking Lubitz to "take over the controls" until he, Sonderheimer, returns from the bathroom outside the cockpit. Instead of answering "Yes," or "Surely," Lubitz answered with the German word *Höffentlich*—"Hopefully".[10] That strange response did not stop Captain Sonderheimer, who was pressured to pee. Was Lubitz's retort a sarcastic response to the Captain, the father figure, something like: "You think I can't fly this fucking airplane?" Or was this sarcastic response from the man who was nick-named "Tomato Andy" by the rest of the crew, just because he had been an airline attendant (like the hostesses) before becoming a co-pilot? ("Tomato" in vulgar jargon implies that he may not be a vegetable, he may be a "fruit" [homosexual]). We recall that police recovered ample evidence of his almost nightly visits to gay porn websites on his computer.[11] Was his resentment for being dubbed "Tomato Andy" the motive for his mass murdering?

But take the word itself, "*Höffentlich*": what was Lubitz hoping for? That his staging, his *mise en scène,* his fascination with sacrificing the whole plane, crew, and passengers, would finally be successful? (We know

[10] "Andreas L. steuerte A320 an den Felsen Das Voice-Recorder-Protokoll von Flug 4 U9525" *Aktualisiert am Montag*, 30.03.2015, 17:28. http://www.focus.de/panorama/welt/andreas-lubitz-steuerte-a320-an-den-felsen-das-voice-rekorder-protokoll-von-flug-4u9525-11-minuten-bis-zum-aufprall_id_4572

[11] "Germanwings killer Andreas Lubitz 'trawled internet for suicide and sexual perversion websites.' Police reported: "he trawled the dark side of the web visiting, among other things, sites containing gay porn, suicide themes and sexual perversions." See http://www.mirror.co.uk/news/world-news/germanwings-killer-andreas-lubitz-trawled-5420880 (accessed 29 March 2015).

now that he had practiced the descent of the A320 when he was alone in the cockpit on the way south from Düsseldorf).[12]

Once Sonderheimer was outside the cockpit and into the bathroom in the cabin, Lubitz firmly locked the cockpit door. The next eight minutes are recorded on the recovered black boxes, one outside in the cabin and one inside the cockpit. What we hear, on the one side, outside in the cabin, is Captain Sonderheimer propelled into a rage, cursing and banging the cockpit door (probably with the stewardess's metal cart—stories of his having an axe or crowbar are misleading: these tools are safely stored only inside the cockpit).

"Open the goddamn door!" is how the German screaming of Sonderheimer is translated. "Goddamn it, open the door!" Sonderheimer continues to scream (to invoke God!), now beside himself with rage, sputtering and battering the impervious cockpit door (since 9/11 cockpit doors have become impregnable). Behind the helpless Sonderheimer, plaintive cries from the passengers fill the air, cries of "O My God!," "Mon Dieu!," "Mein Gott!" "Dios Mios!" in so many languages. All invoking God. These cries of desperation from Sonderheimer and the passengers: what they must have felt in those long eight minutes as the plane now steadily falls, faster and faster because Lubitz has pushed a button to boost the descent speed?

The recovered black boxes register all these protesting voices, a hubbub of prayers and curses, but they register something more: from the microphone in the cockpit. All this cacophony outside the cockpit door: inside the cockpit only the "very calm, even breathing," of Lubitz is discernible. After all, he is only the cool instrument, like the Marquis de Sade, of the *jouissance* of the malevolent God,[13] or conversely, is he deliberately sacrificing all these people to make the Almighty Father very, very, anxious?

This suffering, this trauma, was staged, very dramatically, by Lubitz. He knew the mountainous French terrain by heart from his years in gliders over these very peaks. "Sacrifice," if we may call it that, all these innocents ... Lacan insists on the way in which both sadism and masochism are tri-

---

[12] "Germanwings crash: Co-pilot Lubitz 'practised rapid descent ...'" See www.bbc.com/news/world-europe-32604552 (accessed 6 May 2015).

[13] Lacan, J. (2014). *Anxiety. The Seminar of Jacques Lacan: Book X.* A. Price (Trans.). London: Polity, pp. 146–147.

angulated by reference to the locus of the big Other, like God gazing from above. The sadist, for his part, seeks to make himself the instrument of the big Other's *jouissance* (pleasure and murder), while the masochist submits to pain in service of the larger purpose of inciting the anxiety, the suffering of the big Other. What Lacan insists on is the essential *theatricality* of sadism and masochism,[14] the "staging of torments," while the ultimate spectator of perversion is this gaze of this big Other, the Almighty (hardly) Father. For the sadist, the crucial *jouissance* is not that of the torturer (who, as we see in Sade—or Lubitz!—is virtually mechanical, unfeeling: "the calm, even breathing") but that of the big Other. For the masochist, her submission, far from exciting the anxiety of the torturer, more typically offers to the perverse partner a thrill of power, a complete escape from anxiety. The anxiety is produced not in the human other but wholly on the level of the big Other. It is the big Other (Almighty Father) whose rules are violated, who is scandalised by pain, injury, and death. I quote at length Lacan's words at the end of the *Four Fundamental Concepts*:

> There is something profoundly masked in the critique of the history that we have experienced. This, re-enacting the most monstrous and supposedly superseded forms of the holocaust, is the drama of Nazism.
>
> I would hold that no meaning given to history, based on Hegeliano-Marxist premises, is capable of accounting for this resurgence – which only goes to show that the offering to obscure gods of an object of sacrifice is something to which few subjects can resist succumbing, as if under some monstrous spell.
>
> Ignorance, indifference, and averting of the eyes may explain beneath what veil this mystery still remains hidden. But for whoever is capable of turning a courageous gaze towards this phenomenon – and, once again, there are certainly few who do not succumb to the fascination of the sacrifice in itself – the sacrifice signifies that, in the object of our desires, we try to find evidence for the presence of the desire this big Other that I call here *the dark God* (*le Dieu obscur*).
>
> It is the eternal meaning of sacrifice, to which no one can resist...[15]

---

[14] ibid., p. 145.

[15] Lacan, J. (1994). *The Four Fundamental Concepts of Psycho-Analysis*. A. Sheridan (Trans.). Harmondsworth: Penguin, pp. 274–275.

Lubitz is torturing Capt. Sonderheimer, the pilot, the commander of the ship, the authority. Sonderheimer, the father figure, helpless, bereft of all his power, invoking God to damn the locked door, and damn Lubitz. Sonderheimer invokes "God." And behind Sonderheimer in the cabin: utter pandemonium. "All the demons" are let loose, all invoking: "God!".

According to Roudinesco and Plon, the sadist "transforms himself into an object of *jouissance* offered to God and turns the Law into derision; he unconsciously wishes to annul himself into absolute Evil and into the total annihilation of himself."[16] No wonder such perversions have traditionally been labeled "incurable": the pervert, like the psychotic, disavows reality. But why was not one of the 41 doctors he consulted and treated within the years before the crash able to perceive and treat his perverse structure?[17]

After the crash, the relatives of the dead were summoned to the small French village at the base of the hill, to the chapel where a priest conducted a memorial service marking those lost. The mayor of the village, Monsieur Bartolini, was receiving the sad-faced plodding relatives into the chapel when he was introduced to Günter and Ursula Lubitz, parents of Andreas. It was Bartolini who told them it appeared that their son Andreas had crashed the plane deliberately. Bartolini reports: "Mr. Lubitz totally collapsed, just fell down. He was completely crushed. Desolate, he uttered: 'My life is shattered.'" (we recall that it was Freud who used the expression "the soul is shattered" in cases of trauma).

Bull's-eye! The father crucified.

The pervert, once seemingly powerless vis-à-vis the Other, has triggered "the reversal": now he's the one in power![18]

---

[16] Roudinesco, E. and Plon, M. (2006). *Dictionaire de la Psychanalyse*. Paris: Fayard, p. 810.

[17] We learn that one doctor ("a neuropsychologist") wrote a directive that Lubitz should not be flying on that day, March 24, 2014, and that police found the note torn up in Lubitz's apartment. It appears Lufthansa has been insisting that Lubitz took "the best" psychological tests available, and passed—twice!—"with flying colors". See "Germanwings co-pilot had passed medical tests 'with flying colors'" http://mashable.com/2015/03/26/germanwings-co-pilot-andreas-lubitz/#vF1XFxMYp5qF.

[18] Verhaeghe, 2004, op. cit., pp. 412–413.

Here are Freud's words: "Hate is older than love," hatred of the other (sadism) and hatred of the self (masochism) pre-date any possible 'love' for the other" or the Other.[19,20] We know Freud learned much about the death drive from Sabina Speilrein; her teaching pushed him to make "his dualistic turn" to Thanatos versus Eros after 1920. For Freud, the death drive will be forever "wrapped around" Eros. Freud's saying that hate is older than love survives in Lacan's presentation of the mother's overbearing presence as "a great crocodile in whose mouth you are,"[21] who could devour you at any moment.

One philological note: I have attempted to elucidate the sadism of Andreas Lubitz, and wish to point out that sadism and masochism often follow gender lines, sadism being on the masculine side and masochism on the feminine side. The etymology of our words for "man" and for "woman" in English show this.[22] English, being a German language, derives its words "man" and "woman" from the very early German "Woepman" and "Weibman" (in later German, the "Woep" would be dropped from "man" and the "man" would be dropped from "Weib"). In Sanskrit, "Woepman" described the "weapon-man," that is, the one who kills, and "Weibman" described "quivering, trembling": why? Afraid she would be killed by her man (the Sanskrit "Weib" comes through in Latin as *vibrare*, "to quiver," "to shake"). She is afraid. Man the sadist killer and woman the quivering masochist.

In conclusion, here are "possible motives" for the horrendous crime of Andreas Lubitz. First, he resented his status as "outsider" (*Auslander*): his father was Romanian, never to be mistaken for a "normal German," a fate Andreas shared. Andreas was further alienated from "the norm" by being nick-named "Tomato Andy" (vegetable or fruit?). Could his action be interpreted as an attack on all "the normals"? Second, Andreas resented being "dropped" by his pregnant girlfriend "Maria W." His possibly unwanted separation from her could not be repaired (after an

---

[19] Freud, S. (1915). *Instincts and their Vicissitudes*. S.E. 14: 109–40. J. Strachey (Trans.). London: Hogarth, 1957, p. 139.

[20] LaPlanche, J. and Pontalis, J.-B. (1973). *The Language of Psychoanalysis*. D. Nicholson-Smith (Trans.). New York: W. W. Norton & Company, 1973, p. 99.

[21] Lacan, J. (2007)[1969–70]. *The Seminar. Book XVII: The Other Side of Psychoanalysis*. R. Grigg (Trans.). New York: W. W. Norton & Company, p. 129.

[22] Skeat, W. (1888). *An Etymological Dictionary of the English Language*. Oxford: Clarendon, p. 710.

abortion?), especially after she returned his gift of a flashy new Audi just days before the fated flight. Third, is Andreas "wish to be remembered." "EveryOne will know my name, EveryOne will remember me." Even if it is as a murderer. Fourth is Andreas's wish "to vex the father," be it Captain Sonderheimer, his own successful banker-father Günter Lubitz, or (*tace Lacan!*) to vex the hardly-Almighty Father, God. Fifth, this time according to Lacan, Andreas was sacrificing "to stage possibly convincing evidence" for the presence of this transcendent *Dieu obscure*.[23]

[23] Lacan, 1994, op. cit., p. 275.

Part III

The Fetish and the Feminine

12

Heads Freud, Tails Lacan: The Question of Feminine Perversion

Gérard Pommier

Our knowledge of perversions is still very incomplete. I will first try to show that Freud's conception of perversions is different from Lacan's. Their views extend and complement each other. With this Freudian and Lacanian overview, I will try to look at a problem, that of female perversion. The first list of perversions ever written in the history of humanity was made by the Marquis de Sade, for example in *The 120 Days of Sodom*. It was done long before the nineteenth century sexologists, such as Kraft Ebbing and Havelock Ellis, Freud's contemporaries. Sade's list does not seem complete. For example, he has forgotten his own perversion: his writing itself, which forces his readers to experience the *jouissance* of feeling ashamed of having read it. Much of Sade's conception of perversions is based on transgression of the law and instrumentation of fellow humans, but not by any means, mainly through repressed drives and desires (such as murder). He makes that happen by provoking a

G. Pommier (✉)
Fondation Européenne pour la Psychanalyse

D. Caine, C. Wright (eds.), *Perversion Now!*,
DOI 10.1007/978-3-319-47271-3_12

feeling of shame in the other and, exciting him, he transforms him into a red phallus. The feeling of shame is a very common way to be sexually excited. This is a dialectic that permits movement from being the phallus, to having it, and getting excited, ensuring a grip on a fellow creature, by showing him or her the object of their repressed desire. That is what can be observed in exhibitionism and voyeurism. But this sexual excitement supposes a transgression, a violence that involves sadism and masochism.

I have briefly summarised the central point of perversion for the Marquis de Sade, which is exactly what Freud describes in his paper *Instincts and their Vicissitudes.*[1] From this point of view the central axis of perversion is sadism, and it may be a way for us to understand the perverse dimension of political power. Furthermore, Sade, like Lacan, was not very much interested in fetishism, which was Freud's principal preoccupation in relation to the perversions. For Freud, the fetish replaces the maternal phallus and in this way the perverse subject makes a "denial of castration", first of maternal castration and then of female castration more generally.

But it seems to me that Freud's one-sided point of view on the fetish is stuck in the patriarchal context of his time. For him the fetish is only the symbol of the denial of maternal castration. He does not take into account that there is also a direct link between the fetish and the paternal taboo. Freud wrote in his article on the *Taboo of Virginity*,[2] a paper presented to the Vienna Psychoanalytical Society in 1917, that in some tribes, only a wizard could deflower girls. But he did not write that the young women were protected from men by fetishes of a kind, for example jewellery, clothes in the local fashion, as many charms as correspond to the fetishes imposed, which made them taboo, fetishes imposed by the father of Totemism. Freud only spoke of the fetish as it is used by men (as an ersatz of the maternal phallus) and not of the fetish as used by women (as a sign of paternal taboo). On this issue, as on others concerning girls, Freud was probably blinded by his own father's position, normalised by the patriarchate of his time. He only saw one side of the fetish, as a rejection of

[1] Freud, S. (1915). *Instincts and their Vicissitudes*. S.E. 14: 109–40. J. Strachey (Trans.). London: Hogarth, 1957.

[2] Freud, S. (1918). The Taboo of Virginity (Contributions to the Psychology of Love III). S.E. XI: 191–208. J. Strachey (Trans.). London: Hogarth, 1957.

the feminine, while there exists another side, very easy to see in all public spaces. It is as if the latter were shouting this truth: "Do not approach me, do not touch me! I belong to someone else: 'My heart belongs to Daddy'. Look at these jewels that sparkle! They are emblems of His power to protect my eternal Virginity!"

Once this paternal dimension of the fetish is noticed, some of these features become obvious. Fetishes of this sort over-invest the female body on their luminous side: clothing fantasies, ornaments, high-heeled shoes, twinkling precious jewels set on the flesh. When the anonymous seduction taboo plays its romantic role, it is as if she were saying: "I please you, me that sparkles under the glare from above". By making its peculiarity reflect from above, each woman affirms her eternal marriage with a kind of powerful father of whom she is the daughter. This is the source of men's insatiable excitement. At all times and in all places the universality of this fetish has imposed itself, tattooed on the female body, shining in the high value of jewellery, and if this high value of the gift has been made in exchange for her *jouissance*, this is at the same time the early version of currency. Thus the feminine fetish also opens up a perspective to the fetishism of merchandising.

On this point, we can conclude that Freud has understood only one face of perversion. Lacan was more inventive when he wrote it, like a joke, as *'Père-version'*. It is quite impossible to translate but it means that perversion is on the side of the father. *Père-version* is written with a median indent that reveals its hidden face. This does not invalidate Freud's view: indeed a fetish is first used to deny maternal castration. It triggers excitation according to a simple process: the child first begins to be taken by his mother as a phallus, and he liberates himself from this identification by denying the maternal castration. Then the fetish represents what his mother lacks and, thanks to this exchange, it is no longer his own body. As soon as he is no longer the phallus, he may himself have an erection.

Later, once engaged in a sexual life, if he imposes the use of a fetish on a woman, he hence denies his castration. But will it be enough to excite him? Maybe no! Because he has to impose the fetish by force in a sadistic way, as if he had to communicate his own anguish to his partner. The imposition—by force—of the fetish excites his threatened masculinity because masculinity is anguished by castration. He tries to show himself as at once the provider and the owner of the father's fetish, the same fetish that is used as a taboo. The violence here can be hard, or soft. It is a way to take possession, for example by giving a jewel, or requiring the wearing of certain clothes. The violence of this *Père-version*—in two words—becomes the engine of eroticism. Someone who imposes a fetish almost by force on a woman, is himself no longer the fetish, the phallus of his own mother. And in the same gesture, the sadism identifies him with a father. As I have already said, Freud considered the meaning of the mother/fetish but not the father/taboo. This second meaning includes a transgressive and guilty use of the fetish: using this taboo deserves a punishment, which is a source of excitement. For this sort of royal road, the father of the *Père-version* enters on stage, whip in hand. The whip becomes in this way a sort of queen of the fetishes.

I have described the turn of perversion from Freud to Lacan. The whip shows the double face of the fetish, between the maternal phallus and the taboo symbol of the father. The first face is the launch pad of the second: it is a dislocation of contraries. Maternal anguish gives birth to a mythical Father, dispenser of blows as well as gifts and jewellery. This is the real vertigo of masculine possession, when the gift suddenly builds a jail, when the precious veil is turned into a burka. In its second paternal time, the innocent polymorphous perversion of the child turns into the adult *père-version* which is frightening: it seeks to trade new guilt against the anguish it provokes. Because guilt is unleashed when the teenager becomes a man, when he takes the father's place and suddenly discovers the feminine. To provoke her anguish is his major remedy in the face of this womanhood, before which he seeks to identify with the father. In this sense, it is a fact that forensic psychiatry gives the impression that perversion only concerns male violence. The police almost never arrest women for perversion. And if it seems that a certain form of female seduction or even female exhibitionism has the appearance of a perversion, it does not use the same violence that characterises the male perversion.

I come now to my central question: Does there not exist a psychic violence that would also be a form of *père-version*, but for women? I will try to show how this is the case for the Christian mystics: their orgasm with God renewed a miracle that was true for all the society, and their experience had therefore to be staged and transmitted to the entire world. It had to be exhibited. The mystic was a witch who had turned out well, thanks to the exhibitionism of her orgasm: it had to appear before a witness, before being sanctified by the church. This exhibitionism—organised by the Church—shows the experience of a contre-*jouissance*, which ensures the resurrection of the body without waiting for the day of the Last Judgement. This integration of the mystic orgasm with God has been recognised in theology as a miracle, proof of the existence of God. It demonstrated the power of the Holy Spirit, in spite of the parricide. This is the miracle that everyone could check at night!

The female mystics, seeing visions, tormented, in pain, stigmatised, and anorexic, were fighting all the forms of *jouissance* they could. They refused all *jouissance* and this refusal only became orgasmic in front of a witness. But who can say whether the gaze of the voyeur was itself a *jouissance*, to the extent of soliciting their exhibition, or whether it is rather the mystics who wanted to show off? Since the beginning of Christianity they were exhibiting themselves on their own, screaming for, asking for the help of a priest, of an exorcist, of a witness who could hear them in their debate with the uniting Father, a Father both diabolical and divine. To ensure that the union with God was accepted by the church, a written testimony was necessary. This female exhibitionism was necessary for the glory of faith … and wasn't it a sort of female *père-version* ?

Was the symptom of the perversion of the mystics in their masochism, in some of their really disgusting practices, in the incredible suffering that they inflicted on themselves? No, because this masochist's moment was lonely. It was only a way to pay for their guilt.

On the contrary, the moment of orgasm described by a witness was a universalised exhibition. Through this witness, the exhibitionism asserted its power for centuries to come, to the glory of the divine trinity. It pleaded for an earthly paradise for women, a unique power to end a satanic *jouissance* in favor of a divine relief. The literary exhibition was at the same time necessarily transcribed before being shown to everybody: the painter and the sculptor brought this exhibition to churches, palaces and on the streets. In her writings, Marie of the Incarnation admits of her strange *jouissance* when describing her suffering: "I admit that I delight so much speaking of the happiness of suffering that I think I could write whole volumes without satisfying my desire". Where is the *jouissance*? In suffering or in its transcription? The first is a *jouissance* only because of the second. The mystic woman did not merely satisfy herself with the complicity of a voyeur and a brief exhibition like a vulgar witch. She also needed the reader's confusion or the aesthete's feeling troubled by looking at the statue or the painting. In short, the mystical exhibitionism outperformed the subversion of Sade!

Like most mystics Angela of Foligno wrote her book of visions under the gaze of a young monk: brother Arnaud, man of faith. She called him her "nephew". He witnessed her ecstasies. Other mystics had a confessor, or an inquisitor, or a Doctor of the faith. Is this mystical exhibition an exception? Not really, because for common humanity, lovers of earthly loves are they not also witnesses? The lover is perhaps the architect of carnal love, but at the time of orgasm, he is only a witness. When it is time for orgasm, every man is a voyeur, a shaky witness of the ecstasy. His place is not very different from Brother Arnaud's. *Ewig Weibliche*—the eternal feminine—bears quite well its name of eternity whispered by the Holy Spirit. The soul has always been the wife of God and has spoken in a feminine way: "*Sponsa Christi*", bride of God. In this sense, all ecstasies are feminine, only the female is subject to orgasm. The orgasm of men is only an echo. Every man is a nephew even though he is the lover.

I have just said that proper perversion begins with violence. But is it so sure that this perversion does not concern women? As well as exhibitionism, there are also the various fates of the fetish and the multiple forms of violence. Many men see female seduction as violence, even if it is true that it is their own desire that crucifies them. This is already one kind of female perversion. Some women, or perhaps many, like to make men suffer from their desire.

But do women not make much more extensive use of the fetish when they leave their femininity for motherhood? Motherhood is not a natural destiny for women. There are lots of kinds of mother: the ones who are re-living their own childhood through their children; those who offer their child like a gift to their parents, or to their lover; those who flee their femininity through maternity, and so on. And there is also a desire for motherhood when the child plays the role of a fetish. A child can be assigned to this place, when a woman makes of him a gift to her mother to deny her castration. It is here that there is a type of female fetishism, and where it also dries up. When the hope of becoming a mother carries the prospect of using the child as a fetish, this wish exhausts her desire without serving her lover's excitement. This fetishism looks a lot like revenge, by using the child against the father like a weapon. In this way, a woman takes revenge on the place of object of exchange that has been assigned to her. And so the beautiful child has before him the destiny of the crucified, between the desire of a dead father and a mother's devouring love. This is another trick of repetition! Because women only let men crucify them until it is time to take their revenge. When they make fetishes of their children, is this not a crucifixion, a kind of royal revenge? The crucifix was for centuries a fetish hung above all matrimonial beds. Very exciting! The woman was seen not only as a producer of values—of fetishes—but she was even treated herself as a value. She was herself not only considered as a source of *jouissance* but also as an object of exchange. Motherhood was a prison of femininity, but it could also serve as an instrument of revenge.

When the child is fetishised, it is a form of violence situated between Freudian perversion and Lacanian perversion. I do not know if we can escape from either of these destinies: the best would likely be to run away, but does our desire let us? Or to say it better, maybe our desire is itself a way to escape from this destiny.

13

Queer Theory, Sexual Difference and Perversion

Arlette Pellé

I was introduced to the field of queer studies through several of my patients, who were openly gay and spoke about these theories in relation to their own questions about sexual identity. I therefore became interested in these theories, which address questions to psychoanalysis itself: What has happened that the male and female genders are thought of as categories to be eradicated, as Monique Wittig would have it? How does one deconstruct sexual difference, to which each individual gains access through castration, and arrive at its *queer* use, which includes sexual practices classically thought of as perverse?

"How do I *feel:* as a man, woman, bi, trans…"—a young woman questions her sexual identity, her difficulty around questions of gender. The verb *to feel,* as a man, woman, bi, trans, reminds us of the kind of self-evaluations we use to express our state or mood: "I feel good or bad, depressed or overjoyed". The formulation reduces sexed identity to

A. Pellé (✉)
Fondation Européenne pour la Psychanalyse

D. Caine, C. Wright (eds.), *Perversion Now!*,
DOI 10.1007/978-3-319-47271-3_13

a feeling, which excludes male or female identifications. "It had to be like that," she says about her sexual relationship with her partner: "I was the one to go and buy the 'male prosthesis' and I take on this position in our sexual relationship." I notice the expression 'male prosthesis', which sounds different from the classical "dildo".

As I was to learn later, in the queer movement a prosthesis—a mechanical and imperfect copy of a living organ—has the value of giving a woman an erect penis, as something that is truly hers. It also allows us to think about the body as a hybrid composed of both natural and artificial organs. The notion of hybridity also alludes to the similarities between queer theories and a certain strand of neuroscience which dreams of transforming the human brain and body through sophisticated technology.

Queer theorist Judith Halberstam, cited by Beatriz Preciado, argues: "Real penises are simply dildos that cannot be purchased." And we should add: "that cannot be really detached from the male body." The idea of abolishing the binary of sex by transforming bodies through sex toys, surgery or other techniques, has to do with a theorisation of the body which, as Preciado writes, "defines sexuality as a technology".[1] The dildo then becomes part of the multitude of the mutant and hybrid body.

The young woman associates the phallus which she believes she has, by means of her "male prosthesis", with the satisfaction of the Other's jouissance, namely her girlfriend's, and she tries to show that "it is not true that a woman is not a man". This is what she tells me.

She continues: "I try to have control over sex; I take initiative; I play a role. In the beginning I thought that 'being a man' revealed who I really was. But it is as if I *had* to take on the male role, penetration, so as to be able to be WITH a girl." We find subjective sexed positions that are at odds with anatomy in both straight and gay couples, but here the point is not of taking a masculine position based on identification, but to put oneself clearly on the side of the man, through the real appropriation of the male organ, the "male prosthesis", which enables my patient to penetrate her girlfriend.

Later she says: "I take on this role for the girl. Girls feel more comfortable when they don't have to play the man. It reassures them about their

[1] Preciado, B. (2000). *Manifeste Contra-sexuel*. Paris: Balland, p. 65.

femininity. It's more like I can do anything, I can be both a man and a woman, instead of saying that I am a man." She defines the male and female position in reference to this "doing", with or without the object-organ. This is a deliberate and conscious choice, rather than a subjectivation of a masculine or feminine position.

Several sessions later, the young patient raises the question of her own desire: "I adapt myself – I imitate a man or a woman. When I was a child, they would ask me if I was a girl OR a boy. Now I say that I am a girl AND a boy. But I don't know…I pretend I can do everything, I can play both roles, have both sexes. It protects me from having to be a woman. What is my own desire, if not to satisfy the desire of the other?" she asks. The question of femininity appears together with the question of her own desire. These sessions illustrate the uncomfortable indeterminacy of not belonging to either sex, the difference between imitation and identification, and raise the question of bisexuality.

For some time, the young woman continues to subscribe to the same discourse: "Because my father was my mother, a woman can be a man" (her father took care of the children like a mother, she tells me). In one session, she announces to me, with great enthusiasm: "I've met a 'pregnant man'…" For a split second I believe that medicine has broken new ground!

She then explains: it is a trans woman, who has not undergone surgery and for years has been living as 'Pierre'. Pierre is expecting a child and says "I am a pregnant man". A subjective identification or a deliberate gender choice, "I am a man" takes precedence independently of anatomical sex, so that, as the patient says, her friend is a man expecting a baby. The child will call Pierre daddy, or mommy, or both. If we exclude the biological Real, gender becomes muddled.

Gender studies and queer theory present a programme focused on eliminating the supposedly "natural" female position of "being penetrated". It is a programme that denaturalises gender in order to transform it into a purely socially constructed framework, which can therefore be deconstructed. But can we really do without the biological reality when dealing with sexual difference? From the psychoanalytic perspective, we could say that a man can choose to position himself on the side of women and vice versa, but this position is based on the phallus with anatomy as its reference.

Beyond the issue of gender, queer theory invents mutable, mobile and unstable sexual registers and practices, which tend to subvert the difference between the male and female position in the sexual act. Polymorphous sexuality, the multiplicity of practices and desires, aim to undo not just the binary of male-female but all binary categories, all sexual difference.

It is not a question of "being"—being a fetishist, a sadist or a masochist, a pervert. These clinical categories or structures imply that one is always involved in the same type of sexual acts. Queer is a form of self-determination of those who engage in polymorphous practices and cannot be subsumed under a specific structure; it is understood as something mobile and fluid; it is political and subversive, aiming, among other things, to make the so-called minority sexual practices accessible to all.

It could be argued that regarding the question of gender, queer theory has simply adopted Freud's truly subversive work on infantile sexuality, bisexuality and polymorphous perversion, as well as Lacan's work on jouissance and the formulas of sexuation. One could say that although the postulates of gender theory present themselves as something original and new, these ideas were already identified by Freud.

We could suppose that queer theories simply emphasise the difference between anatomical sex and gender, stressing the bisexuality innate to all human beings, which today we can express more freely than before. However, what they are trying to subvert is something quite different: they are trying to deconstruct heterosexuality and by the same token reject psychoanalysis, which queer theoreticians understand as the guardian of gender normativity, for example by pointing out Freud's and Lacan's claim that "it is the destiny of speaking beings to divide themselves up into men and women." For queer theorists, such arguments equate to a biologisation of sexual difference.

Although it is important to stress that gender theory indeed begins with Freud, it is equally essential to understand that for him, the existence of infantile sexuality in its link to the Oedipus complex must eventually result in the assumption of sexual difference—one becomes a man OR a woman.

But are we either man or woman, or can each of us take on either position at any time? Are we man or woman because of who we identify with "most of the time"? Are we man or woman depending on our relationship to the phallic or other jouissance, or are we man or woman according to the ways in which we couple up? For the queer, bisexuality is an active component of sexual practices, in which either the male or the female body takes on either position indiscriminately.

In this sense, Monique Wittig goes much further than Judith Butler: "The categories 'man' and 'woman' must be destroyed politically, philosophically and symbolically."[2] From this perspective, the queer seeks a redistribution of bodies, of bodies-machines, bodies-organs, bodies-hybrids and bodies-rhizomes, a reengineering of the *jouissances* of the body's parts through subversive bodily acts. In *The Lesbian Body*, Monique Wittig describes what this non-phallic *jouissance* of the body might look like: "the chest the breasts the shoulder-plates the buttocks the elbows the legs the toes the feet the heels the loins the nape the throat … I discover that your skin can be lifted layer by layer."[3]

Each part of the body can become a vehicle for the erotic flows, in a way that liquidates the so-called genital *jouissance*, and with it the sexed masculine and feminine positions, thus also foregrounding infantile sexuality and the utopia of the pre-Oedipal ideal.

Beatriz Preciado—aka Paul B. Preciado—de-centres the anatomical sexual difference between the penis and the vagina in order to promote a sexuality in which the anus and the dildo (with each body part potentially becoming a dildo) are at the centre of sexual behaviour. The anus—the "only universal organ"—is given a central place: seen from the back, there is no sexual difference.

The author is trying to undo anatomy, to denaturalise and reconstruct the body, from a perspective that effaces the real of having or not having the penis as an organ. Queer theory does not argue for the ultimate or potential undoing of the link between biological sex and gender; it rejects biological reality per se.

In trying to deconstruct masculinity and femininity, these movements do not constitute an aberration in contemporary life where we see a tendency to try and rid oneself of all alienation, especially the reference to

---

[2] Wittig, M. (1980). The Straight Mind. *Feminist Issues,* 1(1): 103–111. doi:10.1007/BF02685561.

[3] Wittig, M. (1973). *Le corps lesbian*. Paris: Les éditions de Minuit.

the Other, in favour of returning to the drive, its satisfaction or pleasure. Does this reduce the queer subject to the drive, in line with the modalities of *jouissance* favoured by today's world?

Psychic conflict is thus eliminated; the absence of symmetry or complementarity between the two sexes is seen as a kind of psychoanalytic negative thinking, a disenchantment interpreted as the inability of psychoanalysis to free itself from the heterosexual norm. Of course, psychoanalytic treatment runs contrary to this, provoking a detachment from one's alienation in the Other's desire, in the existing norms; desire and *jouissance* refer each of us to our own irreducible abnormality.

With his formulas of sexuation, Lacan rewrites the Freudian notion of bisexuality and confirms the contingency of gender in terms of *jouissance*. Sexuation upholds difference; it is based on a choice, albeit one that remains in the register of the unconscious. Lacan de-biologises *jouissance*, which is now rooted in the relationship to the Other. He distinguishes between phallic *jouissance*, which is limited for both sexes, and feminine *jouissance*, which is nameless and without limits, a *jouissance* beyond the phallus that orients female sexuality.

Queer theorists such as Judith Butler, but also Donna Haraway, Monique Wittig—the most radical—and Beatriz Preciado, question sexual difference, abolish the category "woman" and at the same time try to defy phallic logic—the phallus as the organising principle of *jouissance* and a "ballast" required by language. They say: psychoanalysts keep telling us that the phallus has nothing to do with the penis, but when I say phallus, I see the symbol of an erect penis, the column on the Place Vendôme, or what remains of the Bastille prison—no matter how you try to explain this to me, I still see it as vertical, upright. How can we then avoid making the link between the phallus and the penis?

Even if we accept the phallus as a differentiating characteristic, not the penis but a symbol of its absence, this symbolic phallus is still a product of heterosexual discourse. Plus, if indeed anyone can have it or not, why do we need to keep this reference, which is after all still an anatomical one? Queer theorists believe that the metaphorical relationship between the penis and the phallus has to do with masculine hegemony, which strives to maintain this phallocentric imaginary. It seems that the phallic reference is intolerable to them because it implies castration.

We can also ask if some of the psychoanalytical concepts are atemporal invariants or signifiers which belong to a particular historical moment in an evolving body of theory. In other words, the criticism is aimed at the law that imposes a duality of sexes and does so using the false phallic yardstick of the penis; the queer proclaims a commitment to do away with the phallus in order to say something about sex and gender.

The queer argument fits in with the modern discourse that rejects the vertical plane in favour of horizontality: equal relations for all, neither man nor woman, the same possibility to employ the multiple expressions of gender—sado-maso-fetishism, lesbian, trans...—the category of perversion collapses. Because these are mutable and deliberate sexual practices, we cannot speak about perversion in the sense of a psychical structure. Polymorphous perversion is idealised because it does not inscribe the subject in a specific sexed position.

13.1 Conclusion

This creates a split, a separation between sexual practices and the subjective gender positions of man or woman, which everyone can continue to hold in their affective or professional lives. In these theories, which are largely elaborated by women, the question of femininity is raised especially vocally.

If, since Lacan, we have been more aware that to position oneself as a woman means leaving the category of the universal, the phallic logic, we could expect these different movements of queer theory to know a bit more about what is this real beyond the phallus. However, by waging war at the front of sexual indifferentiation, queer theorists instead seem to reclaim a position "before" the phallus. Their answer to the question "What is a woman?" is therefore to strive towards the disappearance of femininity and feminine *jouissance*, turning polymorphous perversion into the new norm.

For psychoanalysis, the attempts to define this feminine, non-phallic *jouissance*, as illustrated by the examples of the mystics, of Medea or of women who at a certain moment lose or sacrifice everything to mark what "being a real woman" means, for example to overcome the pain of amorous abandonment, remain rather unconvincing and joyless. Is it because these examples themselves are an interpretation of feminine *jouissance* from the perspective of the heterosexual norm? Could the feminine exception have a different status than to either constantly reappear in these terrifying forms, as we keep seeing in the psychoanalytic literature, or disappear for good, as the queer movement would have it?

14

No Longer a Taboo: Understanding Female Perversion in Motherhood

Estela V. Welldon

After years of clinical experience I have had to acknowledge that there are feelings and activities amongst women that could or must be called perverse, even if the mental mechanisms are different from those found in men. Why is it so difficult to conceptualise the notion of perverse motherhood and other female perverse behavior? Is it because a completely different psychopathology originates from the female body and its inherent attributes?

The study of some of the characteristics of the female libido and of other features which are exclusive to the female inner world might help us to understand the aetiology of perversion in women. We might then see female perversions not as parallels to the psychopathology found in men, but as having their own separate and distinct causes.

There is a dramatic difference in the sense of temporality in males and females. Women have a 'biological clock' that is present and evident from

E.V. Welldon (✉)
International Association for Forensic Psychotherapy

D. Caine, C. Wright (eds.), *Perversion Now!*,
DOI 10.1007/978-3-319-47271-3_14

the moment they are born. From menarche to menopause, this clock dominates women's lifespan and subjects her to the hope/dread of pregnancy. This grounds women firmly in the reality principle. They not only have a different libidinal development from men but they also experience a sense of pressure provided by this inexorable marking of the passage of time which is exclusive to their sex and is intimately related to their reproductive functions.

The first menstrual period—the menarche—heralds the girl-woman's fecundity. Then she will have periods every four weeks—the menses—which are a constant reminder of her hope/dread of it. They will continue for years to come, yet those years are limited. Hence, ambivalence about becoming a mother will in some cases be associated with an enormous amount of anxiety that increases as the years go by. 'Side effects' such as a kind of 'mini mourning' may follow menstrual periods. Then the woman feels bereft of the experience of pregnancy, even though she has asserted her own choice in declining to become a mother for the time being.

For women the act of making love takes on a different dimension than for men since the former are much more aware than the latter of using the same organ for sexual pleasure as for procreation. This awareness grounds them in the reality principle in a much more biological/psychological way than men who, in this context, are more subject to the pleasure principle. Inasmuch as women's drives are object seeking, this dimension leads some women to certain perverse designs that are alien to men. Some women get pregnant in the belief that this is the only way to achieve security with a man, even when the man has asserted his wish not to be part of this process. For others, the wish to be pregnant is born of a desire to inflict revenge on a man they have learnt to hate because they have been deeply humiliated. Still other women do not feel free to enjoy their own bodies, believing that they are exclusively for either procreation or for men's enjoyment.

A patient told me of her hatred for her body, how repulsed she felt even at the idea of being touched by her husband. During sexual intercourse she would only allow him to penetrate her, and then she felt at peace, but she had never experienced forepleasure. During her pregnancies she had felt content with her body and proud of it. It was as if she had never experienced her body belonging to herself for her own pleasure, but only as a 'bridge' for the man's sexual release or for her functioning as a pregnant woman.

In female perversion not only the whole body but also its mental representations are used to express sadism and hostility. Women express their perverse attitudes not only through, but also towards, their bodies, often in a self-destructive way. If we look at the psychopathologies most frequently associated with the female gender we shall find syndromes of self-injury associated with biological/hormonal disorders affecting the reproductive functioning. Such is the case with anorexia nervosa, bulimia, and forms of self-mutilation, where the menses, their absence or their presence, can act as indicators of the severity of the pathological condition. These women experience a feeling of elation from the manipulation of their bodies when they are starving, and which disappears when they start to eat again. They experience a sense of power through being in control of the shapes and forms their bodies take through the physical injuries and abuse they inflict on themselves.

Inasmuch as men had resorted to perversion as a way to deal with the fear of castration, it might be argued that women were left in a position in which perversion was not available to them. But Freud also theorised that the Oedipus complex was resolved in little girls' fantasies about having Daddy's baby. The symbolic equivalence of penis-baby was created. Developing these ideas we could say provocatively that 'Women can't have perversions because they can have babies'. Whereas men's intellectual achievements are viewed as being consistent with their gender, women in parallel situations sometimes find themselves in conflict, on the one hand for intruding into what is regarded as a man's world and on the other for being insufficiently feminine, a notion tied to essentialist implications of anatomy.

Some patients are professional women with considerable intellectual achievements and concomitant financial rewards. As opposed to men in equivalent positions who might easily boast about their successes, these women had difficulties in acknowledging them, and when they did it was with embarrassment and disbelief. It is as if they felt in open rebellion with the traditional expectations. When sexually approached by male colleagues they might find unattractive and uninteresting, they feel humiliated and angry, but also, and despite themselves, secretly reassured and flattered.

In this context, one patient came for therapy because of her difficulties in achieving a high professional standard, despite her outstanding accomplishments as a student. During her therapy she talked about her inability to see herself simultaneously as a woman and as a successful professional. She then explained how she had overcome her disgust about sexual intercourse when she began to 'talk dirty'. She would describe to her lover fantasies about how a strange, 'tarty and smelly' woman was seducing him. This she would do in story telling style, very slowly, using obscene words and filthy scenarios. The 'dirtier' it got the more excited she would become; eventually she would have an orgasm imagining her partner with another woman. This was enacted while being chained to the bed, immobilised and utterly subservient to her partner. Afterwards she would feel appalled, depressed, unworthy of tenderness or love.

During therapy it became apparent that this woman's fantasies had to do with an uncaring and neglectful mother who had made a profitable marriage to a man she despised. She was unable to feel deserving of any man's love, and would conjure up the fantasy of her mother, identifying with her during sexual intercourse, splitting herself into two women. One of them was experienced as a despicable creature who could orgasm when denigrated by making hate instead of love. The other was a professional scholar who would belittle and undermine men while unable to get satisfaction from intimate relationships with them. Professional success was unconsciously linked with killing her mother, who was experienced by her as an 'internal saboteur' who would undermine all her efforts to succeed. We can clearly see in this patient the splitting between her 'libidinal ego' and the 'internal saboteur' described by Fairbairn (1944).[1]

Motherhood can provide a vehicle for some women to exercise perverse attitudes in retaliation against their own mothers. Women's capacity for procreation becoming pregnant and bearing the baby within her own body—provides some of the same emotional characteristics in terms of her object-relations as are found in highly distorted forms in perverse relationships. These include the desire to engulf the other person, to

[1] Fairbairn, R. W. D. (1952a). Endopsychic Structure Considered in Terms of Object-relationships. In R. W. D. Fairbairn (Ed.), *Psycho-analytic Studies of the Personality*. London: Routledge, pp. 82–136.

dehumanise the object, to intrude into, to invade, to be in complete control of and to merge with the other. Whereas in men perverse acts are aimed at external part-objects, in women they are directed against themselves, against their own bodies, or against objects of their own creation, that is, their babies.

I remember a patient who was referred for a psychiatric assessment because of violent behaviour directed towards her second child. Her first pregnancy came as a surprise to her. She proceeded with it as an insurance against a dread of being alone. The child would be dependent on her, under her control. When this first baby was born, she was overcome by feelings of repulsion and revulsion. To overcome these feelings she decided she would fix in her mind the idea of the baby as part of herself. Some days she would choose her right arm as being the baby, and at other times it would be one of her legs. In this way she felt able to master the impulse to strike the child. With her second baby she asserted, "There is no more room in my body for a second one". A strong quality of dehumanisation and the reduction of object to part-object relationship, which are features in perversion, are present here.

My clinical observations confirm this bias. On countless occasions, agencies and establishments have expressed alarm, sometimes verging on panic, when referring male patients to me as sexual abusers. This contrasts strongly with the difficulty my female patients have often had in being taken seriously by some agencies.

I remember a patient who was originally referred from a Child Guidance Clinic where her daughter, aged six, had been sent because of behavioural problems mainly related to school refusal. Following diagnostic assessment there, it was decided that the child's problems were the result of a disturbed family situation, particularly in her relationship with her mother. My patient was described as an inadequate mother who showed exhibitionist behaviour, such as exaggerated demonstrations of affection towards her daughter. However, when she had decided some time to seek help for these preoccupations, she was told not to worry: "It is just natural for a mother to feel very fond of her children, especially if they are single parents". However, she had so closely identified with her daughter that she had come to act like a little girl, expecting her daughter to take care of her needs, including being cuddled and bathed by her.

The little girl defended herself against these excessive demands by a most primitive and infantile acting out.

Mother and daughter had a symbiotic relationship to the extent of sharing the same bed. The mother had initiated the girl in an incestuous sexual relation which involved caressing of breasts and eventually masturbation of her daughter's genitals. The mother had not allowed the girl to attend school because she could not bear the idea of her absence. Nor would the mother let her have her own friends, or life, or allow her to grow up. My patient explained: "I want to be the mother I never had, someone who could be all the time with me and whose attentions could be entirely devoted to me as her daughter instead of being like my mother, hating me so much for being a girl and so involved with the other children and her husband that she never had a minute for me alone. She never forgave me either, that I was born a girl, being the first child. She had so much longed for a boy. I was always the victim of humiliation, and it became much worse when all the other children, five, were born. They were all girls. Then my mother turned to me with even more hatred than ever." (This patient was born in a country where socially and culturally girls were considered as inferior in a more overt way than in the UK and had very little opportunity to make a life of their own.) "As soon as I could I emigrated to this country with the purpose of making my own life as a woman".

Thereafter my patient became a prostitute, a profession which she felt offered her the opportunity of being valued for her female body, whereas previously she had felt degraded because of it. According to her, she felt a kick of elation not only that her body was desired by men but also that they were ready to pay for it. Also, she added another dimension to her job, involving her intelligence, her wonderful command of language and her skilled powers of communication, all of which had been so long overlooked. She became so expert a story-teller that sometimes she could pocket her client's money without it crossing their minds to touch her body. Through such stories she was temporarily able to cope with her intense feelings of depression and low self-esteem. But her despair began to emerge in a way which she felt unable to contain. Eventually she decided to have a child to fulfil her own expectations as a baby. The man chosen for this project was just a token. She had even forgotten who it was or perhaps she felt happier not acknowledging him, scared to have as father to her child someone like her own father, who from her birth had not only ignored her but had also prevented her from accessing an education. She had only contempt towards her mother, primarily because she had felt so rejected by her for being a girl. How could she come to terms with having a body like her mother's, a life like hers? She had experienced her mother as an object of her father's contempt, since her mother could only produce girls, a sex so much underrated by both of them. How could she overcome the feelings of self-deprecation?

She was an intelligent and sensitive woman who had never felt encouraged as a human being, let alone as a girl. She had never trusted anyone and had always kept aloof. Her clients had become "her only friends". Now she yearned for someone she could trust, who could be dependent on her. She gave birth to a girl, in whom she could easily mirror herself and her own needs. She viewed herself, to start with, as an excellent mother. She spent all her time with her daughter. Her working hours never interfered with her functioning as a mother, since she would only work at night, when the child was asleep. So it was only when the daughter began to have emotional problems that the mother started a long and laborious self-questioning of her own motivations.

But why is it so hard to believe in maternal incest, or to regard it as being as serious as male incest? Even in group therapy, which offers a scenario in which this phenomenon is mirrored, men and women alike tend to express not only concern but also shock when confronted with male offenders. Group members seem to identify with the little girls, and experience revulsion and repulsion towards the father's actions. In fact this can prove therapeutic since male offenders are shamed although after a period of intolerance group members often show concern and care. By contrast, the female 'offender' finds other patients minimising her problems. No-one seems to want to hear about her predicament and nobody takes her very seriously. This reaction proves very anti-therapeutic and if the therapist is not ready to interpret the massive denial involved, these women will never have a chance to experience psychic change.

My argument is that motherhood as a perversion occurs as a breakdown of inner mental structures, whereby the mother feels not only emotionally crippled in dealing with the psychological and physical demands from her baby, but also impotent and unable to obtain gratification from other sources. She experiences her perverse behaviour as the only power available to her, through her exclusive emotional and physical authority over her baby. Hence perverse motherhood must be seen as the product of the emotional instability and inadequate individuation brought about by a process that involves at least three generations.[2] But part of the problem lies with society, in that our whole culture supports the idea that mothers have complete dominion over their babies.

The study of power politics might throw new light on the understanding of motherhood functions. Perhaps if women had a longer tradition of belonging to the power structures their attitudes towards men and children would not be governed, as they are now, by a weakness which they strive to turn into possessiveness and control.

[2] Welldon, E. V. (1988). *Mother Madonna Whore*. London: Karnac.

Part IV

Sublimation>Sinthome>Culture

15

The Ball-Joint and the Anagram: Perversion and Jouissance in Hans Bellmer

Michael Newman

If perversion is a structure between neurosis and psychosis, does the conference title 'Perversion Now' imply that the structure, while remaining constant, manifests itself differently at different historical periods, or that the structure itself is transformed or at least contains different possibilities? The perversion I am going to be discussing here—through an approach to the work of the German artist Hans Bellmer—may stand in contrast to perversion 'now' or in our modernity, but I hope will nonetheless suggest the irreducibility of a moment of perversion in the genesis of the work of art, and its relevance for thinking the paradoxical nature of human singularity in relation to law.

M. Newman (✉)
Goldsmiths, University of London

D. Caine, C. Wright (eds.), *Perversion Now!*,
DOI 10.1007/978-3-319-47271-3_15

There are broadly three aspects to the work of Hans Bellmer, who was born in Upper Silesia in 1902[1]: the photos of the two dolls that he made, the first during the mid-30s, the second during the late-30s; drawings, etchings and photographs from the late-30s to the mid-60s (he died in 1975); and in between a series of writings, some around and involving anagrams. Bellmer's work is a practice that through the image, the anagram, and the trait of drawing involves the dimensions of the Imaginary, Symbolic and the Real, with the crucial question of how a singular practice invokes a peculiar relation between them that calls to be explicated through the structure of perversion. This question obviously recalls Lacan's final teaching around James Joyce and the sinthome. If the reversion to the letter gives rise to the linguistic play of *Finnegans Wake*, how does the letter function in relation to the body, in particular the representation of the woman's body, in Bellmer?

While I have no intention of venturing a psychoanalytic interpretation of Bellmer the man, I cannot resist referring to a train journey that he made with his father in 1923. Bellmer's father was a conservative Prussian who had fought in the First World War. He was an engineer by profession, and it was decided that his son would be enrolled in the Berlin Technical College to study that subject. Bellmer has recounted how, in Peter Webb's words 'after the night-time journey he had emerged from his carriage wearing thick make-up and heavy lipstick with kiss-curls drawn in charcoal on his powdered cheeks. The image of open provocation was completed with a black bowler hat on his head and a blood-red pamphlet written by George Grosz brandished in his hand. His father had no choice but to accompany this extraordinary sight across Berlin to their hotel.'[2]

A provocation indeed, but is it not also a scene of seduction, with Bellmer turning himself into a doll? There is also instability in the signifiers of sexual difference: both powdered cheeks and bowler hat. This raises the question, when it comes to Bellmer's making of the dolls in 1934 and

[1] For studies of Bellmer, see Webb, P. and Short, R. (1985). *Hans Bellmer.* London: Quartet; Taylor, S. (2000). *Hans Bellmer: The Anatomy of Anxiety*. Cambridge, MA: MIT Press; Lichtenstein, T. (2001). *Behind Closed Doors: The Art of Hans Bellmer*. Berkeley and New York: University of California Press International Center of Photography.

[2] Webb and Short, op. cit., p. 13.

'35, of the position of identification and relation to the father. If the dolls are Bellmer's object, does he not also identify with them in relation to the father? There seems to be an ambivalence: Bellmer mocks his father while his mother enters into collusion with him—she sends him a box of childhood toys and dolls—but in a roundabout way he follows his father's profession, even in the production of the dolls, given his emphasis on their aspect of engineering. The performance of seduction seems to aim at provoking the appearance of a desiring, obscene, incestuous father, but also to revive a Father that would provide a law or limit on *jouissance*.

The doll has a double character, at once a 'virgin' girl with her short white socks, idealised, but also a knowing woman, in other words before and after some kind of violation. She is at the two poles of base, abject, waste, and remote and pure. Lacan in *Seminar VII* writes of sublimation as raising an object to the dignity of the Thing.[3] The doll is at the two limits of the object: below as cast-off, and above as pure. At either extreme, she would be out of circulation, outside the chain of signifiers and substitution of objects governed by the Symbolic.

The photos and drawings are also traps. As Jean Clavreul argues, the pervert is the one who traps, because "the relationship between the fetishist and his fetish is sustained only when this fetish has the power to fascinate the other."[4] Clavreul contrasts the illusion (or representation) which for the neurotic is the means of access to the truth with the fetish of the pervert: "This fetishization is marked by the fact that the activity, the knowledge, and the interests of the pervert must above all be *rigorously of no use*, to lead nowhere. Anything validated by the pervert is marked with the seal of uselessness."[5] Apart from making the pervert sound already like an artist, this uselessness indicates a relation to the Real. Indeed I think it would be possible to re-read the history of modern art in terms of its relation to perversion. Let us take a feature of Bellmer's doll photographs as a starting point, their relation to forensic photographs of crime scenes. Henry Bond suggests, "An essential quality of the perverse

[3] Lacan, J. (1992)[1959–60]. *The Seminar of Jacques Lacan, Book VII: The Ethics of Psychoanalysis.* J.-A. Miller, Ed. & D. Porter (Trans.). London: Routledge, p. 112.

[4] Clavreul, J. (1980). 'The Perverse Couple', in *Returning to Freud: Clinical Psychoanalysis in the School of Lacan*, Stuart Schneiderman (Ed.). New Haven: Yale University Press, p. 218.

[5] ibid., p. 225.

fantasy is that it is a fundamentally built image. It is portable and can be remapped in any new setting, like a series of instructions (a scalable diagram) that can be deployed as required."[6] There is an intrinsic relation between photography and perversion—photography is not a realist but a perverse medium, because it freezes and stops time (and creates tableaux).[7] As Bond writes, "the problem of 'not knowing' is resolved—in a state of duress—by simply, and so brutally, freezing the action: producing a 'frozen moment' which, above all, restores certainty."[8]

As Lacan says vis à vis Joyce, the artist's knowledge is a 'savoir faire'.[9] Four key procedures in what we might describe as Bellmer's perverse making involve the mirror, the ball-joint, the anagram and the trait.[10] In one of his own writings, 'The Ball-Joint', Bellmer describes the procedure of placing a mirror on a picture of the body—we might suppose a photograph—and angling it. There is an obvious anamorphic dimension to this to induce a division and a gaze in the field of the visible, but the axis also creates a limit or vortex where the body is 'sucked up into nothingness'.[11] This produces a sense of horror, which Bellmer describes according to the metaphor of a candle melting into its own wax (a catastrophic collapse of the phallus into an "informe"—formless—blob). If the mirror divides and doubles, the solution is the whip, which 'unites the top into a new reality', a spinning top which thereby forms a cone, which reminds Bellmer of the multi-breasted Venus of Ephesus. The joint of the symmetrical division—a figure of the female sex?—is unified by a whip which produces the maternal or Imaginary phallus.

---

[6] Bond, H. (2009). *Lacan at the Scene*. Cambridge, MA: MIT Press, p. 58.

[7] Metz, C. (1985). 'Photography and Fetish'. *October*, Autumn, 1985, pp. 81–90.

[8] Bond, 2009, op. cit., p. 71.

[9] Lacan. J. (2005)[1975–6]. *Le Seminaire de Jacques Lacan: Livre XXIII, Le sinthome.* J.-A.Miller, (Ed.). Paris: Seuil, pp. 61–64; Lacan, J. (1975–6). *Seminar, Book XXIII: Joyce and the Sinthome.* C. Gallagher (Trans.), http://www.lacaninireland.com/web/published-works/seminars/ (accessed 13 August 2015), 13.1.1976. See also Harari, R. (2002). *How James Joyce Made His Name: A Reading of the Final Lacan.* New York: Other Press; Thurston, L. (Ed.). (2002). *Re-Inventing the Symptom: Essays on the Final Lacan.* New York: Other Press; Thurston, L. (2004). *James Joyce and the Problem of Psychoanalysis.* Cambridge: Cambridge University Press.

[10] Masson, C. (2000). *La Fabrique de la poupée chez Hans Bellmer: Le "faire-œoeuvre perversif", une étude clinique de l'objet.* Paris: Harmattan.

[11] Bellmer, H. (2005). *The Doll.* London: Atlas Press, p. 66.

Effects of symmetry in the female body were made possible by the introduction of a ball-joint at the position of the stomach, to which, for example, a second set of legs could be attached in place of the upper torso, arms and head. Bellmer writes in some detail of the history of the 'Cardan' joint where the centre is in a state of equilibrium while the outside shell is turned (thus, for instance, an ink pot could be rotated while always having it's opening at the top, so that the ink never gets spilled). Bellmer wonders what would happen if the outside were at the centre, answering 'two fundamentally conflicting demands….concentricity and eccentricity'.[12] Effectively the outside would become the inside, and *vice versa*. *Extimité*, as J.-A Miller writes, is used by Lacan to designate the Real in the Symbolic.[13] Bellmer discusses the outside inside as a problem at once of engineering (the Cardan joint and the ball joint), and of the body.

Bellmer then turns to the discussion of the body in terms of tropes of language, but subject to rules that are not those of grammar. He writes of the body as a 'physical alphabet' which may be organised according to condensations, superimpositions, proofs of analogies, ambiguities, and puns. This "accords completely with the way the body unconsciously creates symbols".[14] Having established the way that the body functions as language in this sense, things take a different turn.

In "The Anatomy of the Image", Bellmer again describes doubling the image of the body by holding an angled mirror against it, but now he compares the 'axis of reversibility' to 'mirror writing' and 'reversal of syllables', which he compares to palindromes. In other words, he moves from mirror inversion to that of sentences or phrases where the operation is not at the level of metaphor and metonymy but rather involves the reversal of letters generating a play of meaning but also nonsense. What this involves is a shift from relations of signifiers, whether metaphoric or metonymic, to the letter extracted from the word and the chain of signi-

[12] ibid., p. 60.

[13] Miller, J.-A. (2008). 'Extimity' in *The Symptom*, 9, Fall 2008, http://www.lacan.com/ symptom/ (accessed 13 August 2015).

[14] Bellmer, 2005, op. cit., p. 68.

fiers. What are the implications of this for the relation of the body to the signifier?

Bellmer describes

> a certain photographic image that has remained an unfading memory, a man had haphazardly bound his victim's thighs, shoulders, chest, back and belly with strong iron wire in order to deform her. Tightly criss-crossed, it produced swollen cushions of flesh, irregular, spherical triangles, incising her body with long creases and impure lips, creating hitherto unseen multiplications of breasts in indescribable places.[15]

It is, in fact, the description of a series of photographs he made of his partner Unica Zürn, one of which was published as the cover of *Le Surréalisme, même*, no. 4, 1958.

This procedure involves effectively parcelling up the body by drawing lines on it with wire, as if incising traits into it. Again he compares the effect to Diana of Ephesus, which draws attention to the repetition or multiplication of the traits (maybe also the marks of the whip, going back to the idea of the top). He writes of the new, 'synthetic Eve':

> She is born of division, subtraction and multiplication, but also of that interchangeability that mathematicians call 'permutation' and philologists 'anagrams', and whose significance is this: the body resembles a sentence that seems to invite us to dismantle it into its component letters, so that its true meanings may be revealed anew through an endless stream of anagrams.[16]

The meaning of the body here does not work through metaphor and metonymy (as in hysterical conversion) but rather through a surface (indeed topological) conversion of body parts and segments into letters which may then be subject to an endless combinatory, producing phallic *jouissance*, which Bellmer describes as 'language's pleasure in creating such forms'.[17] However according to the rules of the game, the letters in

---

[15] ibid., p. 129.

[16] ibid., p. 133.

[17] ibid., p. 115.

their new combinations must form words and sentences, thus subjecting themselves to an already existing dictionary and grammar, preceding the act of creation.[18] The basis is the applicability of the letter to the body through the trait, which is in effect a cut.[19] Lacan speaks of the trait in relation to the cuts the Marquis de Sade made on his bed-head to commemorate his ejaculations with his valet,[20] inscribing in relation to the signifier the repetitive count of *jouissance.*

It is clear from Bellmer's writing—particularly the description of the abyss of the mirror-hinge, and the melting candle—that the production is related to anxiety. The absence of a signifier of sexual difference (vagina and penis are interchangeable and merge) requires an alternative set of procedures to organise *jouissance*. Through these procedures, the artist takes the place of the failed father who is at once the overbearing Nazi and a pathetic invalid, obscene and inadequate.

In this respect, the move is similar to the artist 'making a name for himself' compensating for the inadequate father in Lacan's Joyce.[21] Effectively, what we see in Bellmer's oeuvre, from the doll to the drawings via the trait and the anagram is the very move from sublimation to sinthome. What this involves is a shift from a conception of art engaging with the Thing of the Real to 'the' Symbolic, to the relation of the Real

---

[18] See Zürn, U. (1994). *The Man of Jasmine*. M. Green (Trans.). London: Atlas Press, pp. 115–6, on breaking the rules: For her, in the making of an anagram, there are always letters that are left over. She reports that for the first anagram she makes this summer, she takes the phrase "the imaginary madness" (*Der eingebildete Wahnsinn*). The result:

'Your ways into the hiterland B.

Where it rains in blindly.—We—

Woe—Deliriums are prayers. N—N—N—

...

Will it never end?

No G—B—L—I—H—Who?—'

...

But she adds:

'The result is poor and imperfect. The rule for anagrams is that each anagram must use up all the letters contained in the initial sentence. Some letters have been left over, and that is forbidden.'

[19] Lacan, J. (1961–2). *Seminar, Book IX: Identification.* C. Gallagher (Trans.), 22.11.1961, pp. 11–18.

[20] ibid., 06.12.1961, pp. 28–37.

[21] Lacan, 2005, op. cit., p. 94; Lacan, 1975–6, op. cit., 17.2.1976.

to the creation of 'a' symbolic, namely in Bellmer's case the law of the anagram.

What is at stake in this is the singularity of the subject. Nothing internal to the Symbolic, Imaginary or Real can give that singularity. And if it is a 'relation' as a fourth thing, that is paradoxical, since singularity is precisely that which is not reducible to relations. So the subject is held together in a singular way by the relation of a non-relation. This must also apply to the Real and to *jouissance*, such that singularity has not to do with a special hotline to *jouissance* (a supposition which is the source of the neurotic's pervert-envy), but the particular form that a non-relation takes which, as generative or productive, is both non-relation and relation. How may this be articulated?

I want to consider the surface of inscription, that which receives the mark, or the surface of the etching plate, with the possibility that we might thereby locate a second level to fetishism, and thereby another implication of perversion. According to Henri Rey-Flaud's discussions of fetishism, the phallus as signifier of difference requires a prior difference, '*la différence brute indifférenciante*' (the brute undifferentiated difference).[22] This is a primary difference referred to the space of the Thing, which doesn't inscribe any temporality, any ordinality—'*un brouillonnement palpitant, un grouillement saccadé*' (a trembling muddle, a jerky swarming). Without the intervention of the name of the father or its initial *trait unaire* (unary trait), this structure would be psychotic. The brute difference is the condition for the first symbolic metaphor. The *Urverdrängung*, the primal repression that will found the representative system, depends on the difference between difference and non-difference. Difference has to be attributed before it can be a matter of something—such as the maternal penis—existing or not existing. According to Rey-Flaud, the denial involved in the phallic lack of the woman, the expression of the denial of symbolic difference, is but the metastasis of a primordial denial bearing on brute difference.[23]

This is the level not of presence/absence (Imaginary) or of the disavowal of knowledge (of Symbolic castration) but rather the level of inscription.

---

[22] Rey-Flaud, R. (2002). *Le Démenti pervers: le refoulé et l'oublié.* Paris: Aubier, p. 148.

[23] ibid., p. 149.

What makes the difference between difference and non-difference is the inscription of the trait. Insofar as this is the 'trait unaire' (before the difference between signifiers) it is the primordial inscription of—or being inscribed with—the Symbolic of the Father that opens up the very possibility of a relation, in the sense of a passage rather than a negation (it is 'pre-negation' as it were), rather than a fusion, with the Real of *jouissance* (the Real that is not a falling away from the Symbolic).[24] The *trait unaire* (*einziger Zug,* unary trait), which in the *Seminar IX* on Identification Lacan associates with marks or cuts, is also a primary identification of the ego ideal, hence both a first difference and a first alienation which marks the subject, and is associated with both the symptom and the proper name.[25] We could say that the trait meets the letter insofar as both are singular: the unary trait differentiates itself from non-difference not from another signifier; and the letter falls out of the chain of signifiers. The single Letter is the step between the *trait unaire* and the difference of (at least two) signifiers. The overlapping of the trait and the Letter is the meeting point of the Real and the Symbolic.

What it at stake here, I would add, is once again a relation with the non-relational, this time as pre-differential. If the Symbolic is ultimately relation, the question then becomes: What would the Symbolic need to be that which would enable the relation with brute difference, the denial of which underlies second order fetishism which may thus be seen as a symptom of defence against psychosis? In Lacan's earlier model of sublimation, that relation would be that of 'falling away'—the Real as that which falls away from the Symbolic. In the later conception which gives rise to the sinthome the Real is, as Colette Soler puts it, 'outside of the Symbolic'[26]; it has a specific valency of its own, so can contribute actively to the formation of the—or a—Symbolic. If perversion involves the construction of a relation to *jouissance*, this need not remain stuck at the Imaginary maternal phallus, but may also involve an intervention into the Symbolic, such as Joyce's creation of polyvalent or equivocal words from lalangue—engendered, according to Lacan, by 'the totality of women...

[24] Soler, C. (2014). *Lacan—the Unconscious Reinvented.* E. Faye & S. Schwartz (Trans.). London: Karnac.

[25] Lacan, 1961–2, op. cit.

[26] Soler, op. cit., p. 3.

before a tongue that is decomposing'—in *Finnegans Wake*.[27] In Bellmer the 'active' relation to the creation of a symbolic involves the anagram and the trait. While the anagram is based on letters separated from words to make new words, the trait will concern, indeed institute, the difference in difference of difference and non-difference. Thus the perverse refusal of the signifier for sexual difference leads to a regression (in the logical sense) to the separation from non-difference via the (paternal) *trait unaire* meeting up with the doubleness of the Letter between the Real and the Symbolic of the signifiers. The relation takes place not through the constituted Symbolic (from which the Real can only be conceived as having fallen away), but through the Letter. The Letter connects the signifier to *jouissance* and allows for the creation of a Real-Symbolic. The inscription of the body by the trait as seen in Bellmer's photographs of Zürn, and his drawings, allows for the relation to the body—the woman's body—as non-difference but on the basis of a violent delimitation. To treat the body as an anagram implies the non-distinction of words and things characteristic of psychosis, but this is recuperated by the rule of a perverse scenario which becomes the law of a work of art, based in this case on the sacrifice of the feminine *jouissance* that is not-All, where the letter would fall out of the word.[28] The defence against psychosis becomes confused with the defence against the feminine.

Nonetheless it may still be possible to make a distinction between a fixating repetitive perversion, and a perversion that is transformational and productive. This is at least one of the things I think Lacan was getting at with his notion of the 'sinthome' as a fourth term or knot that holds together the Real, Symbolic and Imaginary. It locates the singularity of the subject not in a substance or essence, but in a way of relating or holding together which opens up the possibility of a generative relation to *jouissance* and the Real. Bellmer's work hovers on a strange edge between symptom and sinthome, between a repetitive acting out and a generative production, between the fixity and repetition of the phantasm and what disrupts it and opens it up to change (and thus, one might add,

[27] Lacan, 2005, op. cit., p. 117; Lacan, 1975–6, op. cit., 9.3.1976.

[28] For the feminine as 'not-All', see Lacan, J. (1972–3). Seminar, Book: XX: *Encore*. C. Gallagher (Trans.), http://www.lacaninireland.com/web/published-works/seminars/.

between originality and kitsch). It can thus be read as both a generative perversion as relation without relation to primary in-difference, and as a symptomatic perversion that defends against psychosis. Perhaps that is a reason why his work may be paradigmatic of 'perversion now'. On this edge perversion becomes a kind of *pharmakon*, at once a disavowal of difference and the means of a transformation of the Symbolic of the singular subject through a regression to in-difference where it is marked by the trait as a first One that will come via the Letter to hold the dimensions of the subject together in a unique way.

The Unary Trait, the trait of a primary and singular identification of the Other is the place where *jouissance* and the Symbolic are connected. The trait comes from the Other as a point of identification that marks an invasion of *jouissance* in the body. The repetitions through which *jouissance* insists lie at the origin of the signifier. As Paul Verhaeghe suggests, *jouissance* thereby becomes the gateway to the signifier.[29]

This helps us to account for the law-like character of a work that does not fall under the already given law of a Symbolic Order (what art and literary criticism tried to grasp under the notion of 'style'). It provides a basis for the invention of a law, a savoir-faire that finds its source in *jouissance* (the being-marked by a trait of the irruption of *jouissance*) that through the making as a form of repetition is simultaneously promulgated and lost in the back and forth between the singular trait or letter and the treasure of signifiers and general knowledge. Therefore there are two perverse moments here: first, not giving up on the connection between the trait and *jouissance*, which involves the 'regression' to the level of inscription and the letter extracted from the system of language (this is not a disavowal insofar as the association of *jouissance* with the trait is constitutive of the signifier—in this sense the pervert reveals a truth that the neurotic has given up on or repressed); and second, the insistence that this relation to the signifier through *jouissance* can be turned into a law (evident in sadism and masochism). This arguably involves disavowal of

[29] Verhaeghe, P. (2006). 'Enjoyment and Impossibility: Lacan's Revision of the Oedipus Complex', in J. Clemens and R. Grigg (Eds), *Jacques Lacan and the Other Side of Psychoanalysis: Reflections on Seminar XVII.* Durham: Duke University Press, p. 32.

the separation that makes desire possible, at the cost of the abandonment of *jouissance*.

What we are faced with, in at least some works of art, is a distinction between the repetition of substitutions involved in desire and the repetition of the return of *jouissance*. The savoir-faire of art articulates these alternate kinds of repetition in the institution through practice of a paradoxical law of the singular oeuvre.

16

Neither Loss nor Mourning, but Perversion

Diana Kamienny Boczkowski

My attention has been drawn to certain instances of artistic production where *jouissance* seems to derive from losses that have not been symbolised. The hypothesis we can make about some of these cases is that loss can lead to the creation of a *jouissance* that could be linked to perversion. In these cases there is a pure and simple denial of loss, a loss not symbolised through the introduction of the accounting function of the phallic symbol. When this function is denied, the subject might create a real substitute for the phallus, which—though not allowing the loss to be symbolised—can take its place, characterised in Lacan's later work as the sinthome. Does the case of Joyce, in his use of the letter, especially in his letters to Nora, not show us such *jouissance*?

In the *Écrits*, Lacan detects a connection between loss and the fetish. Writing about the burning of Gide's correspondence by his wife Madeleine, he notes that with this act there were two losses: one for

D. Kamienny Boczkowski (✉)
Association lacanienne International

D. Caine, C. Wright (eds.), *Perversion Now!*,
DOI 10.1007/978-3-319-47271-3_16

Gide himself and the other for the world. Lacan writes, "The letters in which he placed his soul [...] had no carbon copy. When their *fetishistic nature* appeared it gave rise to the kind of laughter that greets subjectivity caught off guard" (my emphasis).[1] For Gide, these letters are a fetish; for the world their disappearance provokes laughter, for it is at this moment the phallic value insinuates itself. Added to this is the further loss of which Lacan writes: that of Gide's father, leaving Gide to the mercy of his mother.

Many definitions of perversion appear throughout Lacan's seminars. One of them elaborates the proximity between perversion and sublimation, both of which can engender *jouissance* in the Other. This authorises the exploration of artistic productions from this dual point of view. It is the relationship between the denial of loss and the emergence of a perverse and often obscene *jouissance* that I am going to look at here.

16.1 Loss and Mourning

Why do we miss someone when we are grieving? According to Lacan, the fact of missing them is determined by what we were for the lost person; the part that we have been for the other, the loved one who has disappeared. What do we mean when we say that the unrepresentable death has not been symbolised? We mean that the subject does not engage in the process whereby, little by little, libidinal attachment is withdrawn from the loved object, described so eloquently by Freud in 'Mourning and Melancholia'.

The void of loss can be raised to the dignity of a structural loss. Religion has its relics; the history of art is full of objects that are part of the process of grieving by virtue of their role in the elaboration that takes place around this void. The history of photography as an art form in its own right contains a large chapter intimately linked to mourning.

[1] Lacan J. (1958). "Jeunesse de Gide ou la lettre et le désir", in *Écrits*. Paris: Seuil, 1966, p. 739.

16.2 Neither Loss Nor Mourning: Two Cases

The first case I want to discuss is that of the French Surrealist painter and photographer Pierre Molinier, whose life is full of moments of *passage à l'acte*, as well as numerous demonstrations of his sexual position and his taste for cross-dressing. It is well-known that Molinier had a sister whose legs he greatly admired and who died when he was 15 years old. What is somewhat less known is that after the sister's death Molinier experienced an orgasm while caressing her legs during the wake. He becomes the inventor of Surrealist photography. In his works, legs proliferate: both his own, in drag, and those of other people. He stages these legs, identifying with the body of his dead sister. While this identification bears witness to a denial of loss, there is no other trace of the loss he suffered in the biographical material available to us. Here, mourning is political: it reminds us that our fate is determined by the other and by his or her disappearance.[2]

This reading suggests that the denial of loss can function in precisely the same way as the disavowal of the lack of the phallus of the mother/sister. This is key to understanding certain clinical cases. The example of Molinier reminds us that the image that becomes fixated in the place of the denial, of the *Veleugnung*, is the last image preserved after the traumatic recognition of the mother's castration. The fetishisation of the legs, elevated to the status of an *objet d'art*, is a possible outcome of the foreclosure of mourning or loss. It would appear that the separation carried out by the grieving subject,[3] did not take place for Molinier. On the contrary: the loss was denied. In its place—and this is my argument—we see the emergence of an object of *jouissance* hinting at perversion. By the way, Molinier's relationship to the death of his father was also quite particular: he kept the father's bones in a suitcase in his workshop.

The scene he used to repeat in this workshop was organised around a mirror, a bed, the body in very precise positions, the legs, and often a photo taken in this moment. He dressed like a seductive woman for these artistic photographs; and he committed suicide in the same place.

---

[2] Butler, J. (2005). *Vie précaire: Les pouvoirs du deuil et de la violence après le 11 septembre 2001.* Paris: Broché.

[3] Allouch, J. (2011). *L'érotique du deuil au temps de la mort sèche.* Paris: Broché.

16.3 'Melancholia' by Ryū Murakami

The second case is the novel *Melancholia* by Ryu Murakami, where the title refers to the melancholia of the main character, Yazaki. Themes of sadism and denial resonate throughout. The second character in the book is a female journalist who, while interviewing Yazaki, becomes identified with the place of the object in his fantasy.

Yazaki used to be a film producer; Reiko, a woman he lost, was an actress in one of his films. It was the loss of Reiko that prompts the impossible mourning that continues throughout the book. And yet we somehow cannot detect the register of mourning. In losing Reiko, Yazaki lost an object of *jouissance* rather than a love object.

In his loss, Yazaki takes on the status of a "pseudo-homeless" person, without a fixed abode. We could call this melancholia: an identification with the object as waste, outside all discourse. Yazaki does nothing to keep Reiko. The dimension of desire is completely absent. He behaves exactly as he did in his childhood when, by his father's decision, he was separated from a little dog to which he was strongly attached. It is only during the interview with the journalist that Yazaki speaks about his loss, which indirectly lets us see the prior loss of the dog. Indeed, in his answers to the journalist's questions, he brings up a series of losses, which begin with the dog and continue with the loss of his father in his childhood, the loss of a child at birth and the loss of Reiko. There is also an account of Yazaki's nightmare, in which Reiko calls to him in the same way that the abandoned dog called for his father.

In the series of Yazaki's losses we should also include the loss of another homeless man, Mr Johnson, who functions as a figure of knowledge, particularly knowledge about the Aztecs (Johnson tells Yazaki that the Aztecs enjoyed imposing anal torture on their enemies). When Johnson dies of HIV, Yazaki decides that he no longer needs to be homeless.

From the series of losses beginning with the dog and including Reiko and the women, described on all fours, an interchangeability of object attachment can be deduced. The logic of the losses and the mourning Yazaki described to the journalist, exert a kind of fascination on her, a fantasmatic construction which eventually brings her, like an abandoned object, to a distant land, where she is taken by car, just like Yazaki's little dog was taken in his childhood.

Taken to a faraway place, the journalist is transformed into separate organs, disassembled into objects that are intended for the "international organ trade". Yazaki identifies with the Aztec torturer and is no longer homeless. Yazaki's father, a chemical engineer, had committed a professional error, which created an earthquake in the family's life. A connection can be made between the father's fault and Yazaki's own drug addiction. He can neither love a woman nor enjoy her—his *jouissance* is intimately linked to cocaine, a chemical product representing the father's fault. He cannot but repeat the abandonment of the dog under the guise of abandoning this woman, whose position as a piece of waste echoes his own previous homeless existence.

Is not the use of organs without the victim's consent in this story, an allusion to the generalisation of the Sadian maxim, bringing about what Lacan calls, in his Écrits, an "odious social order"?[4]

16.4 What Is the Link with Now?

The emergence of the obscene is something we see in both Molinier's work and in the novel by Murakami Ryu. The word 'obscene' itself, derived from the Latin *obscenus,* is commonly translated into French as "what cannot be shown on the scene".[5] It is also part of the language of divination; its presence suggests bad omens.[6] In both of their works, the obscene figure appears in the place of mourning; the organ trade in its relationship to *jouissance* in Murakami, the various perverse practices in the place of unsymbolised loss in Molinier.

In today's world, we are witness to the increased presence of the obscene in social space. Lacan also defines perversion as the universal law of a right to *jouissance*, a law that, contrary to the Kantian maxim, puts

[4] Lacan, J. (1962). "Kant avec Sade" in *Ecrits*. Paris: Seuil, 1966, pp. 765–90.

[5] ibid.

[6] Desanti, J.-T. (1983). "L'obcène ou les malices du signifiant" in *The Dado Syndrome: Dado's Virtual Anti-Museum*, available from http://www.dado.virtual.museum/dado-artwork-desanti.php.

an emphasis on self-love. Today, the obscene is increasingly put on show, to the extent of creating its own aesthetics. It is displayed as an ordinary characteristic as evidenced, for example, by a series of recent opera productions: *Guillaume Tell* in London,[7] Daniel Slater's reimagining of *Aida*[8] in Holland Park or Katie Mitchell's *Alcina* in Aix-en-Provence,[9] which revolves around a perverse scenario. What is the function of these productions and why are they suddenly so numerous? Why was Slater subject to such ferocious criticism this summer and why was the Royal Opera House director Damiano Michieletto forced to actually change several minutes of his production of *Guillaume Tell*? We could argue that these productions show a critique of, rather than apology for, perversion. How could we be surprised? Even Lacan in his seminar *Encore* said that all art is obscene.

16.5 Loss and *Jouissance*

In contrast with perversion that is well defined—that provokes the *jouissance* of the Other, that is repetitive and clearly connected to the denial of castration, that has a clearly established fantasy—there is also a perverse *use* of *jouissance*, which is much less well-defined. This perverse use can be limited to a specific object or person, or to a form of relationship to the Other. In our two cases, loss appears to be the negative counterpart of a certain use of *jouissance*, where not only is the loss *not* symbolised but it remains absent from the subject's imaginary. What results is artistic production that can take the form of a perverse practice.

---

[7] Donizetti, G. "Guillaume Tell", Royal Opéra House, London, September 2015.

[8] Verdi, J. "Aida", Holland Park Opera, London, July 2015.

[9] Handel, G.F. "Alcina", Théâtre de l'Archevêché, Aix en Provence, July 2015.

17

Perversion and Sublimation

Luigi Burzotta

One hardly need knock thrice on the set in order to announce the curtain call: we are already in *The Balcony* of Jean Genet. What happens in this play? *The Balcony* is a brothel and its regulars: the little old man, the employee of a credit institution, gentlemen who indulge themselves by dressing up and playing the role of certain characters. The most sought after are those that represent human functions which bear on the symbolic through the power conferred upon them by society: the Bishop, the Judge, the General.

> All of these figures represent functions in relation to which the subject finds himself in some way alienated, these are functions, of speech, of which the subject finds himself (sic) to be the support, but which go well beyond his particularity.[1]

[1] Lacan, J. (1957–8). *Seminar, Book V: Formations of the Unconscious*. C. Gallagher (Trans.), http://www.lacaninireland.com, 05.03.1958/p. 190.

L. Burzotta (✉)
Laboratorio Freudiano, Rome; Fondation Européenne pour la Psychanalyse

D. Caine, C. Wright (eds.), *Perversion Now!*,
DOI 10.1007/978-3-319-47271-3_17

In *The Balcony*, by way of the artifice that is a house of illusions (*maison d'illusions*), Genet shows us what it is to enjoy (*jouir*) these roles, with the purpose of making us appreciate that within the different forms of ego-ideal found in society, "the formation is always accompanied by an eroticisation of the symbolic relationship", to the point where "an assimilation can thus be made between he who, in the position and function of bishop, judge or general, enjoys [*jouir*] his position" and the "little old man" known to the landlords of houses of illusion, who comes to satisfy himself there. That is to say, that what leads the pervert to seek satisfaction in the pleasure of this image is "that it is the reflection of an essentially signifying function."[2]

It is the same clandestine site of the ego-ideal that produces the perversion of the young André Gide, who "could constitute himself only through asserting himself in the place occupied by his cousin…who constructed a personality within her, through her, and in relation to her. This is what puts him, with regard to her, in a position of mortal dependence."[3] Later, I will return to the subject of André Gide and Lacan's treatment of it, delivered alongside his analysis of *The Balcony* during the seminar *Les formations de l'inconscient* (5th March 1958).

But, for now, from the point of view of perversion, we shall stay with *The Balcony*, where Genet shows us "all the confusion that establishes itself in the relations, however fundamental, of man and speech", which, according to Lacan, "we can crudely call, on the day of general disorder, the whorehouse (*bordel*) in which we live."[4] At this liminal moment in his analysis of *The Balcony*, Lacan arrives at this conclusion: "Society, indeed, knows only how to define itself in relation to a more or less advanced state of cultural degradation."[5]

This definition of society anticipates what Lacan will later develop in the final lesson of his seminar, *Le désir et son interpretation* (1st July 1959)[6] where, specifying culture as "a certain history of the subject in its relation

---

[2] ibid., p. 191.

[3] Ibid., p. 188.

[4] ibid.

[5] ibid.

[6] Lacan, J. (1958–9). *Seminar, Book VI: Desire and its Interpretation*. C. Gallagher (Trans.), http://www.lacaninireland.com.

to *logos*", he explains that due to a kind of social inertia our relationship to *logos* remains masked and "it is for this reason that Freudianism exists in our epoch".[7] Lacan distinguishes between this "history of the subject in its relation to *logos*" and "that which presents itself in society as culture", defining the relation between the two "as an entropic relationship, for all that passes for culture in society always includes some function of disaggregation". The affinity between that which Lacan advances in his analysis of *The Balcony* and that which he proposes during his seminar of the following year is based upon a dialectical relation between society and culture, a dialectic "that leaves open the same gap inside which we situate the function of desire".[8]

In this gap lies the reason for Lacan's argument concerning perversion in relation to identification:

> What is produced as perversion reflects, at the level of the logical subject, the protest against that which the subject suffers at the level of identification, insofar as it is this relation that establishes and orders the norms of social stabilisation of different functions.[9]

In *The Balcony*, through a series of debasements, Jean Genet presents us with these functions in their most sacred variations, namely the bishop himself, the judge and the general, here positioned as "specialists" of perversion, whilst all around outside the revolution rages—everything that unfolds on the inside is accompanied by the staccato of machine-guns from the outside. The town is in the full throes of revolution.

At the apogee of the crisis a "diplomat of pedigree", the *envoy* from the royal palace, arrives to enlighten the amiable group at the heart of the brothel as to what is happening at the palace. There, in the most perfect state of legitimacy, we discover a deranged Queen utterly absorbed in the pursuit of futile activities: "she embroiders, she doesn't embroider… she snores, or she is not snoring."[10] But if the Queen, in her rosewood casket (*coffre*), "snores or doesn't snore", in the eyes of the diplomat, delighted

[7] ibid., 01.07.1959/p. 344.

[8] ibid.

[9] ibid., p. 345.

[10] Lacan, 1957–8, op. cit., 05.03.1958/p. 192.

by her imposing silhouette and resolute character, there remains only one thing to do: to entrust power to the superb and haughty landlady of *The Balcony*. And so, like that, power is immediately embodied in Irma, the landlady of the brothel. Wholly transformed into symbol, she assumes, "and with such superiority", the duties of *The Queen.*[11]

We arrive, then, at both the regimentation of the perverts seen flaunting themselves throughout the first act, and their full and authentic ascension to the mutual roles they were performing in their varying amorous frolics. Called upon by the *Envoy* to occupy the positions of power vacated by the previous fallen order, the perverts hesitate: how, indeed, can one truly assume a function in place of the Other if they are themselves on the side where the Other exists? As perverts, each of them has been devoted to flaunting themselves in the clothes of the Other, in the role of "singular auxiliary." This awkward situation is easy to comprehend. If they are perplexed at the idea of following the project of the diplomat, it is because, even if they do not know it, they have already devoted themselves to "filling the hole in the Other" and have proven to be specialist "defenders of the faith."

On the other hand we have the real and actual *Chief of police*, good friend and powerful protector of the landlady of the brothel, who worries that no one has yet recognised his grandeur and asked to dress up as the *Chief of police* whilst making love. This becomes his torment and the problem of all, because, having succeeded in demonstrating that he alone is order and linchpin, someone coming and asking to be *Chief of police* would be the event that would sanction his elevation to the order of functions that are respected. Naturally, if somebody comes and asks to be *Chief of police*, this role could be entrusted to all comers now that the *Chief* is elevated to the level of *Hero* next to Irma—*the Queen*. To this end he consults his entourage on both the subject of the appropriateness of some sort of uniform and a symbol to represent his position; somewhat shockingly to those listening, he proposes a phallus.[12]

However, the question of the uniform is usurped by events as the character of the *Plumber*, well known in this establishment, finally arrives

[11] ibid. p. 193.

[12] ibid.

asking to play the role of the *Chief of police*; Carmen, the prostitute, helps him don all that is necessary to enter into character, including the wig. With the transformation complete, and in heated discussion with Carmen who pushes for him to leave and eventually succeeds in imposing her will, the virtuous *Plumber* makes a gesture towards castration. According to Lacan, this means that in order to become fully integrated, this man, who has fought for the brothel to find its new order (*sa nouvelle assiette*), must be castrated, ensuring that the phallus is again promoted to the level of the signifier.[13]

Could we call sublimation this reversal that sees the character played in perversity become a replacement for a legitimate function in society? This is perhaps the hypothesis, here caricatured, of the comedy. Lacan articulates something similar in the final lesson of *Désir et son interpretation*, where he advances the idea that from perversion—here understood "in its most general form as that which, in the human being, resists all normalisation – we can see this discourse produce itself, this apparent empty elaboration that we call sublimation, and which, in both its nature and its products, is distinct from the social valorisation subsequently conferred upon it."[14]

This movement from perversion to sublimation is represented by Lacan as a dial (*cadran*) where "something establishes itself as a revolving circuit between, on the one hand, conformity… – all of culture which monetises itself and alienates itself in society – and, on the other hand, perversion, representing at the level of the logical subject and through a series of debasements, the protest which, with regard to conformity, elevates itself to the dimension of desire, insofar as desire is the relationship of the subject to its being. It is here that this famous sublimation inscribes itself."[15] As it is true that we sublimate with the drive, this passage from perversion to sublimation is legitimated by the very nature of the drive as "reduced to the pure play of signifiers"; Lacan would make special mention of this reduction to pure "grammatical montage", from

[13] ibid., p. 194.

[14] Lacan, 1958–9, op. cit., 01.07.1959/p. 345.

[15] ibid.

where the subject is constructed as perverse, during *Seminar XI* (1964).[16] For now, he articulates sublimation as "that by which desire and the letter can be made equivalent", and thus "situates itself as such at the level of the logical subject, there where it establishes and unfolds all that is, properly speaking, the work of creation in the order of *logos*."[17]

I wonder if this movement from perversion to sublimation exists also for André Gide, because it is true that his perversion "is not necessarily the fact that he can only desire small boys, the small boy he had been for an instant in the arms of his aunt", as object of seduction for his aunt who had caressed his shoulders, his neck, his chest, a seduction from which he escaped. Rather, he is perverse insofar as he cannot constitute himself in the ego-ideal, "only through asserting himself in the place occupied by his cousin, Madeleine." On the other hand, however, it must be noted that being "he whose thoughts all turn to her, he who literally gives in each instance that which he has not,"[18] is only possible through the act of constantly telling himself, of submitting to a correspondence which is the heart and root of his existence as a man of letters, a man entirely within the signifier.

Lacan reminds us of the cry of despair when the poet discovers the disappearance of the letter chest in which he kept his correspondence with Madeleine: "My money box! My dear money box"![19] We cannot better conceive of "the anatomy of the vacuole", this "forbidden centre" of the self that we find on the outside and which Lacan speaks of in his seminar *D'un Autre à l'autre,*[20] than through this precious box with a world of letters, in both senses of the word "letter", echoing from the inside; an image of "sublimation at the level of the drive" that we also find in the work of Jean Genet.

With all the agitation on the inside, the whorehouse (*maison des illusions*), the grand *Balcony*, the phantasmagorical brothel (*bordel*) takes

---

[16] Lacan, J. (1964). *Seminar XI: The Four Fundamental Concepts in Psychoanalysis*. A. Sheridan (Trans.). Harmondsworth: Penguin, 1994.

[17] Lacan, 1958–9, op. cit.

[18] Lacan, 1957–8, op. cit, p. 188.

[19] ibid.

[20] Lacan, J. (1968–69). *Seminar, Book XVI: From an Other to Another/the Other Side of Psychoanalysis*. C. Gallagher (Trans.), http://www.lacaninireland.com.

the form of a “small bell” (*grelot*), something round which envelopes the inexhaustible eruption of colours and sounds whilst the revolution, which rages outside, might as well not exist: compared to the creative richness found in the rooms of the brothel, it is merely a sterile fiction represented by the monotonous sound of a machine-gun. Returning to the “schema of the relation between perversion and culture, as distinguished from society” in *Seminar VIII* Lacan states: “If society leads, by its effect of censorship, to a form of breakdown called neurosis, it is in a sense counter to elaboration, construction, and sublimation – let’s admit it – that perversion can be conceived when it is produced from culture.”[21]

This detail, in confirming the affinity between perversion and sublimation, distinguishes perversion once more by its capacity of elaboration and construction, a quality specific to the perverse subject; the opportunity to constitute himself in the ego-ideal which follows exactly from his refusal. If the neurotic has no difficulty in constituting himself in the ego-ideal, “where the illusion of a retroactive primary narcissism inscribes itself,” on the other hand, hooked by this lure, “the subject as neurotic is precisely doomed to the failure of sublimation.”[22]

[21] Lacan, J. (1960–61). *Seminar, Book VIII: Transference*. C. Gallagher (Trans.), http://www.lacanireland.com. 23.11.60, p. 24.

[22] Lacan, 1968–69, op. cit., 26.03.1969.

18

The Piano Teacher

Jean-Claude Aguerre

Today, the concept of perversion can no longer be understood in the same way that Krafft-Ebing[1] described it in 1886 and Freud adopted it in the first of his *Three Essays on the Theory of Sexuality.*[2] And yet for many people, the notion continues to refer to sexual deviation, despite the criticism from both psychoanalysts and the wider public. Homosexuality and various kinds of sexual play have obviously been detached from this label, but perversion still connotes something dysfunctional, something outside the sexual norm. However, addressing perversion in terms of normality and deviation poses a number of difficulties. In Krafft-Ebing's view, any sexual relationship without reproduction as its aim was perverse. In the 19th century,

[1] Krafft-Ebing, R. (1886). *Psychopathia Sexualis: Eine klinisch-forensische Studie*, first edition. Stuttgart: Enke.

[2] Freud, S. (1905). *Three Essays on the Theory of Sexuality.* S.E. 7. J. Strachey (Trans.). London: Hogarth, 1953.

J.-C. Aguerre (✉)
Espace Analytique

D. Caine, C. Wright (eds.), *Perversion Now!*,
DOI 10.1007/978-3-319-47271-3_18

all sexual deviations were considered simply immoral, but soon the idea of morality was replaced by that of health: is the pervert immoral or ill?

Thus the law calls upon medical discourse to decide on the potentially perverse subject's responsibility, on whether we are dealing with moral perversity, linked to Victorian morality, or pathological perversion. The psychiatrist is asked to decide what is normal and what is pathological. The pervert becomes a patient in need of treatment. It is only with Freud that we arrive at the idea of a structure. Among the different approaches to the concept, I find that Freud's 1927 text on Fetishism[3] and Lacan's rereading of it in the *Seminar IV on The Object Relation*[4] are the two key texts that can help us account for perversion today.

As Freud defines it, the fetish is an object that takes the place of the mother's missing penis. Lacan tells us that the fetish represents the phallus as absent. The castration anxiety, provoked by the observation that the mother does not have a penis and therefore must have been deprived of it, is relieved by this denial: she does not have the phallus, but she has it anyway. The pervert would then be an individual who remains in this state of denial, of *Verleugnung*. In fact, the pervert might go one step further. Instead of looking at the pervert as someone who does not give up his belief in the existence of the mother's pseudo-phallus, I would suggest that we take into account the notion of knowledge. In the beginning, the child's reality testing confronts him with what he sees and what he learns. The child learns that there is a world of *jouissance* from which he is excluded and which the mother accesses through the father. This new knowledge becomes material for all fantasies of castration. It is said that the pervert is desperately searching for a substitute object—the fetish—that would allow him to mask the fact of castration. As I have said, I think we could go further. The pervert is well aware that this object, the so-called fetish, lacks in consistency. He knows that it is *not* the mother's phallus, but he is able to make do with it anyway.

Lacan speaks about the fetish as the symbolic phallus and, coming from him, I find this formulation slightly too trivial. In any case the fetishist has access to the Symbolic, otherwise he would be on the side of psychosis.

---

[3] Freud, S. (1927). *Fetishism*. S.E. 21: 147–157. J. Strachey (Trans.). London: Hogarth, 1961.

[4] Lacan, J. (1994a) [1956–7]. Le séminaire, Livre IV: La relation d'objet et les structures freudiennes. Paris: Seuil.

Thus the fetish—the female shoe in the *Diary of a Chambermaid,* the women's lingerie or any other object functioning as a fetish—comes to represent the phallus as missing and gives the pervert access to *jouissance*. The moment of exultation, when the pervert can laugh his head off, is when he manages to make someone *else* believe that he believes in it. The denial of maternal castration functions for the pervert as a masquerade.

The masquerade consists in masking, hiding this maternal lack. The pervert *knows* it is a mask—and a very useful one because it not only gives him access to a *jouissance*, but also makes it possible to make a generalisation: the mother does not have the phallus and, by the way, ultimately no one has it. Of course, some people have a penis, but the phallic function is outside everyone's reach. Except for the pervert himself. This knowledge which cannot be subject to doubt—this is what brings the pervert close to the paranoiac—gives him power over the classic neurotic. Pierra Aulagnier writes: "The purest position of the perverse subject is precisely this claim, which makes his actions the consequence of a choice he considers justified and supported by a knowledge about the truth of what is both good and evil in their fundamental link to the register of desire."[5] The first perverts would thus have been those who ate the fruit from the Tree of Knowledge of good and evil in Genesis.

Michael Haneke's film *The Piano Teacher,* based on a novel by Elfriede Jelinek[6] (2014 Nobel Prize for Literature), shows a particularly violent relationship between the two main characters played by Isabelle Huppert and Benoît Magimel. It seems to me that Haneke—if not Jelinek herself—must have studied the characteristics of perverse subjects as they might be described by a psychiatrist and is trying to convey them through the character of Erika Kohut, played by Huppert, a piano teacher at a prestigious conservatory in Vienna. The character does manifest a number of sexual deviations that indeed seem strongly pathological. First of all, her quite sordid voyeurism: we see her hiding in a drive-in at night to spy on the couples that come here to have sex in their cars. At the sight of this spectacle she urinates on the ground. When she is surprised by a man having sex with his girlfriend, she runs away. Later she is watching

[5] Castoriadis Aulagnier, P. (1967). *La perversion comme structure in L'inconscient 2,* La perversion, 11–41. Paris: PUF.

[6] Jelinek, E. (1988). *The Piano Teacher.* J. Neugroschel (Trans.). London: Serpent's Tail.

a porn film in the booth of a sex shop. She takes out a dirty tissue from a rubbish bin, smells it and smears it on her face. She lives with her mother in a large apartment, but they share the same bed. The relationship with the mother borders on the incestuous. At one point, Erika starts touching her mother, who pushes her away, saying something like "stop bothering me", but she does not leave the bed.

Erika's life is peaceful, if we can call it that, until the arrival of Walter Klemmer (Benoît Magimel), an extremely gifted young pianist. In order to be accepted into the conservatory's master class, Klemmer must pass an audition in front of all the teachers. Everyone is dazzled by his virtuosity; Kohut alone expresses serious reservations against his admission, which are dismissed. And yet it is precisely she that Walter Klemmer asks to be his teacher. We could say that Kohut has not separated herself from her mother; they form a unit. The mother leaves her no freedom: Erika is over forty years old, but must go straight home after her lessons have finished; the mother calls regularly when Erika is asked to play at a concert at her friends' house.

Jelinek's book develops the theme of Erika's relationship with her mother and her mother's mother much more than does Haneke's film. In the book, Erika has been completely isolated from the world by these two women. All of her desires must belong to them exclusively, or rather she simply should not have any. The only narcissism permitted to her, or in fact imposed on her, is to become a piano virtuoso. And yet it is in just this that she fails: after a disastrous examination performance, she had to give up on becoming a concert pianist. She manages only to secure a teaching position at a prestigious conservatory, a post which carries the recognition of a certain talent. Klemmer, the young pianist, has a power over his teacher; despite his youth, he is already a great virtuoso. He holds the phallus Erika's mother lacks, the phallus she desired for her daughter.

Walter Klemmer falls in love with Erika. We never really understand why: she is not at all likeable. She is not ugly, but she is not really pretty either. Furthermore, she is extremely rigid, disdainful of her students and even openly sadistic towards them. She could not treat Walter more coldly and tells him that she was the only one of the five teachers to have voted against his admission to the master class. In spite of all this, he makes open advances to her, which she flatly refuses. A young female student at the conservatory is asked to accompany a baritone singer on a piano. During their lessons, Erika is violent and sadistic towards the young woman, bringing her to tears each time. At a rehearsal, Walter encourages the young woman, consoles her and offers to turn the pages of her score. Erika observes the scene and although she does not seem to pay any attention to it, she subsequently enters the cloakroom and hides shards of glass in the young girl's coat pockets. When the young woman screams with her hands covered in blood, Erika hides in the toilets. It seems to me that Walter immediately understands who is behind the act. He enters the toilets and, as if he was incredibly excited by the event, instead of his previous insistence on seduction he simply throws himself at Erika: what follows is practically a rape scene. Yet Erika continues to push him away, although she engages in a series of humiliation scenes in which she dominates him, and announces that she will offer him a contract: "I will make a list of all the things you can do to me. My wishes will be jotted down and available to you at any time."

In her article on perversion published in the journal *l'Inconscient* in April 1967, Pierra Aulagnier points out the importance of the contract in the perverse relationship:

> Both partners are to make a mutual and most rigorous commitment to respect and blindly adhere to a series of rules that will invariably define their erotic actions. They make a promise to obey this law or these rules regardless of what their desires may be at the moment when they must apply them [...] The point of the enactment of this ritual seems to be a kind of repetition or a phantasmatization of a scene of castration [...] we should add that this contract shows that the victim is supposed to – even obliged to – enjoy the pain that he inflicts on himself.[7]

Erika Kohut's text is the paradigm of a sadomasochistic contract:

> Stuff the old nylons I have prepared into my mouth as deep as you can and gag me so cunningly that I can't emit the slightest peep. Next take off the blindfold, please, and sit on my face, and punch me in the stomach to force me to stick my tongue up your ass. In case you witness a transgression on

[7] Castoriadis Aulagnier, op. cit.

> my part, please hit me, with the back of your hand, slap my face [...] Nothing in this type of contract reminds us of a declaration of love. It resembles a notarized deed. In other words, it is a discourse pronounced in the name of the law, rather than in the name of love.[8]

Walter reads aloud the contract Erika has handed to him in an envelope. At this point, Erika pronounces perhaps the only humane words in the film: "I have been longing to be hit for many years now. I have been waiting for you, you know." In this sense, I would perhaps take some distance from Aulagnier. I think that the contract, at least the contract depicted in the film, could in fact be read as a declaration of love. In the film, faced with this expression of Erika's manifestly genuine pain, Walter answers: "You are sick, you need treatment, I wouldn't touch someone like you with a ten-foot pole." It is almost a joke: the masochist is asking the sadist to hurt her, and his answer is 'No'. If indeed this were love—as Walter has been swearing for as long as he has been trying to seduce her—the two partners might have been able to make the contract work, albeit with some difficulties. Mr and Mrs Robbe-Grillet functioned with a similar agreement, the so-called "Contract of Conjugal Prostitution", all their life; it was drafted by Alain and remained unsigned by Catherine, as her signature would have destroyed the "illusion of being forced". She writes that they were "not really into accessories" and only used a couple of whips. She explains: "If someone were to judge our sex life based on solely the number of penetrations, they would have found it pitiful. Luckily that was not where things were happening for us, but rather elsewhere, on those empty shores where pain and humiliation are the sources of pleasure and love." Catherine and Alain Robbe-Grillet's love story lasted throughout their life and I don't think that we could classify them as perverse. Though devastated by her husband's death, the 83-year-old Catherine continued to act as a dominatrix during the sadomasochistic parties she organised at her home, a flat in the posh Parisian 16th arrondissement.

Walter at first explicitly refuses the contract, but ultimately he succumbs to it. One night he storms into Erika's flat, locks the mother in

[8] ibid.

her room (which was included in the contract), rapes Erika, beats her violently and leaves her bleeding on the floor. He insults her, telling her that she has managed to contaminate him, that she has entrapped him in her perverse game. That because of her he comes to masturbate under her window. Everything is in place to describe the woman as a paragon of perversion. But I think that Haneke pushes this too far (if it is not Elfriede Jelinek herself). At the beginning of the film, we see Erika cutting her labia with a razor. Her mother sees the blood on her thighs and thinks she is having her period. The mother's domination and the way Erika is treated, as a child, by her mother and grandmother would have driven anyone mad. Thus I imagine the character of Erika more on the side of psychosis than perversion.

In the novel, the two women—Erika's mother and grandmother—are described as completely phallic. They are in possession of the phallus that could be fetishised as the magic of music. Walter knows that music is not the phallus and that Erika does not have it; he has understood that neither Erika nor her mother have the phallus. His *jouissance* comes from having this knowledge in the face of Erika's scorn. He knows that she believes in the fetish, while he knows that there is simply nothing there. One of Erika's students could succeed—and what is more, succeed in an examination where Erika herself has only proved to be an accompanist, never the virtuoso. And she cuts the student's fingers. At the beginning of the film, Walter attends private concerts where Erika is playing. He knows that he is a better pianist than she, but still he asks her to give him lessons. Erika does not want to train virtuosos; what could be worse than to see one of her students succeed where she has failed? In Jelinek's book, it is the mother who says this clearly: "You didn't make it – why should others reach the top? And from your musical stable to boot."

It is Erika's gesture—the criminal act she commits by cutting her student's fingers—that plunges Walter into an exalted state. His *jouissance* revolves around a woman who believes in her fetish; it derives from confronting her with the void of castration that she refuses. It consists in playing with the naiveté of a woman who imagines that any representation of the phallus could actually function. Had he not been perverse, he could have accepted the contract and begun a love story. Erika is the Snow White waiting for her Prince Charming to awaken her to love—or, in more simple terms, to save her from her mother's total domination. However, he is only looking for a *jouissance*. He knows how to enjoy the phallus as absent, with a woman who believes in it. When he attacks her in the toilets, after previously having rejected her, she furiously masturbates him, as if to check that this thing really exists. She masturbates him, but he does not ejaculate. This is not where it happens for him.

The day after being raped and beaten by Walter, Erika is expected to give a concert at the conservatory. Before leaving home, she takes a kitchen knife. Everything suggests that a real castration is imminent. She hides in the entrance to the conservatory and we expect her to stab Walter. The latter arrives and walks past her, telling her "I can't wait to hear you, Professor." She keeps the knife in her bag. 'Can't wait to hear' what, a mediocre pianist? Walter enters the concert hall. Erika stabs herself in her shoulder and leaves the conservatory. Her castration stems from the fact that the fetish can no longer hold. The wound is bleeding, but she does not seem to notice. She leaves the building with a firm step, as if nothing had happened. I will finish with another quotation from Aulagnier: "The perverse subject speaks reasonably, sometimes even brilliantly, about the folly of desire. He justifies his perversion in the name of a surplus-of-pleasure, which he claims to authenticate based on a surplus-of-knowledge about the truth of *jouissance*."

Erika Kohut offers us an image of perversion, primarily in terms of sexual deviation, but given her experience of being totally controlled by her mother and grandmother, the two women doing their best to separate her from the field of desire, we should situate her on the side of psychosis rather than perversion. There is no doubt that music as a fetish could replace the maternal phallus for her, a phallus of which she herself is deprived. Walter intuitively perceives Erika's illusion; his *jouissance* stems from both this illusion and his knowledge, making him ultimately the one truly perverse character in the film.

19

Human Versus Mechanical in Lacan: Fetishistic Strategies of Death and Intensity

Željka Matijašević

19.1 Introduction

This paper which, in its title, amalgamates the human, the mechanical, Lacan, fetishism, death and intensity, starts with the articulation of the subject in Lacan's *Séminaire II*,[1] where the subject's dependence on the death drive, which is not biological but symbolic, plays a prominent part. Lacan's subject as 'subject(ed) to death' relies heavily on the mechanicist paradigm, which raises a necessary question of the relation between vitalism and mechanicism, or between life and death. I look into the taste for death in fetishistic denial, typical of perversions, which I interpret as

[1] Lacan, J. (1954–5). *Le séminaire, Livre 2: Le Moi dans la théorie de Freud et dans la technique de la psychanalyse*. J.-A. Miller (Ed.). Paris: Seuil, 1978.

Ž. Matijašević (✉)
University of Zagreb, Croatia

D. Caine, C. Wright (eds.), *Perversion Now!*,
DOI 10.1007/978-3-319-47271-3_19

circulating around the denial of the border between life and death. The second part of the paper analyses and proposes the culture of intensity as one offshoot of the mechanicist paradigm. The border between life and death is interpreted as just one of many borders defining the 'borderland'.

19.2 The Man Machine in Lacan

There are several deaths in Lacan, multiple ways to die. The first is in the Imaginary, as the fascination with the mirror-image is laden with aggressivity and suicidal tendencies. It is also in the Symbolic, in the structure of obsession, as opposed to life; the 'aliveness' of the subject reposes in the intensity with which he manages to run his mechanical structure insofar as he is the subject, intensity which comprises the risk, the danger of undergoing a short-circuit, supplied by *jouissance*. Which explains a third death: death in the Real.

Lacan's ego, inhabiting death, is closely related to the narcissistic specular image with its associated fictionality, falsity, aggressiveness, duplicity and lethality, the lethality of the visual. In Lacan's view, the roots of aggressivity are intrasubjective, resulting from *méconaissance*, the misrecognition through which the ego comes to being at all by taking the place of the imaginary other. The alienation, on which the ego is based, bears similarities to the structure of paranoia, inasmuch as the Imaginary is fictitious, illusory. The narcissistic structure of the ego is also connected with Freud's primary masochism and the death drive.

In his essay "The Mirror Stage"[2] Lacan points to the semantic latency of the word narcissism which includes two important moments: in the myth, Narcissus falls in love not with himself, but with his image; and, secondly, this fascination with his own image leads Narcissus to his death. This suicidal tendency is related to the identificatory process and its aggressive consequences.

The Symbolic order, as a stabilising order, comes to the rescue by separating the subject from the image, by forcing the subject to renounce its

---

[2] Lacan, J. (1949). "Le Stade du miroir comme formateur de la fonction du Je, telle qu'elle nous est révélée dans l'expérience psychanalytique", in *Écrits 1* (Sélection). Paris: Seuil, 1966, pp. 89–97.

symbiotic relation with the *objet petit a*. It is an act of symbolic castration/creation. Lacan's pivotal "Rome Discourse"[3] emphasises the perilousness of the word, the words which define us, the names which exist for us before we are born and persist beyond our death, the words which make us "faithful" or "renegades". Lacan oscillates between the restorative power of the Symbolic and its linguistic dimension—language, on the one hand, while on the other hand, the words which create/define us have a deadly power of annihilation. This is Lacan's true debt to Hegel. It is the second death: through the process of symbolic castration we are subsumed under the deadly, annihilating power of the word.

It is with the introduction of the Thing into Lacanian theory, in his seventh seminar, *The Ethics of Psychoanalysis*,[4] that the subject comes to measure itself against the third term of the 'Real'. The symbolic order will be modified into an agency exclusively keeping the subject at a distance from the Real. The death drive is posited in the dangerous liminal zone which separates the world of symbolic objects from those of the Real, and the danger is presented by *jouissance*, intense, enlivening, yet lethal for the subject's structure. This appears as a third death in Lacan. Too little and too much *jouissance*, the state which is already defined as 'too much', as a surplus. We die, then, in the Imaginary, in the Symbolic and in the Real.

In the article "Lacan Iconoclast", Jean-Joseph Goux explains how Lacan "deduces the autonomy and transcendence of the Symbolic … from scientific and technical data that were not available to Freud".[5] The pure signifier is on the side of the Law, "the best examples of which are axiomatic mathematics and computer functions",[6] so that the Lacanian symbolic order is foreign to humanity, higher than it, outside of it, and humanity must submit to it. Goux names it "the sin of the Imaginary"

[3] Lacan, J. (1953). "The Function and Field of Speech and Language in Psychoanalysis", in *Écrits 1 (Sélection)*. Paris: Seuil, 1966. Also *Ecrits: A Selection*. A Sheridan (Trans.). New York: W. W. Norton & Company, 1977.

[4] Lacan, J. (1959–60). *Le séminaire, Livre 7: L'Éthique de la psychanalyse*. J.-A. Miller (Ed.). Paris: Seuil, 1986.

[5] Goux, J.-J. (1991). "Lacan Iconoclast", in *Lacan and the Human Sciences*, A. Leupin (Ed.). Lincoln and London: University of Nebraska Press, p. 115.

[6] ibid., p. 116.

and proposes that Lacanian thought is "a technological iconoclasm".[7] According to Lacan, as Goux suggests, Freud obeys this iconoclastic prescription in one book, namely *Beyond the Pleasure Principle*. Why? Because of "the automatism of repetition", that is "the mechanical insistence of the signifying chain".[8] Goux concludes that this is the reason the death drive is a manifestation of our subjection to a symbolic order: "The machine is nonliving. It is inanimate. The death instinct is the machine inside of man."[9] Lacan's approximation of the structure of the subject with the machine is most clearly articulated in his recourse to the age of the machine as something separating Hegel and Freud, to the advantage of the latter, in the second seminar, *The Ego in Freud's Theory and in the Technique of Psychoanalysis*, in "L'Univers symbolique", "Freud, Hegel et la machine" and 'Le Circuit'.

> *There is in Freud something of which we speak, and of which we do not speak in Hegel, which is energy.... Energy, I remarked on it to you the last time, is a notion which can only appear at the moment when there are machines.... The founder of modern biology... Bichat... knew that we had entered a new period, and that life was going to be defined from then on in relation to death. That converges with what I am in process of explaining to you, the decisive character of the reference to the machine for the founder of biology.*[10]

> *The first question posed to us, analysts, and perhaps we can in this way resolve the controversy between vitalism and mechanism, is the following – why are we led to think about life in terms of mechanism? How are we, actually, as humans, parents of the machine?... In relation to the animal, we are machines, that is to say something decomposed.*[11]

Libidinal energetics as the Freudian discovery par excellence will, in Lacan, be modified into the energetics of the symbolic order itself (by

---

[7] ibid.

[8] ibid., p. 117.

[9] ibid.

[10] Lacan, 1954–5, op. cit., p. 95.

[11] ibid., pp. 43–4.

which means he also dispenses with the libidinal character of Freudian energetics): "*The machine incarnates the most radical symbolic activity of humans*"[12] and will thus justify the introduction of the Symbolic order itself, by presenting the pattern of fundamental functioning.

> *I am explaining to you that it is inasmuch as humans are engaged in the game of symbols, in a symbolic world, that the human subject is decentred. Indeed, it is with the same game, the same world, that the machine is constructed…the symbolic world is the world of the machine.*[13]

Lacan's reliance on mechanicism is directed against Hegelian organicism and evolutionism, that is, against an organicist conception of consciousness. It is, for Lacan, an anthropomorphic illusion proven by his recourse to the world of the inanimate, strictly rejecting what he calls "delirious anthropomorphism". Thus, the Freudian problem of "beyond the pleasure principle", which some might have wrongly interpreted as the conflict of two drives, is in Lacan's view a purely symbolic problem.

> *Freudian biology has nothing to do with biology. It's a question of a manipulation of symbols to resolve questions of energetics, as the reference to homeostasis makes manifest, which makes it possible to characterize as such not only the living being, but the functioning of our principal apparatus.*[14]

By opposing energetics to organicism, and by approximating mechanicism to symbolicism, Lacan is able to justify his articulation of the 'subject'.

> *What does analysis unveil – if not the fundamental, radical discordance of conduct that is essential for humans in relation to everything that lives? The dimension discovered by analysis is the opposite of something that progresses by adaptation, by approximation, by becoming more perfect. It is something that moves by leaps and bounds.*[15]

---

[12] ibid., p. 95.

[13] ibid., p. 63.

[14] ibid., p. 96.

[15] ibid., p. 108.

However, Lacan's explanation of the way in which the subject-as-machine progresses suggests that, in order to 'perfect' itself, the subject-as-machine insofar as it is a structured subject, can progress only if its very structure undergoes a fundamental transformation.

> *It is always the 'apprentissage'* (training) *of someone who will do better the next time. And when I say will do better the next time, it is that something quite different will have to be done.*[16]

Doing something completely different signifies doing something entirely different from that which is known, familiar, functional, highly adapted and adaptable, but also highly mechanical and fetishistic, so that the mechanical as functional comes to be replaced by the process through which the subject must necessarily outgrow its mechanical structure, even if it necessitates existing temporarily as a dysfunctional subject.

Another important and very well-known manifestation of the death drive is the question which structures obsessional neurosis: "Am I dead or alive?" a question closely related to the contingent character of existence, and which the obsessional answers by always positioning himself on the side of death. The obsessional neurotic's attitude to time can be, in Lacan's words, one of "perpetual hesitation and procrastination while waiting for death, or of considering oneself immortal because one is already dead."[17]

Louise J. Kaplan in the *Cultures of Fetishism* (2006) pinpoints five fetishistic strategies of modern culture, deduced but also emancipated from, their origin in sexual fetishism. Clearly, the fifth and the final one is a corollary to the necrophilic principle, the most extreme form of sexual fetishism, and an extension of it, "that exposes the death drive hidden in the folds of the erotic object",[18] the principle which is closely related to aggression and destruction, and which is, in Kaplan's view, "the key to the strategy of fetishism".[19] Fetishistic strategies in Kaplan's work are also exposed in the zone between living and non-living matter, when we

---

[16] ibid.

[17] Evans, D. (1996). *An Introductory Dictionary of Lacanian Psychoanalysis*. London: Verso, p. 126.

[18] Kaplan, L. J. (2006). *Cultures of Fetishism*. New York: Palgrave-Macmillan, p. 7.

[19] ibid.

are confronted with mechanical creatures that are made to seem alive and human. Kaplan's penultimate chapter is about robots and androids[20] where she explains how the fantasy about machines which acquire, or which are endowed with human qualities, always provokes and evokes a counter-fantasy that humans can become machine-like.

Freud's essay "The Uncanny" provides another clue to the exploration of fetishism. In the first part of the essay, Freud suggests that the uncanny is a subspecies of all horror-inspiring things which originate in the familiar and well-known. No wonder that Freud, following Otto Rank's excellent work *The Double*, highlights the motive of the double as the most uncanny, while also enumerating other manifestations of the uncanny in the form of ghosts and phantoms but also mechanical dolls and marionettes.

19.3 Borderline Intensities: Jouissance and Death

Our cultural uncanny is a mechanical doll, a marionette, a living puppet or a mortified human being, while the borderline subject, i.e. 'the inhabitant of the borderland' is the name given to our incapacity to negotiate, in our interiority, the relation between the mortifying and mortified machine on one hand, and enlivening and life-bearing forces on the other hand. So, what I propose is that the principal anxiety of contemporary culture is that we will burn out from our intensities, like a candle that burns at both ends. However, there is also a complementary anxiety that boredom, generated through the narcissistic feeling of mechanical omnipotence and immortality, will kill us, that we will end up bored to death, literally.

The borderline category is, in contrast to narcissism, extremely confusing so that, before proclaiming the onset of the borderline culture, the term itself must be subjected to close scrutiny. The most enlightening theoreticians of the borderline are Otto F. Kernberg and Heinz Kohut. In his pathbreaking work *Borderline Conditions and Pathological Narcissism*

[20] ibid., pp. 155–173.

(1975), American psychiatrist and psychoanalyst Kernberg analyses the main characteristics of borderline personality organisation: the fragility of the ego; the regression to primary processes instead of secondary thinking processes; the regression towards more archaic defence mechanisms (splitting, projection, projective identification and reality denial); a pathological stance towards any object including the inability to integrate competing attitudes towards the one object.[21] In line with the internal splitting, then, every object is classified as either bad or good.

Freud established the difference between transference neuroses (hysteria and obsessional neurosis) and narcissistic neuroses. In defining and discerning psychopathological categories based on Freud's work, Lacan also remained, as Soler suggests, "rather faithful to classical diagnoses, borrowing paranoia from Kraepelin, schizophrenia from Bleuler, and perversion from Krafft-Ebing", in a striking contrast with "…IPA psychoanalysts who try to avoid these classical formulations with categories such as 'borderline' or 'narcissistic personality'."[22]

Lacan's work, which omits the borderline category, paradoxically provides a perfect articulation of the contemporary borderline structure. Thus the psychoanalyst who refused to use the borderline category, is the one who has been the most successful in articulating something which we are witnessing today—the borderland. If the borderline describes, in the first place, a personality structure or organisation, and thus a clinical category, it can also be thought of as a cultural category, characterised by an intensity of emotions and affects, and an anxiety of fragmentation. To that extent, the notion of the 'borderline' can be replaced with the idea of a 'borderland', an array of highly idiosyncratic, individualised structures which have to be approached one by one. The definition of borderline culture should also imply the theme of immortality related to narcissistic omnipotence which is, in turn, related to the anxiety of life gone eternal.[23]

---

[21] Kernberg, O.F. (1975). *Borderline Conditions and Pathological Narcissism*. New York: Jason Aronson.

[22] Soler, C. (2003). "The Paradoxes of the Symptom in Psychoanalysis". In *The Cambridge Companion to Lacan*, J.-M. Rabaté (Ed.). Cambridge: Cambridge University Press, p. 94.

[23] An excellent article on the difference between clinical and social categories is Diana Diamond's "Narcissism as a Clinical and Social Phenomenon". In J.S. Auerbach, K. N. Levy, C.E. Schaffer

One example of a pervasive intensity that comes to replace, or subsume, all previous attributes of life, is the extremely popular new vampire genre. What the new vampire and the inhabitant of the borderland have in common is intensity, which makes it possible to establish an equivalence between the new fictional vampire and the real-life 'borderline subject' for whom the border is represented as an unsure positioning between life and death. Stefan, the good vampire from *The Vampire Diaries*, a vampire soap opera, apart from successfully fighting his inherited hunger for blood in the best possible manner of recovered addicts, repeatedly explains to his loving Elena how the life of a vampire, and the becoming of one, necessarily involve an extreme intensification of both positive and negative emotions. This emotional and erotic intensity is closely connected to the death drive, a mandatory trait of the new dark, vampire, borderline romance. The sinister prospect of erotica suddenly turning into thanatica is always present, accompanied by the glorious cry: "I have experienced love at first bite".

Neo-vampirism reinterprets the old vampire tradition. The new vampire, the positive pole of the old, emerges as a deeply troubled and tortured being, structured through the neurotic repression of his hunger for blood in endless conflict with his inherited intensities. His evil counterpart, the bad vampire, belongs to an outdated tradition. Such popular representations of the vampire should be considered in relation to borderline culture, culture which promotes intensity as the measure of aliveness. In this light, the popularity of neo-vampirism is, on a deeper level, related to the narcissistic sense of immortality and the glorification of emotional intensity and fulfilment or self-fulfilment through emotional vampirism. The new vampire is very humane, human, troubled, tortured, anguished, in the best tradition of *poètes maudits* (cursed poets).

Anne Rice with her *Vampire Chronicles*, and in her earlier works *Interview with the Vampire* (1976) and *The Vampire Lestat* (1985) created a new vampire code, in which her anxious and lonely vampire is more

(Eds). (2005). *Relatedness, Self-Definition and Mental Representation: Essays in Honor of Sidney J Blatt*. New York: Brunner-Routledge.

similar to Hamlet than he is to Dracula,[24] but this humanity causes his inability to provoke horror. The location of evil is a common question in the texts on the late Victorian Gothic and it is the question which is always raised in relation to Stevenson's *Jekyll and Hyde*, and Bram Stoker's *Dracula*. Brian A. Rose in his work on Jekyll and Hyde, *Jekyll and Hyde Adapted: Dramatizations of Cultural Anxiety*[25] points out that all American adaptations of that work are related to the shifting form of anxiety, the anxiety of fragmentation. Therefore, he claims that related to the location of evil, in Victor Fleming's otherwise very bad adaptation from 1941 a shift was made towards Hyde as distinctively human, where all animalistic undertones disappeared. Hyde has become one of us and his expression of evil is pure psychosexual sadism.

The new vampire is a construct which mediates the most troubling anxieties of contemporary culture. Here, we need have recourse to the crucial distinction in psychoanalytic theory between the pleasure principle and pleasure as ecstasy, most clearly defined through Lacan's concept of *jouissance*: the level of intensity where pleasure turns into pain and happiness becomes unbearable. On the other hand, neo-vampirism also touches upon the other facet of the contemporary borderline subject where, in contrary to ecstatic happiness, it promotes pain and suffering as emotions that are the guarantees of our identity. Pain guarantees life while the horrifying void represents death, and self-fulfilling negative and destructive emotions are once again the measure of aliveness.

The phrase "I am wounded, therefore, I am" continues the romanticist tradition of the cursed genius and later the cursed poet, up to today's extreme popularisations. Self-mutilation is, on the one hand, a physical substitution of emotional pain as the diversion of attention; it is also an imprint made through self-inflicted wounds, the necessity to leave the traces of existence on one's own body in the act of lethal self-confirmation. While showing his Spring-Summer Collection of 2012,

---

[24] Wood, M. J. (1999). "New Life for an Old Tradition: Anne Rice and Vampire Literature", in *The Blood is the Life: Vampires in Literature*, M. Pharr and L.G. Heldreth (Eds). Bowling Green: Bowling Green State University Press, p. 65.

[25] Rose, B. A. (1996). *Jekyll and Hyde Adapted: Dramatizations of Cultural Anxiety*. Westport Greenwood Press, pp. 88–107.

a famous fashion designer Yohji Yamamoto opted for "the aesthetics of disfigured faces" with models covered with bruises, scars and wounds. After heroine chic, we are witnessing the aesthetics of *The Fight Club*: wounds, bruises and scars serve, paradoxically, as patches for the internal void, through the compulsion to repeat this primary, but highly exciting experience of pain.

Part V

Social Discourse, Politics and the Law

20

What Does Sade Teach Us About the Body and the Law?

André Michels

The study of perversions represents a particular challenge for analytical discourse. This is not only due to the difficult task of defining perversions but also to the questions they raise, so radical that they sometimes compel us to reconsider the foundational principles of our practice, and to produce a new version of the analytical discourse. If one acknowledges the *Freudian moment* in psychoanalysis as the exploration of the territory of neurosis, and the *Lacanian moment* as the study of psychosis, would the next step go back to the investigation of perversions?

Indeed, it is not certain that we have exhaustively evaluated their excessiveness (*dé-mesure*): in order to do that, it might be necessary to reconsider what has been said about them until now. The perversions refer to an abyss of human "nature" which, in order to be taken in account, implies a reorganisation of the actual discourse that constitutes it. Besides, considering the crime as both the foundation and the condition of the law

A. Michels (✉)
Espace Analytique

D. Caine, C. Wright (eds.), *Perversion Now!*,
DOI 10.1007/978-3-319-47271-3_20

implies an inversion of the latter: an investigation in which Sade is not the first actor, but the first theorist. The horror that it inspires in us is part of the Sadean action itself, which is essentially an act of writing. In order to recognise its true value, it is necessary to place it first in its context.

20.1 Science and Ethics

Sade is a child of his time: he has been deeply affected by the French Revolution, by the end of the *Ancien Régime*, by the T*erreur*, and by the reformulation of the penal code. He is also influenced by the Enlightenment that has prepared the ground on which, on the one hand, a political and social movement like the Revolution could bloom; and on the other, the simultaneous emergence of a great discursive and epistemic apparatus of the scale of German philosophy could emerge. Its main protagonists considered it to be a major contribution to the transition of the epoch—and to the epoch of transition—as important as the political action of their French neighbours. Hence the idea of reading Sade in the context of the time, considering the issues of the Revolution, on the one hand, and of the Enlightenment—and especially Kant's interpretation of it—on the other.

Adorno and Horkheimer were the first theorists to make this connection. Still under the influence of the horrific events of WWII, they published the *Dialectic of Enlightenment* (Dialektik der Aufklärung) in 1947.[1] They deal with a double question: first, how were these events possible at that exact moment in history, among the people who have been at the heart of the process of the Enlightenment and who have been at the cutting edge of the scientific and technological research? And secondly: if they were possible in this context, and no other, in these conditions, and no other, does it mean that this outburst of violence and brutality, unequalled in the history of civilised humanity, is inherent to the project of the Enlightenment and to its other side, reason itself? This is the path chosen by Adorno and Horkheimer who call unexpectedly as witnesses

[1] Adorno, T.W. and Horkheimer, M. (1947). *Dialectic of Enlightenment: Philosophical Fragments*. G. Schmid Noerr (Ed.) & E. Jephcott (Trans.). Stanford: Stanford University Press, 2002.

the wandering of Ulysses– a mythical character—and the writings of the marquis de Sade—a disreputable character.

The authors have been harshly criticised for the correlation they make between knowledge and power, particularly, by their main follower, Jürgen Habermas. The latter aims specially at their arguments and methods; but as Marcel Hénaff highlights, he never, symptomatically or otherwise, mentions Sade.[2] Is it through modesty or because Habermas does not know what to do with this reference that does not fit within the frameworks that are familiar or seem legitimate to him? Even if he were right regarding the arguments, and the obvious errors in reasoning, he would nonetheless be a far cry from the brilliance of their thesis. It will be up to philosophy to take up its principal ideas, on the one hand the relation between reason and power—opening the field that will become the basis of Foucault's work—and on the other, the relation between reason and violence. It is this relation that would bring them the greatest criticism, despite the fact that it seems to the authors to be a precondition to any possible thought about the Nazi crimes. Their reference to Sade does not present him as a precursor of those crimes, as many have thought, but allows them to fix a date to a process that emerges in his writings, but which is absolutely unclassifiable.

Lacan's text "Kant with Sade",[3] written about fifteen years after, does not follow necessarily the path of the *Dialectic of Enlightenment*, which some people consider as the inaugural text of contemporary philosophy, but it indicates that Lacan's epoch is ready to understand some things: the censorship of the Sadean texts had been recently removed. Besides, it is from the analytical experience that a discourse can be heard and elaborated that, since its emergence, has not stopped interrogating the reason for an under-lying violence. The most surprising fact is that the latter functions as its Other, as its "treasure trove" (*trésor*) of signifiers. Half a century earlier, Freud already remarked prosaically that we are all born of a long lineage of murderers, to indicate what continues to speak in us. Reason never comes first, but takes its signifiers from what precedes it or exceeds it, and which we could therefore call 'un-reason' (*dé-raison*).

---

[2] Hénaff, M. (2014). *Violence dans la raison? Conflit et cruauté.* Paris: L'Herne, pp. 40–43.

[3] Lacan, J. (1962). *Kant avec Sade. In* Écrits (Sélection). Paris: Seuil, 1966e, pp. 765–790.

Similarly, one can say that the law has its roots in a state of non-law (*non-droit*), namely the violence inherent in the state of nature (*status naturalis*). We can thus suppose that questions of law and of norms, in other words of *jouissance* in its legal dimension, lie at the heart of our consideration of the clinic of perversions.

In 1962, Lacan returns to a problem posed in previous seminars, especially in *The Ethics of Psychoanalysis*, on the relationship between pleasure, desire and *jouissance* concerning the problematic of ethics. From the beginning, he compares the "Sadean boudoir" with "the schools of Ancient philosophy" to argue that: "Here, as there, one prepares for science by correcting the position of ethics."[4] Is it not a bit much, to present Sade as witness of ethics? Or perhaps, he has another idea on this subject that needs to be clarified. He not only considers Sade as a representative of the violence that occurs during the Enlightenment, which is even inherent to reason, but he also suggests that one must consider him from the point of view of ethics, and what the latter represents with regard to science. He highlights particularly the intrinsic link between science and ethics or, rather, he raises the question of their relationship; in order to know how it has changed in Modern Times (*les Temps Modernes*). If this is the case, if it has really changed, what is to be expected from the reading of Sade? This is why Lacan suggests reading him "with" Kant, his contemporary, who in the same epoch had pushed thinking on ethics as far as possible in order to differentiate it, precisely and contrary to ancient and medieval philosophy, from that of science.

It is thus important for us to know what this question says about the specific moment of the Lacanian creation and what it means for analytical discourse itself. To what extent does the latter permit us to realise the change that has taken place in the relation between science and ethics? To what extent does the latter concern the study of perversions, beginning with the idea we have of them, the status we accord them and—because it is for us essentially a psychoanalytical concern—their epistemological and heuristic function in the elaboration of analytical discourse?

---

[4] ibid., p. 765.

20.2 Perversion and Knowledge

The Lacanian formulation raises some important questions. First of all, if there is a change in the relationship between science and ethics at the time of the Enlightenment, that is to say with the emergence of modern sciences, we can suppose that not only is psychoanalysis concerned with it to the highest degree, but that it emerged from it, beyond what it has been possible to say about it until now. It is perhaps, more than any other discourse, called upon to speak the "truth" about it, or at least a substantial part of it. Then, what place and what function does this change have for the perversions—in all their forms, as they emerged for the first time with hitherto unsurpassed violence—under Sade's pen? Lacan warns us nonetheless against the hypothesis of seeing in Sade a precursor of Freud: "It is silly to consider that Sade's work anticipates Freud's, even with regard to a catalogue of perversions…"[5] Even if some thinkers contradict him on this point,[6] to claim this position would be a methodological mistake and a failure to take into account the extremely precise timing to which any discursive production is subject. Lacan insists on this point about Sade: "…a clearing occurs which continues over a hundred years in the depths of taste in order to make Freud's approach possible. We need sixty more years to say: why so?"[7]

If Sade is fundamentally engaged in his time, it does not mean that his contemporaries were ready to welcome his scandalous message, or even understand it. After an underground existence of more than a century, the perspicacity and the sensitivity of some poets– first Apollinaire, and then the Surrealists—were necessary to give him an audience. Lacan suggests that it is from his own opening up (*frayage*), that is to say from a certain progress of analytical discourse, that it is possible to say something more, to clarify the status of Sade, of his work, and of what his name symbolises. He gives us an idea of the time necessary for this subversive and unfathomable work to find its way to us. One can justifiably

[5] ibid.

[6] Roudinesco, E. (2007). *La part obscure de nous-mêmes: Une histoire des pervers*. Paris: Albin Michel, p. 133.

[7] Lacan, op. cit.

ask what remains of it now, exactly two centuries after the death of the "divine marquis"? Even if it is a mistake to place Freud as following on from Sade—it is known that Freud had none of the latter's works—he did nonetheless establish a practice and a tradition of thought that, perhaps better than any other, made it possible to fully appreciate the Sadean abyss—its true value, if I may say so—or to extract from it the excessiveness (*dé-mesure*) of what we call "perversion." Nor does this exclude the fact that, in order to accomplish this, the psychoanalytic tradition has to adjust its instruments to the Sadean scale.

If there is an influence, it goes both ways. It is linked with the elaboration of a context which, retroactively, makes it possible to determine the conditions of emergence of what is *new*. So it is the analytical discourse, particularly in its Lacanian version, that allows us to take account of the Sadean excesses (dé-raison) as coextensive with the reason of the Enlightenment, of Evil as the Other of Good, that is to say as its very condition, of crime as the foundation of the Law. This makes of Sade not a "prince" of perversion but rather its first theorist, and of his work the depositary of a knowledge that only demands to be recognised as such and thus to be elaborated. One could argue that it should be philosophy, or law in its ethical dimension, to pick up the torch, that should be destined to think about Sadean subversion. But have we not seen Habermas who in going back to the founding text of his masters gave Sade a miss, thereby closing a barely opened chapter? It would only have disturbed too much his way of thinking, his ethics of a "communicative action" (*kommunikatives Handeln*) that is certainly more suited to the psychotherapies than to psychoanalysis. Can we imagine a next step in philosophy that will be inspired by the Sadean excesses (*dé-raison*) as a consubstantial with reason itself?

Psychoanalysis will have the task of reconsidering the ethical registers in relation to a knowledge produced by the clinic of perversions that, while imposing itself at the heart of our practice, also goes beyond it in being widely talked about, and in infiltrating the political and religious domains. Therefore, it is important to identify the epistemic function of the perversions, as it expresses itself in the Sadean text, such that it reveals itself to our attention and our reading, prepared by the already long tradition of psychoanalysis, while we have just emerged from a century of uninterrupted horrors. Those started with the beginning of WWI and are marked by a series of acts implementing new forms of violence, first in Europe, by destroying what was most dear to an ancestral tradition, before going global and engaging progressively with other cultural areas.

We are witnessing unprecedented violence, linked with the development of a new technique: an organ of construction as well as destruction; instrument of knowledge, but also of its perversion. As with the old technique, the new one is in essence an extension of the body. However, while giving it an unprecedented power (*jouissance*), it instrumentalises it, subjugates it and is eventually likely to crush it in turn. The modern technique adds to the body a dimension of another order, a violence that is not easily "convertible" into a norm: whether an epistemic, legal or social norm. So that Étienne Balibar talks about an "inconvertible violence",[8] which is understood by Marcel Hénaff as "a violence that is not led to any rationality able to transform it into an organised, instituted power – such as the State – but remains pure aggression, unlimited hatred, destructive rage as we have observed in the case of ethnic cleansing operations."[9] We can also talk of a brutal cruelty that while being devoid of any meaning or of aiming to abolish it, is based on an excess of meaning that only fanaticism can produce.

Another reading would say that all discourses are affected by a hole—a hole of meaning, of reason, of knowledge—which compound the violence; that it is all the more important to think it through, and for lack of the ability to grasp it, to try to determine what is inscribed in it. For however inhuman it may be, the violence in question is fundamentally human. More than ever, it raises the question that Kant placed at the heart of his thought: "What is Man? (*Was ist der Mensch*?)." What is the man who is capable of committing such actions? The current and future clinic must take into account the pressure on the threshold of humanity that spares no discourse, but confronts them all with a form of dehumanity (*dés-humanité*) which seems to impose another "order" that is an "invention" of our time. What is new, as Freud already observed, is

[8] Balibar, E. (2010). *Violence et civilité*. Paris: Galilée, p. 96.

[9] Hénaff, ibid., p. 209.

that for the first time in its history, humankind has at its command the technical mean to annihilate all its representatives up to the last.

20.3 Crime and Law

To pronounce judgement on perversions leads us to radicalise our thinking including that of the psychoanalytical clinic. It compels us to take the measure not only of the inhumanity that is in mankind, but also to consider it as being an essential part of it. "Essential" here means: not by accident, but by reason, not by contingency but by necessity. That gives a rightful place to the coruscation, the fury of a Sade. Contemporary thought collides at the threshold (*seuil*) of humanity, which escapes it and is always repelled, not by malice, but according to the order of reason; or in other words, by the order of the reason we call science. In its name, our modernity continues to transgress the most firmly established norms that the law is convoked to rewrite according to principles that are themselves subject to caution.

To evoke Evil as a necessity or, to speak as Sade does, of the necessity of Evil, enables engagement not only with a morality that refers to an idea of "sovereign good," but also, even more fundamentally, with the notion of the "Banality of Evil" (Banalität des Bösen), proposed by Hannah Arendt, for the want of any better category to think the Nazi horror. Her observation accords with those of Primo Levi and other witnesses in remarking that those who enacted the extermination were not, in the great majority, either monsters or sexual deviants, but people who were apparently normal. Subsequently, one may ask what does *normal* mean? Are we not challenged to think like Sade that the greatest monstrosity is to be found in this "normality", just as the greatest cruelty is that of the law? The specificity of the Nazi crime is precisely to have been committed in the name of the law—of a law perverted by a criminal State.

The taking into consideration of perversions, as the law does, implies the need to rewrite not only a clinical chapter, but also its founding principles. Before being able to determine the sources of knowledge that constitute the perversions, it is useful to address the issue of the relationship between crime and law, in particular, of what law owes to crime. In this respect, it is interesting to cite the example of Gilles de Rais, companion of Joan of Arc, who became *maréchal de France* and was famous for the many sexual offenses he committed, especially on children: he is said to have killed as many as 300 children, a worthy character for a Sadean novel. He is close to it, except for the fact that he enacted unimaginable violence that Sade worked like a slave to try to keep in the realm of fiction only.

Georges Bataille, in his presentation of the minutes of the trial of Gilles de Rais, writes about him: "Crime is a creation of the human species, it is even the creation of this species alone, but it is mostly a secret aspect of it."[10] An aspect, in any case, that says a lot; maybe especially because it is a secret and has to remain as such. The crime, particularly if it is a sexual crime, would say something about the *truth* of humankind: this signifies neither legitimation nor justification, but is rather a reference to censorship and repression, which can never be completely lifted.

Bataille tries to demonstrate the intimate link between truth, censorship and repression: "Crime obviously calls for the night; crime without the night would not be the crime. But, profound as it is, the horror of the night aspires to the radiance of the sun".[11] Here as elsewhere, the act (the crime) is all the more radical the more profound is the repression. "Every act, *acting out* or not, analytical or not, is related, is somehow linked with the opacity of the repressed. And the most original act, to the most original repressed, to the *Urverdrängt.*"[12] This formulation highlights the similarity and the difference between the *maréchal* and the marquis. The action of the first is reproduced by the second in a long elaboration of his fantasy by an act that is transformed into writing, by an act of writing that is submitted, astonishingly, to the requirements of the Enlightenment. It is the advent of these requirements that has changed the situation, following the order of reason that they have permitted to be established or recognised in everything, including the field of crime,

---

[10] Bataille, G. (1959). *Le procès de Gilles de Rais*. Œuvres complètes X. Paris: Gallimard, 1987, p. 277.

[11] ibid., p. 279.

[12] Lacan, J. (1960–1). *Le Séminaire, Livre VIII: Le transfert*. 2ème édition. Paris: Seuil, 2001, p. 397.

instituted as a "discipline"—to be named criminology—and in all kinds of behaviour considered abnormal, aberrant or perverse.

Sade is in the paradoxical situation of fighting the order of reason with the very means of reason. Only human passion, which is firstly of a sexual order, can resist this order. Yet, if Sadean sexuality is intended to subvert order—whether political, religious, legal or moral—is it not to establish, at the same time and in the same way, rules that are even more constraining and restrictive? It is for this reason that Foucault speaks of a "Sade, Sargent of Sex,"[13] "promoter of a disciplinary eroticism that accompanies the extension of an instrumental rationality."[14] Foucault, understandably, sets himself against "the literary sacralisation of Sade:" "…he bores us. He's a disciplinarian, a sergeant of sex, an accountant of the ass and its equivalents."[15] The "honesty" (*tout dire*) that Sade is so proud of—to the point of making a system out of it at the service of an "absolute" of knowledge and *jouissance*, is it not terrifying because of this very "absolute"? Since it is never guaranteed of its foundation and is always subject to an entropic process, a process of loss, the Sadean figure is obliged to resort to increased violence, always deeper, more cruel. What logic does it follow, if we suppose that it is not purely arbitrary?

Crime is not the other side of law, as one would suppose, but it has an ambiguous relationship with it, to say the least. Crime needs law, law needs crime. The crime of Sade is inseparable from the aim of theorising it, of establishing its founding principle. It is raised as an imperative to which only an act can respond; an *imperative to jouissance* so powerful and ferocious that it crosses all the stages of life of the individual, that it manifests itself in each of his acts. They themselves are subjected to such rigour that it seems to Lacan that he can approach them only through Kant's ethics, to which the latter wanted to give a basis as solid as the laws of nature. The Kantian imperative is "categorical" because its aim is universal, which is reformulated by Lacan into a Sadean version—established as a "*right to jouissance*". It is relevant because it breaks

---

[13] Foucault, M. (1975). "Sade, sergent du sexe". In *Dits et écrits*. Vol.2. Paris: Gallimard, 1984, pp. 818–822.

[14] Foucault, M. (2013). *La grande étrangère. A propos de littérature*. Notes des éditeurs, Paris: EHESS, p. 147.

[15] Foucault, M. (1975/1984), op. cit., p. 822.

with a secular tradition, with an ethics dependent solely on the pleasure principle (*Lustprinzip*). "In the very moment of *jouissance*, [the pleasure] would not be part of the game, if fantasy did not intervene to support it from the very discord where it falls. In others words, fantasy creates the very pleasure of desire (*le fantasme fait le plaisir propre au désir*)."[16] The Lacanian reading, inspired by the clinic, orientates itself from a "beyond" of the pleasure principle, from a beyond which Sade establishes in action and which takes the appearance of a crime. It lays claim, in relation to the very demands of the right which is, first and essentially, the right to *jouissance*.

The Sadean action, whatever one might think, is firstly an act of writing. What gives it all of its radical character is that it does not have any physiological, moral or social limit. This gives it a theoretical rigour, without diminishing its practical value, of being inscribed in a quest for the real, far beyond the improbable reality of his characters, towards a truth that only fiction can claim or have access to. Foucault insists on this in his reading of *The New Justine*, a story set "entirely, totally under the sign of truth."[17] It is indispensable to Sadean writing to which it gives its brand and its pertinence: "…this is not a novel, it is the truth: therefore, you have to believe me".[18] But, which truth? "The truth that Sade is speaking of… it is not really the truth of what he is telling, it is the truth of his reasoning".[19] In other words, it is the truth according to the order of reason which nevertheless must guarantee an action which is the writing. We could say that it is a truth that refers to the impossible writing of the sexual relation or to a necessary sexual disunion, so that "it is on the condition of breaking a communication that limits it that the true violent nature of eroticism is revealed, whose translation into practice alone corresponds with the sovereign image of man."[20]

If this violence implies "the denial of the partners (*la négation des partenaires*)," as "an essential part of the [Sadean] system"[21] then is it not a

---

[16] Lacan, 1962, ibid., pp. 773–774.

[17] Foucault, 2013, op. cit., p. 149.

[18] ibid., p. 150.

[19] ibid., p. 153.

[20] Bataille, G. (1957). *L'érotisme*. Paris: Minuit, p. 186.

[21] ibid.

way to write negatively about them, to minimise them? The question of the aim of the action remains unsolved. As mentioned earlier, Sade is looking for the most deeply repressed, the most authentic truth, which is undoubtedly sexual. He is looking for the most unsayable unsaid thing, the most unbearable, not only for the society of his time, but for all societies of all times. This is why his action is based on a principle that claims to be universal and on a writing style that transcends the categories of time and space: "I would like to find a crime whose effect continues indefinitely, even when I am no longer there, (…) that even beyond my life, its effect would still persist."[22]

The objective of a never-ending *jouissance* aims also towards a *jouissance* that can only be reached at infinity, that is to say asymptomatically. Sade would like to make of it the foundation for his own writing, the only way to guarantee a place for the unsayable, when the subject has vanished or disappeared, that is to say a place from which no one can any longer respond. Is it not a way to trace the horizon where he can inscribe the structure of his fantasy and build his plural fiction?[23]

20.4 Body and Law

Lacan ends his contribution on Sade in this way: "Our verdict upon the submission of Sade to the Law is confirmed." He even assumes that it is one of the motives that pushed him to the crime: "The apology for crime only pushes him to the indirect avowal of the Law. The supreme Being is restored in Maleficence."[24] Is it a way to reassure oneself? The fact remains that the Sadean action is writing on the edge: always pushing further, transgressing, challenging the limit. Can there be a better way to overcome it, to push it back still further? Implicit is the question: what is the limit beyond all the possible transgressions, given that it is the limit of the Other, the Other body? Is it necessarily death or rather its erotisation?

[22] de Sade, D.A.F. (1797). *Histoire de Juliette.* Œuvres Complètes, tome 8. Paris: Gilbert Lely, 1986–1991, p. 298.

[23] Lacan, 2001, op. cit., p. 398.

[24] Lacan, 1962, op. cit., p. 790.

It is as if the Sadean action, transgressive by nature, had as a principal objective to explore the field of the Other, with evil or rather the doing of evil as the main operator. Its aim would thus be to access, through the *jouissance* that he snatches—sometimes literally—from the body, the knowledge of which he is depositary. Action as a *malum facere* never stops transforming the other's body into the body of the Other, even an absolute Other, after having removed it from the body or by reducing it to remains, in preference to the lone voice. The radicality of the Sadean approach is fuelled by the context of that time, more particularly by the *Terreur*, which both horrified him and inspired his most pertinent contributions to the political and juridical debate that accompanied the Revolution.

Maurice Blanchot who considers "solitude" as the foundation of the "Sadean moral"[25] does not take into consideration the fact that it applies, even more fiercely, to the exploration of the field of the Other according to its own logic and that needs to be elucidated. It is present in his text and in action in his writing. Lacan gives us a lead when he says about *Philosophy in the Bedroom*, which was published eight years after *Critique of Practical Reason*, that "it completes it, we will say that it gives the Critique its truth."[26] For they both ask questions of the subject in the face of his action and the object of this action, at the time when the idea of Good, sovereign or not, seems to be very uncertain. How can one obstruct particular interests to give ethics a more solid basis? For Kant, this can only be a maxim with a universal value. "Therefore its weight only appears in the process of excluding drive or feeling, everything that makes the subject suffer in his interest for an object: what Kant designates for all that as 'pathological'".[27] Would Sade be then the representative of this "pathology," which appears in his relationship with desire and the drive? It appeared in a letter addressed to his wife, written long before the Revolution, in November 1783, when he was already in prison: "My manner of thinking, so you say, cannot be approved. Do you suppose I care? A poor fool indeed is he who adopts a manner of thinking like

[25] Blanchot, M. (1963). "La Raison de Sade". In *Lautréamont et Sade*. Paris: Minuit.

[26] Lacan, 1962, op. cit., p. 766.

[27] ibid.

others! My manner of thinking stems from my reflections; it holds with my existence, with the way I am made. It is not in my power to alter it; and were it, I'd not do so. This manner of thinking you find fault with is my sole consolation in life; it alleviates all my sufferings in prison, it composes all my pleasures in the world outside, it is dearer to me than life itself. It is not my manner of thinking but that of others that has been the source of my unhappiness."[28]

Sade shows here a bit of suffering, of pathos or passion, usually unnoticed, inaccessible to the law that he finds "cold." When he is set free on the day after the Revolution, after being transferred from Bastille to Charenton, he has already spent about fifteen years in prison for a series of offences, probably less because of their seriousness than their scandalous character that struck the imagination of his contemporaries. He started his series of crimes with a *fait divers:* the flagellation of a young prostitute. It gained a legal, political and poetical dimension thanks to her allegation and most likely by the details mentioned. Sade is eventually sentenced for having flogged the young victim until she drew blood, for making incisions on her body and finally for having poured wax on her wounds. It is the statement and the introduction on a third appeal, announced in the verdict of the judges, which transforms this petty crime into an inaugural act, not of a series of scandals, which would not have deterred the marquis, but of his writing. This founding moment can only be reconstructed after the fact and its status, its real weight, can only be measured in the achievement of his work, considered as a whole. The Sadean action finds its base there as a function of the legal dramatisation, which as he tries to demonstrate, is structured as a perverse scenario. It is the law and its application that, literally and against his will, transform him into a monster.

The witnesses hasten to denounce the excesses of the legal system, its arbitrariness and the corruption of the judges under the *Ancien Régime*. They become the central characters in Sade's writing of fantasm. According to him, fantasm finds its consistency only in its reference to the real that constitutes the *jouissance* of the "judging thing" (*chose jugeante*).

[28] A Mme de Sade, début novembre 1783. Cited in Jallon, H. (1997). *Sade. Le corps constituant.* Paris: Michalon, 1997, pp. 15–16.

He became the absolute master in the elaboration of fantasm that has been so striking that until today it has been accepted at face value. That is the reason that he, that is to say his writing, has fallen victim to the most drastic political, legal and cultural censorship until the recent past, till just after WWII, a period of a century and a half. The legal system never let go of Sade, who responded to it by putting on stage the most perverse, the most repugnant judges reduced to their strict corporeity, always vile and disgusting. "Corrupted, so will be the magistrates of the *Ancien Régime* also in their body: the president de Fontanis is described as someone 'commonly emaciated, long, thin and stinky like a corpse.'"[29] What matters, beyond the description, of which one could cite many other examples, is the logic at stake: referred to as "the truth of bodies",[30] what I have called: the *jouissance* of the judging thing. "Justice is not this abstract figure placed above human contingencies. It is incarnated in a series of sick and repulsive bodies".[31]

Sade suggests that the truly perverse action occurs at court, that the law itself is perverse and that those who pronounce it are necessarily compromised by it. Sade becomes the "author" or the reporter of it, par excellence. He dedicates, even sacrifices his life to his writing. For this, some considered him a "saint." This writing work is a necessity to him, since it protects him from falling into madness, into the most complete despair. It particularly allows him to question the *jouissance* at work in the apparently most formal, most dispassionate, and therefore most disembodied act of judgment. Sade brings the body to the very heart of justice, of its practice, to interrogate as much the judges as the victims in their corporeity. To know more, one must act. Hence the necessity of crime: more than contingent, it becomes necessary, the necessary challenge to the law, whose *truth* the crime will tell. The less law there is, the less crime there will be, states Sade; just like Saint Paul who thinks that with "accomplishment" of the law, which implies its abrogation, "sin" will disappear from earth and humankind will be saved.

[29] ibid., p. 24.

[30] ibid., p. 25.

[31] ibid.

I have said that it is the legal scenario, and the sanction that comes with it, that will transform a minor event into an inaugural action. And simultaneously, the young prostitute's flagellated body—cut, ticked, stamped with wax, used to mark with a seal the official or confidential document, by way of signature—is transformed into the "constituent body" (*corps constitutant*) of Sadean writing. It is firstly, essentially, writing directly on the body, directly on the "*jouissance* substance" (Lacan). The body becomes the place of the Other, the place of writing par excellence, of the determining marks that constitute the matrix of fantasm. Sade never stops elaborating its logic and interrogating its truth that he strives to say "totally" (*la dire "toute"*): he makes a duty of it at the cost spending half his life in prison, and then in an asylum.

21

Perversion and the Law: From Sade to the 'Spanner Case' and Beyond

Colin Wright

In what follows, I will first say a few words about why there might be an intimate link between modernity and perversion. Then I will extract some co-ordinates from what Lacan had to say about the Marquis de Sade, concentrating on the relation between the law and the body in perverse structure. This will pave the way for a discussion of the relevance of these Lacanian co-ordinates for our era, when the social link, post Sexual Revolution, is characterised by a sort of marketised polymorphous perversity. Against this backdrop, it is tempting to argue that perverse transgression has been nullified by a permissive turn in society, as if it is now impossible to read *120 Days of Sodom* properly because it appears on the shelf next to *50 Shades of Grey*. I will nonetheless argue that Lacan's structural approach to perversion—rooted in analytic practice rather than in observable behaviour, and in the ethics of psychoanalysis rather

C. Wright (✉)
University of Nottingham

D. Caine, C. Wright (eds.), *Perversion Now!*,
DOI 10.1007/978-3-319-47271-3_21

than in any shared morality, 'liberal' or otherwise—is a crucial bulwark against this generalised 'perversity' which has itself become a superegoic law. I will explore these issues finally by engaging with some examples of the encounter between law and what I will call the 'body of jouissance', focussing in particular on the ruling on sadomasochistic practices in the so-called 'Spanner Case'.

21.1 Modernity and 'Perverting the Course of Justice'

If psychoanalysis has been able to show that modernity and perversion are structurally linked, it is because it has emerged from and shaped this very link. However one defines modernity, some kind of iconoclastic break with the putatively *pre*-modern is always implied. Indexing a certain enjoyment in transgression then, it is no wonder modernity has provoked questions about, and practices of, perversion. After all, isn't the Enlightenment's challenge to religious dogma already a sort of double-act between the hysteric and the pervert, with the former pointing out the flaw in God's authority while the latter tries to prop it up (often, paradoxically, via blasphemy)—both asking, in their different ways, what kind of father can guarantee the law now?

This perverse interrogation of the authority of the father was a precondition for the Freudian revolution. As Lacan points out *apropos* of Descartes, psychoanalysis owes its very existence to the emergence of *modern* subjects, riven by doubt yet dreaming of a flawless certainty guaranteed by an honest God. It is the divided modern subject, burdened by a question, who classically comes to analysis, and it is the supposition of a knowledge capable of alleviating doubt that sustains neurotic transference. But if the modern subject doubts himself, isn't it because he already began to doubt the law of the father? Modernity is thus entangled in a great tumult in the field of ethics which de-links the question of the good from its Christian opposition to sin. The libertine tradition, of which Sade can be considered the high point, vividly testifies to this.

But for us as psychoanalysts, it is Freud who was able to de-imaginarise the Sadean fantasy and demonstrate its imbrication with modern civilisation. To be extremely reductive, one can identify three interventions on perversion in Freud's work. Firstly, in the *Three Essays on Sexuality*, he breaks with the psychiatric discourse of 'deviancy' by showing that there is no biological reference by which to measure sexual 'normality' or its opposite in human beings: rather, there is a polymorphously perverse core only contingently 'normalised' by the mechanisms of socialisation. This aspect of Freud was taken up in the twentieth century 'liberalisation' of sexual mores whose signposts include the famous Kinsey Report and all the iconography of the sexual revolution in the 1960s. However, it is crucial to note that this was largely Freud 'lite', obscuring his more fundamental insight that the encounter with sexuality is itself *traumatic*, a confrontation with the real that makes a hole in psychic representation—*troumatique* in Lacan's apt neologism. By contrast, the 'polymorphous perversity' associated with the sexual revolution was straightforwardly hedonistic and easily recuperated by capitalism. Sexuality could thereafter be conceived as a lifestyle choice and a consumer right: far from being an unwritable, non-relation at the core of the human condition, *The Joy of Sex* became simply another bodily practice, not radically different from yoga, or going to the gym. If Freud is seen as a champion of instinctual pleasure in this way, rather than a theorist of jouissance, psychoanalysis threatens to become completely absorbed into, and indeed complicit with, the market-based service of goods ….

This is why Lacan's Freud is more important today than ever. Lacan foregrounds the importance of two other 'moves' in Freud's thinking around perversion. Firstly, in *Beyond the Pleasure Principle,* Freud isolates, in the death drive and its link to the repetition compulsion, a pleasure in pain of which Sade had been the literary witness and advocate over a century before. Secondly, in *Civilization and its Discontents*, Freud recognises a perverse dimension to the superego and the sublimation of desexualised libido demanded by civilisation.[1] He therefore challenges the Aristotelian and then Christian tradition that had equated doing good with feeling good, exposing not simply the potential enjoyment in behaving badly

[1] See Vadolas, A. (2009). *Perversions of Fascism*. London: Karnac.

('sin' already named this) but, much more scandalously, the 'evil' kernel of the good itself.

It is ironic, then, that English law retains the crime of 'perverting the course of justice'—meaning to deliberately obstruct a police investigation, for example—given that Freud revealed the course of modernity to be a progressive *intertwining* of perversion and justice. He even intimates in *Civilization and its Discontents* the connection between the aggressivity of modern morality and Kant's categorical imperative, which Lacan would take up so provocatively in his famous écrit.[2]

21.2 Law and the Body in Perverse Structure

Lacan locates the Marquis de Sade at the crux of this quintessentially modern problem of law in the wake of the decline of symbolic authority. His life and work—both in their way imprisoned—testify to modernity's tendency to both make law a regulatory, administrative tool of normalising discipline on the one hand, and to drain law of the sovereign absolutism that once guaranteed its authority on the other. Sadean perversion, then, represents a response to existence on this cusp which Lacan names, in *Seminar VII*, 'contemporary life'.

Whereas the neurotic subordinates himself to a symbolic law underpinned by a paternal function that ultimately does not require an actually authoritarian father, the pervert refuses to recognise the lack in the Other that would enable the law to operate via a phallic signifier circulating in the social link. Instead, the pervert aims to restore to the Other of law its absolutist omnipotence. The body of the law must be full, non-lacking, un-castrated, immune even to the symbolic inscription of sexual difference. One sees these themes very clearly in Sade's writings. Man-made laws are continuously mocked, derided and demoted in favour of a cosmic law that operates far above merely social values: in Nature, Sade insists, crime and destruction are the sovereign laws of life in its true vitality. The cancellation of sexual difference, classically through the maintenance of

[2] Lacan, J. (2006). 'Kant with Sade', in *Écrits: The First Complete Edition in English*. B. Fink (Trans.). London: W. W. Norton & Company, pp. 645–668.

a phallic mother by means of fetishistic disavowal, is discernible in Sade's text in the predilection for sodomy common to so many of his characters: the anus is better suited to reducing the series of victims to a substitutable list of undifferentiated stand-ins. Beyond the petty, sexuated laws of men then, perverts only recognise the authority of what Lacan identifies very precisely as '*a will to jouissance*'.

Despite what neurotics imagine about the pervert, this is very much the *jouissance* of the Other, with the 'of' here in its genitive mode: the Other enjoys, not the pervert. The masochist, for example, is active in orchestrating a scenario that extracts *anxiety* from the Other, as a sign of their *jouissance* that does not deceive. As Lacan shows in *Seminar VII*, Oedipalised law makes desire and its prohibition one and the same thing. Far from being outside this dialectic in a lawless zone of pure abandon, as the neurotic likes to imagine, the pervert repeatedly stages a transgression that is paradoxically rule-bound in order to make the superegoic kernel of law appear on stage. Again, this is evident in Sade's writings: despite his inclusion in the *Pléiade* since 1990, in truth he is really a terribly tedious writer, circling around variations on the same scene again and again. Michel Foucault captured something of this when he referred to Sade, disparagingly, as "an accountant of arses and their equivalents".[3]

But the analyst will always be interested in the 'programme of jouissance' that combines arses and accountancy! Psychoanalysis demonstrates that the question 'what is a body' is a central concern for every *parlêtre*, whose being by definition derives from the real traces of language. As Lacan's early work on the mirror-stage shows, a complex operation is required to bring a chaotic bundle of drives within the bounds of a coherent bodily imago. Psychotics remind us that this imaginary body can easily disperse into fragments when symbolic quilting points are lacking. Equally, *having* a body is a similarly complex phenomenon dependent upon the effects of the signifier, as conversion symptoms in hysteria classically indicate. Being a body and having a body are not the same thing. Autistic subjects sometimes show us that a prosthetic device is needed to supplement the organism so that it can fabricate a body with manageable rhythms and borders. So what is the Sadean pervert's relation to

[3] Foucault, M. (1994). *Dits et Écrits*. Paris: Gallimard, p. 822.

being/having a body? Again, if we mistake jouissance for pleasure, we risk taking Sade's libertine philosophy too literally: although the pervert *appears* to be the staunchest advocate of hedonistic sensual indulgence, in fact, his body is reduced to a mere instrument serving the *Other's* will to jouissance. This is one meaning of the inversion of the matheme of neurotic fantasy with which Lacan formalises perverse structure in 'Kant with Sade'. The object is not on the side of the Other as in neurosis, but on that of the subject: the pervert's body is prostituted to the Other's enjoyment. In *Seminar XVI*, Lacan implies a masochistic core to all perversion for this reason: the body as *object a* is instrumentalised as a means of turning S (A̶), signifier of the lacking Other, into S (A). The body's capacity for pleasure, by contrast, constitutes a limit to this instrumental jouissance-function: hence, again, the inexhaustible, permanent erections in Sade's men and the women who display cartoon-like indestructability as a way, in fantasy at least, of evading this limit.

These two dimensions, law and the body, come together in the famous 'maxim of jouissance' Lacan extracts from *La Philosphie dans le boudoir*, "I have the right to enjoy your body, anyone can say to me ...'. As opposed to the Kantian moral imperative which remains within the orbit of a psychological notion of individual conscience, Sade's maxim, in its very syntax, situates the moral law in the 'Other's mouth'. Bodies are certainly to be enjoyed then, but not by individuals deluded enough to think they 'own' them.

21.3 The Spanner Case and Beyond

Let us now explore the relevance of these perhaps familiar co-ordinates for our own conjuncture (which many have defined as post-modernity or liquid modernity). This is important, because the legal Other is not what it was in Sade's day ... or Lacan's for that matter.

I am not a lawyer or legal scholar, so I can only comment on the broadest of tendencies. Nonetheless, I think it is right to follow Foucault in saying that there has been a general move away from disciplinary forms of law organised around punishment and a related paternal limit, and towards law as a more 'horizontal' or indeed 'democratic' tool of *normalisation*. At the international level, we saw in the 1990s the emergence of 'restorative' as opposed to 'punitive' models of justice, and the centrality of notions of forgiveness in various truth and reconciliation commissions such as in South Africa and Chile (supported by a kind of 'cod' psychoanalysis, incidentally). At a more domestic level in the UK, we also saw in the 1990s the development of Anti-Social-Behaviour-Orders, or ASBOS, which turned behaviour from criminal transgression as such into the object of legal control. ASBOS have been served for everything from having sex too loudly to playing football in the street to inconveniencing local emergency services by repeatedly attempting suicide. And of course, the law has also come to register turbulence in the field of sexuality: employers are now enjoined to cater for 'gender dysphoria' and pre- and post-op transgender workers. Very recently in the UK, it has been deemed necessary to formulate new legislation for so-called 'revenge porn', by which ex-partners exact revenge on their former lovers by distributing explicit video clips or photographs of them on social media, suggesting the centrality of the digital semblant in a new arrangement of the voyeurism-exhibitionism couplet which Freud had already linked in his *Three Essays*.

Without judging such developments (for from where but their 'other side' would psychoanalysis do so?), it is nonetheless interesting to wonder whether all this makes life difficult for the pervert today? How frustrating to find the law on your side! Reflecting on time spent in Hitler's Berlin just before the outbreak of the war, Jean Genet observed that "it is not very interesting to be a perverse man in so perverse a land". Perhaps the contemporary pervert faces a neoliberal version of this same dilemma? Because we don't see many in analysis, we might even be tempted to imagine that the pervert is now as extinct as the Dodo. But as Serge André has argued "the sadist is more likely to frequent the magistrate's than the analyst's consulting room".[4] And if we look at the so-called 'Spanner Case',[5] it seems magistrates continue to find the presence of the pervert challenging.

---

[4] André, S. (2013). *Les perversions No. 2: Le sadisme*. Lormont: La Muette.

[5] See Thompson, B. (1994). *Sadomasochism: Painful Perversion or Pleasurable Play?* London: Continuum International Publishing Group.

Legally, the Spanner case pertains primarily to a ten year period between 1987 and 1997, although as a controversy it is ongoing. It began when video tapes showing apparently lethal sadomasochistic acts found their way into the hands of the British police. The police immediately began a murder investigation which they called 'Operation Spanner', only to find that all the filmed protagonists were not only alive and well, but had willingly consented to these acts as part of an underground gay S&M scene. The criminal investigation proceeded nonetheless—the course of justice would not be 'perverted'!—and despite the key element of consent being present, prosecutions resulted: sixteen men were found guilty of 'assault occasioning bodily harm', with no significant distinction being made between those who were giving and those who were receiving the harm. This surprising verdict stands to this day, despite the case going to the British High Court in 1993, and then the European Court of Human Rights in 1997, and despite a well-organised activist campaign led by the *Spanner Trust* which continues to lobby to prevent consensual BDSM activities, gay or straight, being criminalised. In fact, cases involving sadomasochistic acts between consenting *heterosexual* couples, including ones with fatal results, have been successfully defended on the basis of consent, strongly suggesting a degree of homophobia in the original ruling (in 1996, for example, the British Court of Appeal overturned the conviction of a man for branding his wife on the grounds that private, consensual activity could not be a criminal matter).

Of course, we cannot assume the men involved in the Spanner case were perverts structurally speaking, since we do not pin our diagnoses on behaviour, and it is well-known that Lacan is very critical of the composite term 'sadomasochism' which even Gilles Deleuze called a "semiotic howler".[6] Nonetheless, the legal response to the case still demonstrates that the *common* discourse of perversion now revolves around two conceptual axes which go against the grain of analytic discourse: namely, 'consent' and 'harm'. While the reification of these concepts explains the prominence of the figures of the paedophile and the sexual psychopath in the popular imaginary, they also signal law's perplexity before what

[6] Deleuze, G. and Sacher-Masoch, L. (1994). *Coldness and Cruelty and Venus in Furs*. New York: Zone Books, p. 134.

might be called *the unruly body of jouissance*. Lacan said several times that 'jouissance is real', and that 'the real is without law'. It follows that bodies embodying jouissance will remain, not outlaws (the law busies itself with naming those, making them in-laws of sorts), but more radically, 'extimate' to the law.

Consent is of course a keystone of liberal law which holds the subject to be a rational, well-informed decision maker who enjoys autonomy over a life lived in pursuit of a fundamental right to happiness which must be constitutionally and legally protected. The subject of consent knows what it wants and what it does not want. In other words, we do not meet him in our consulting rooms! There, subjects generally do not know what they want, other than *not* wanting what they still want nonetheless: such is the 'law' of the symptom. Because consent is such a fundamental concept in everything from marriage to medical intervention, the law struggles to legislate for those whose consent cannot be clearly demonstrated: children, people with learning disabilities, people under the effects of drugs and/or alcohol, the mentally ill considered to be *non compos mentis*, and so on. The discourse around abortion, too, has largely shifted from a religious framing to a legal one, so that the foetus represents less the miracle of life over which only God should have dominion, and more a legal entity with a right to life but no agency to give or withhold consent.

More difficult than these figures incapable of consent, however, is the short-circuiting effect of those subjects who can and do give their consent but to practices from which the law believes citizens must be protected. This is indicated by the recent debates about 'assisted suicide' and clinics that facilitate it, such as *Dignitas* in Switzerland. But it is also central to the Spanner case, where consent was freely given to 'occasion bodily harm'. Now, the BDSM scene does have accepted conventions for establishing consent, from 'role-contracts' to 'safety words'. However, for our purposes, emphasising BDSM as a 'lifestyle choice' one should be free to pursue in private actually nullifies the challenge thrown down by perversion: it reduces the unruly body of jouissance to the more governable body of pleasure, the Other's will to jouissance to a reciprocal agreement among imaginary others. As we saw, the Sadean maxim in fact demands a radical asymmetry, even as it facilitates a certain 'turn-taking'.

Inextricably linked to the notion of consent, harm has similarly deep roots in the liberal tradition. From Adam Smith to John Stuart Mill, the body is effectively framed as a possession, a property, a commodity that has a place on the market as labour power for sale. Jeremy Bentham placed the body within his 'felicific calculus', submitting it and policies governing it to a cost-benefit analysis of the ratio between pleasure and pain. In such circumstances, 'bodily harm' is figured as an impairment of a body's ability to either produce or consume. One can see this today in related legal concepts like 'damages', which show the extent to which the body has been financialised: as the etymology of the word already implies, 'corporations' are legally constituted as bodies that can suffer 'damages' and claim monetary recompense accordingly. So the crime of 'occasioning bodily harm' at the centre of the Spanner case suggests that liberal law tries to govern the body of pleasure by protecting it against the risk of unpleasure, but it also demonstrates that it does not know how legislate for the body of *jouissance* that enjoys beyond the pleasure principle. Only psychoanalysis can support a know-how with the latter kind of body.

Lacan in his later, Borromean period seemed to move away somewhat from the structural co-ordinates of perversion I have been using. But it is interesting to note there, in *Seminar XXIII* on Joyce for example, both a pun which brings out a new emphasis—*pére-version*, a turning toward father substitutes precisely because the paternal function is increasingly inoperative—and the following statement, which seems to imply that an *ethics* of perversion—as opposed to moralistic discourse judging types of behaviour said to be perverse, or indeed not perverse enough—still has something to teach us in the era of post- or liquid modernity: "you can do without the Name of the Father, as long as you make use of it."[7]

[7] Lacan, J. (1975–6). Le séminaire: Livre *XXIII: Le Sinthome*. Paris: Seuil, 2005.

22

Narratives of Perversion in the Time of the Psychoanalytic Clinic

Ian Parker

22.1 The Time of Perversion: Machinery and Representation

Opening *Seminar VI, Desire and its Interpretation*[1] Lacan, referring to 'the metaphor of the factory' (*'la métaphore de l'usine'*), says 'certain conjunctions of the symbolic and the real are necessary for the notion of energy even to subsist' (*'certaines conjonctions du symbolique et du réel sont nécessaires pour que même subsiste la notion d'énergie'*) (12 November 1958). This is in line with a historical materialist account of what he elsewhere referred to as the invention of the unconscious. That account grounds

[1] Lacan, J. (1958–1959). *Le séminaire, Livre VI: Le désire*, http://staferla.free.fr/S6/S6.htm (accessed 10 February 2016).

This paper is in two parts; first a theoretical framing, and second, an intervention.

I. Parker (✉)
University of Manchester

D. Caine, C. Wright (eds.), *Perversion Now!*,
DOI 10.1007/978-3-319-47271-3_22

the concepts on which psychoanalysis operates in conditions of industrial production and clock-time; psychoanalysis works on the 'subject of science' in capitalist society. So, what is the place of perversion in these technological conditions, and in the narratives of perversion which psychoanalysis then elaborates in its own practice, practice in the clinic and as political practice?

Perversion in psychoanalysis is, paradoxically, on the one hand configured as a kind of narrative, which is a narrative of 'development', even for those of us who do not explicitly employ developmental-psychological notions. On the other hand it also functions as a static repetitive scenario of which the non-perverts dream, particularly obsessionals who obediently reproduce the social relations necessary for capitalism to function. 'The phantasy of perversion' (*'Le fantasme de la perversion'*), Lacan says, 'is in space'(*'il est dans l'espace'*); 'it suspends some essential relationship or other' (*'il suspend je ne sais quelle relation essentielle'*), and while it is 'not properly speaking atemporal' (*'Il n'est pas à proprement parler a-temporel'*) he notes that 'it is outside time' (*'il est hors du temps'*).[2] Lacan thus indicates that to grasp the material conditions within which that fantasy works we need to move from the metaphor of the factory to that of cinematic representation in capitalist culture.

Toward the end of *Seminar VI* Lacan notes that 'the fantasy of the pervert presents itself as something which one could call a sequence' (*'le fantasme du pervers se présente comme quelque chose que l'on pourrait appeler une séquence'*), one which is 'cut off from the development of the drama' (*'coupée du développement du drame'*), and he then associates this sequence with 'what appears to us on the screen under the name – I am not sure of the term – of "trailer"' (*'quelque chose comme on voit apparaître sous le nom – je ne suis pas sûr du terme – de "rush"'*).[3] His claim is that 'what is seductive in these images, really depends, in effect, on this aspect of their not being inserted into the chain' (*'Ce qu'ont de séduisant ces images tient bien, en effet, à leur côté de désinsertion de la chaîne'*).[4] This claim raises questions about what the psychoanalyst today assumes to be

[2] ibid., 15 April 1959.

[3] ibid., 17 June 1959.

[4] ibid.

the temporal process to which the subject is expected to adapt in order for them to function, a temporal process which Lacanian psychoanalysis then subverts. The time of psychoanalysis should be grasped in its relation to visual representation, including representations of the narrative of the clinical 'case'.

In contrast to the popular cinematic forms of visual representation which perversion inhabits, (in which we should now include internet pornography) and of narratives of perversion, the temporal movement of psychoanalysis is to reduce signifiers in the clinic to non-sense and to extract the phallus from the narratives which instate it. That is, the phallus as privileged signifier is removed from the chain of signifiers which accords it its power. Psychoanalysis consists in a series of narratives with a commitment to particular notions of time which perversion resists, Lacan notes, as 'that which in the human being resists every normalisation' (*'ce qui dans l'être humain résiste à toute normalisation'*).[5]

Resistance to normalisation is for our psychoanalysis, of course, politically ambivalent. At one moment perversion appears to subscribe to a narrative of the subversion of the subject, one which is against adaptation. It then seems allied to a progressive politics which questions reigning social relations, including, perhaps, that of the nuclear family, which relies upon binary oppositions of sex, and of generation much beloved by certain traditions in psychoanalysis which pathologise what they think they know to be perversions. At the very same moment perversion resists castration by the signifier as a form of normalisation, castration to which our psychoanalysis is committed. Now the subject of perversion's attempt to make an Other exist, an Other to which it will then conform, is effectively allied to a reactionary politics.

It is with these considerations in mind that we need to explore the ambivalent political function of fantasies of perversion in the time of psychoanalysis. That is, both the historical time in which psychoanalysis emerges and functions, and time as the form of narrative which frames an account of perversion and responds to the resistance perversion pretends to enact. I focus on the politics of paedophilia, the way that politics

[5] ibid., 1 July 1959.

positions itself today, and the way the politics of psychoanalysis intersects with it. It is not because paedophilia is characterised as a perversion by psychoanalysis that I frame it in that way here, but because in this 'case' a subject speaks of their identity as paedophile as if they were a pervert, and they position themselves in relation to an Other that they then describe as anxious, divided. The place of the paedophile in the clinical structure of perversion is thus to be explored in their own account rather than presumed by us.

I will take a quite specific 'case' which, as you will see, is nonetheless embedded in some general debates about the nature of paedophilia, politics and psychoanalysis. There has been a remarkable shift of concern over the last four decades, from a concern with the rights of children and paedophiles directed toward sexual liberation to a concern with protection of children subject to relations of power. This has meant that those who were once able to position themselves as championing the freedom of children to have sex, including with adults, and including those who actually took on the identity of paedophile, are now positioned as abusers or as naively or deliberately complicit in abuse. This shift of attention toward the prevalence and traumatic consequences of child sexual abuse entails a shift of claims to identity by those involved, claims that are bound up with the role of 'identity politics' in left and feminist debates.

I will now describe in more detail the local context for the case, and this next part of the paper is also my response to a demand for political engagement with the issue from one of the participants in what we should also understand to be one of the latest events in a series of crises of the Left. My reply is a private communication which I make clear would also be a public statement. So, it has the status simultaneously of being a description, a response, and an intervention, perhaps also as an interpretation which I frame in my response as a demand that this attempt at a political engagement stop now.

Further analysis of the linkage and disjunction between the clinic and politics, and of the relationship between psychoanalysis and perversion as mediated by forms of temporality in the narrative representation of clinical cases, will have to be for another time. I now present the intervention.

22.2 Identity: Uses and Abuses of Power

Identity is a weapon against power, and the oppressed makes this so either by discovering a name for their experience or by seizing a name used against them to turn it against the enemy. This is why the turn to 'identity politics',[6] notwithstanding the third wave queer feminist critique,[7] was crucial to the development of the women's movement and of Black feminism. Identity discovered or seized by the powerless is hard won, but also carries with it the bitter traces of the times of silence, hatred and often enforced self-hatred of victims. No more so than when those speaking their own history of the violence wrought against them are survivors of child sexual abuse.

That double-history is one of historical time—of children disbelieved and made passive, that is, of their oppression running alongside and reinforcing that of women in the family—and of personal time in which the survivor gathers the courage and resources to speak of what happened to them and who they are. It is a personal question that is also a political one, and this is why political organisations that are both socialist and feminist have put campaigns against child abuse on their agenda for change.[8]

This is a burning question at a time when sexual violence on the Left is so visible, and when some groups in transition from the left to 'anti-establishment' politics[9] are keen to disparage what they call the 'victim lobby' response to 'paedo panic'.[10] Such groups overlook the key difference between a victim organising themselves to speak against power and

[6] Combahee River Collective. (1977). 'History is a weapon: Combahee River Collective Statement', http://historyisaweapon.com/defcon1/combrivercoll.html (accessed 10 February 2016).

[7] FIIMG. (2015). 'Queer: Excitable speech on tinternet', http://fiimg.com/2015/04/07/queer-excitable-speech-on-tinternet/ (accessed 10 February 2016).

[8] Left Unity. (2014). 'Crime and Justice Policy', http://leftunity.org/crime-justice-policy/ (accessed 10 February 2016).

[9] Farage, N. (2015). 'I'm taking on the establishment and they hate me for it', *Spiked Online*, http://www.spiked-online.com/newsite/article/im-taking-on-the-establishment-and-they-hate-me-for-it/16758#.Vml5j14zpQK (accessed 10 February 2016).

[10] Hewson, B. (2015). 'How "recovered memories" fuelled the paedo panic', *Spiked Online*, http://www.spiked-online.com/newsite/article/how-recovered-memories-fuelled-the-paedo-panic/16850#.Vml77V4zpQK (accessed 10 February 2016).

someone with power speaking as if they too were a victim, which is a key difference between progressive and reactionary uses of 'identity'.

In fact, paedophilia has long been a battle-ground of identity, with attempts by paedophiles declaring their identity then attempting to ally with the Left in campaigns against age of consent laws in the 1970s (which succeeded in getting support from leading intellectuals, including the historian Michel Foucault, existentialist philosopher Simone de Beauvoir and the Catholic Lacanian child psychoanalyst Françoise Dolto).[11]

A new attempt to open a 'debate' about this 'identity' in the Left included a link to a 2006 Guardian newspaper interview.[12] In this case the pseudonymous individual who sent appeals for a debate about the issue is clear that they are 'non-abusing', that they have never acted on their desires. So, there is a deliberate and bizarre attempt to shift the question from the domain of the law to that of identity. The Guardian interview describes an experience of what the interviewee calls his 'morally abominable desires', and the 'triggering incidents' in his own childhood of being abused which were discovered, he says, during his psychoanalytic treatment with the then head of the Portman Clinic in London (an NHS forensic psychotherapy service specialising in 'sexual perversion'). The analyst was an International Psychoanalytical Association (IPA) psychoanalyst who allegedly told his patient after two and a half years that he should sleep with a woman, at which point he surmised that he had been 'cured'. Except, what seems to have remained is a need to speak about a category of identity which is based on what is named as a 'sexual orientation'.

One of the bones of contention between the IPA and traditions of psychoanalysis after Jacques Lacan has been the goal of strengthening the ego, and hence personal identity, in the former tradition, as opposed to subversion of the ego in the latter. There have recently been some quite different ways of puzzling over memories of child sexual abuse using Lacanian ideas; written for the Left but without attempting to configure Left politics in line with what happened. These explorations draw

---

[11] See, e.g., Foucault, M. (1978). 'Sexual Morality and the Law', http://www.geocities.ws/foucault_on_age_of_consent/ (accessed 10 February 2016).

[12] Aitkenhead, D. (2006). 'The shadow that refuses to disappear', *The Guardian*, http://www.theguardian.com/society/2006/feb/25/socialcare.familyandrelationships (accessed 10 February 2016).

attention to the role of the 'guilt of the abused', a form of self-hatred which usually reinforces their silence and isolation. In contrast, in the particular case in question here, something is driving a declaration of identity and a compulsion to speak about it.[13]

Difference in clinical orientation has sometimes led to the assumption that the Lacanian option is necessarily more politically subversive, which is belied by the reactionary stance of some Lacanians and the progressive activity of some IPA analysts, including this psychoanalyst (political participation in the struggle against Apartheid is noted by his 'cured' patient). In fact, the extrapolation of personal therapy into politics is part of the problem here; memories, narratives, ideas about the development of the self that may have been arrived at and functioned as a source of consolation and strength in therapy do not then operate in the same way outside it.

There is a double-effect of a discourse of perversion as a pathology which here is tangled up with the identity of a 'paedophile' still compelled to speak from within a category assigned to him. The first is the cutting out of the social fabric of a type, the perverse 'paedophile' as one about whom psychiatric knowledge has much to say in terms of character, development and the predisposition to offend, but little to say in terms of the sexualisation of gendered power relations under capitalism. The second is the compulsion to speak about the self within the disciplinary terms of psychiatry and psychoanalysis such that there is a contribution to that knowledge—the incitement to speak about the pathological self is exactly what the 'psy' wants so that it can know more—but also with the effect that the individual believes that they are supplying valuable information.

The two aspects of this double-effect—between psychiatric knowledge of perversion and self-knowledge of the identity it assigns—are linked. Through a process of reification they circulate, on the one hand, in the discourse of society as commodities and, on the other, in the discourse of the clinic, both inside the clinic itself and in the *society* which needs the clinic as a separate space to 'cure' people so that they adapt to society.

[13] Seymour, R. (2015). 'The Guilt of the Abused', *Lenin's Tomb*, http://www.leninology.co.uk/2015/03/on-guilt-of-abused.html (accessed 10 February 2016).

These paedophiles are then 'things' that speak; and if they speak, they also speak the language of power, seizing back and, as it were, perverting the claim for a right to speak that was made by the oppressed.

It should be clear that support for 'survivors' of child sexual abuse should not be taken up within the discourse of rights in such a way that someone who identifies as a 'paedophile' (even if it is as someone who has never committed an offence) can also present themselves as a 'survivor' who must be supported, as if they too must be supported as one of the 'oppressed', battling 'dehumanised references' to what they are. That would not be a 'contribution' to 'an open and inclusive debate'; instead of being in 'solidarity with demonised groups' it would be dangerous to those who really are abused and oppressed.

What this kind of plea for the recognition of identity overlooks is the way the discourse itself operates within relations of power. Someone making this kind of appeal is, on the one hand, disconnected from those social relations, compelled to speak about identity, and, on the other hand, also repeating the psychiatric categories that psychoanalysis could have disturbed, could have broken him from. If he were really 'cured', then surely we would expect that he would not remain so attached to the very terms within which he was categorised and expected to speak.

So, our response to appeals of this kind to open a debate should be to continue the analysis by stepping back from those terms, by insisting that he give up on the attempt to use them to structure the political movements he wants to participate in. This response is in line with warnings made by Black feminists against those who, in the sphere of academic debate, want to speak of their 'whiteness' and thus colonise the voices of those who have been tracing its contours as a form of resistance.[14]

Identity is double-edged: this is why even those who claim it also suggest that it should be used only strategically,[15] and why they worry about

[14] Ahmed, S. (2004). 'Declarations of Whiteness: The non-performativity of anti-racism', *Borderlands e-journal*, http://www.borderlands.net.au/vol3no2_2004/ahmed_declarations.htm (accessed 10 February 2016).

[15] Spivak, G. (2014). 'Herald Exclusive: In conversation with Gayatri Spivak', *Dawn*, http://www.dawn.com/news/1152482/herald-exclusive-in-conversation-with-gayatri-spivak (accessed 10 February 2016).

how it often becomes a kind of commodity.[16] This is a danger for the oppressed themselves in speaking against power, but it is an even bigger danger for the oppressed when it is claimed and spoken by those with power.

22.3 Concluding Comments

This intervention treats the 'case' as one which must be located in narratives of the psychoanalytic clinic, the place where the normalisation of 'perversion' as category of pathology and of 'paedophile' as category of subject is to be resisted, by the patient and by the analyst. It treats the demand to speak publically, outside the clinic, as an instance that must be located in political narratives where pathology and identity are handled quite differently.

Here, the role of the clinic needs to be marked, marked out, remarked upon, including the way it functions as a machinery of representation, an apparatus running alongside the factory and cinema. Each apparatus provokes characteristic narratives, fictions, and particular regimes of truth. A psychoanalytic approach to perversion responds by specifying in which domains it might be possible for personal truth to be spoken, and in which domains that truth is corrupted and betrayed.

[16] Alcoff, L. M. (n.d.). 'Whose afraid of identity politics', http://www.alcoff.com/content/afraidid.html (accessed 10 February 2016).

23

Sectarian Discourse: Form of Perversion in Action in Our Modernity

Monique Lauret

In the exchange with Einstein, published in July 1932, under the title *Why War?* Freud suggested that civilisation is only conceivable at the price of a renunciation by individuals of some of their most violent impulses. In Freud's view the tendency towards aggression can be sufficiently deflected (but not eliminated) by means of culture, a theme that he had developed in *Civilization and its Discontents*, submitted for publication in 1929, just a week before Black Tuesday on Wall Street. But the deflection towards culture may not suffice. At the end of his essay Freud remains pessimistic and poses the question, as decisive for the destiny of the human race, of "whether and to what extent their cultural development will succeed in mastering the disturbance of their communal life by the human instinct [Trieb] of aggression and self-destruction."[1] Thus also Lacan who, at the

[1] Freud, S. (1933). *Why War?* S.E. 22: 195–216. J. Strachey (Trans.). London: Hogarth Press, 1964.

M. Lauret (✉)
Espace Analytique

D. Caine, C. Wright (eds.), *Perversion Now!*,
DOI 10.1007/978-3-319-47271-3_23

end of his *Ethics* Seminar in the 1960s, offers a radical depiction of our Western societies as a civilisation of hate which, caught in a technocratic ideology, inevitably runs up against a wall of hatred and destruction.

While Freud opposes the death drive to culture, Lacan situates the death drive in its inherence in the symbolic and makes of it the *ex nihilo*, whence language and the speaking subject originate. *Mitteleuropa*, the most refined and culturally advanced part of Europe, with Vienna as its capital in the late 19th century and early 20th century, at the hinge of a world that was about to disappear—the *World of Yesterday* that Stefan Zweig took as the title of the last book before his suicide—gave birth to our modernity with Freud's psychoanalysis, the literature of Schnitzler and Zweig, and the music of Mahler and Schoenberg, but it was the same *Mitteleuropa*, which, at the opposite extreme, nurtured the rise of nationalism, anti-Semitism and the unprecedented mass extermination of the concentration camps. As if an expansion (*Erweiterung*) of the cultural potentialities of a people or group went hand in hand with an expansion or extension of its destructive potential; an evolution parallel to the couple of union and atomisation.

After World War II a normative notion of extremism has emerged in the discourse of Western democracies. The renunciation of violence, called for by the two "pacifists", Freud and Einstein, in order to achieve political ends that would ensure peace and the development of culture, is still not recognised by constitutional states. Toleration of war is an offshoot of the destructive impulse. Everything that can act against it, on the side of Eros, will fight against destruction. Freud emphasises the importance of the libidinal bond, the establishment of ties of sentiment between members of a group—whether by attachment to a love object (not necessarily with a sexual goal) or by identification—in order to generate a community bond, which can provide a solid foundation for the edifice of human society. Violence is kept in check by unification and the power of those who are united constitutes the Law, the power of a community that has overcome its earlier violence by means of its affective and identificatory bonds and whose discourse structures the real of our world.

But the creation of ties of sentiment can also be a means of perverting the speech that brings truth and life. This can happen when such ties are hijacked by sectarian discourse, which is well acquainted with and knows how to utilise the mechanism of mass psychology, of the "group mind". As Freud wrote in 1921 in *Group Psychology*, where he commented on a classic text about the group mind by Gustave Le Bon: "love relationships [...] constitute the essence of the group mind."[2] Our modernity is marked by the harmful and deadly effects of sectarian ideology, fanatical totalitarianism, which proliferates in times of crisis—crises of values, political crises, identity crises. A sect (the word comes from the Latin "secta", related to "sequi", meaning "to follow") is a specific group, which cuts itself off from the body of society in order to constitute itself as a micro-community with its own rules, laws and institutions, and whose practices may be deemed extremist in a democratic society. Sectarians are primarily followers of a master, S1, in whom power and supposed knowledge are concentrated. The sectarian group may simply be a group of eccentrics, people living on the fringes of society, or people with non-standard religious beliefs, such as various Protestant sects; but a sect may also be a group that constitutes itself in opposition to the law of the community and functions in a perverse manner. It is this type of group function that will interest me: dangerous groups that are founded on subjugation of their members by means of a "sectarian discourse" for the aggrandisement of destructive or perverse and dangerous leaders, people who disguise as law what is fundamentally a negation of law by means of a sectarian discourse, which is the real weapon that gives them power.

23.1 The Group and the Sectarian Position

In *Group Psychology*, which pursues a train of thought that began in *Beyond the Pleasure Principle* of 1920, Freud follows Le Bon in noting the suggestibility of groups, which allows and nurtures "contagion". Under the influence of this "contagion" an individual in a group undergoes a profound and complete alteration of his psychic activity. "His liability

[2] Freud, S. (1921). *Group Psychology and the Analysis of the Ego*. S.E. 18: 65–144. J. Strachey (Trans.). London: Hogarth Press, p. 90.

to affect becomes extraordinarily intensified, while his intellectual ability is markedly reduced, both processes being evidently in the direction of an approximation to the other individuals in the group."[3] These two notions of the growth of affect, the most remarkable and most important phenomenon of group formation, and of the inhibition of thought can explain the mutual suggestion between individuals and the particular sensitivity to the prestige of leaders, which prevails in groups. The leaders must themselves be fascinated and fanaticised by a strong belief, or otherwise possessed of extreme cynicism, in order to be capable of awakening such belief within the group. The strength of this belief then produces in the individual a sense of unlimited power and invincibility, a regressive sense of omnipotence.

The group can, Freud tells us, "replace the whole of human society, which is the wielder of authority, whose punishments the individual fears, and for whose sake he has submitted to so many inhibitions."[4] But when a part of the group feels threatened in its identity, when it no longer recognises itself in what constitutes the basis of the identification, this faction may fall back on a sectarian position and indulge in unlimited violation of laws, drawing to itself adherents who "hunt with the pack" like hordes of savage barbarians. All individual inhibitions fall away and all of the cruel brutal and destructive impulses, which slumber in the individual as hangovers of a primal period, are awakened with a view to free satisfaction of the drive in a runaway, maniac mode. The human being can then tumble downwards several rungs on the ladder of civilisation. Freud quotes Le Bon: "Isolated, he may be a cultivated individual; in a crowd, he is a barbarian – that is, a creature acting by instinct. He possesses the spontaneity, the violence, the ferocity, and also the enthusiasm and heroism of primitive beings."[5] The subject of temperate *jouissance* regresses to the subject of the drive, to a *jouissance* that is acephalic, annihilating.

Any group can fall back on a "sectarian position", a position understood in its Kleinian sense as a momentary stage of psychic organisa-

[3] ibid., p. 87.

[4] ibid., p. 84.

[5] ibid., p. 76.

tion, corresponding to the points of fixation that can mark the start of a process. This is the hypothesis developed by Bernard Chouvier.[6] The installation and putting down of roots in a sectarian position causes a loss of moral sense, of logical thinking and of a sense of reality, thereby cementing subjection of the individual to the group, the abandon of the self to group control. Reality testing is totally eclipsed by the group ideal. The ideal ego takes over from the ego ideal. In this resurgence of the ideal ego the sectarian position thus constitutes for the group a psychical closure and an ultimate narcissistic regression.

Freud poses the specific problem of how this neo-reality of the group comes about and he attempts to find a way of thinking about the psychical processes that lead to submission of the individual to the group, based on the analysis of two groups that are constitutive of our societies—the army and the Catholic Church. The two psychical functions specified by Freud are identification and the libidinal bond. The ultimate cement that holds the group psyche together is a libidinal drive, and the deeper the regression the greater the power of the group bond. In its most archaic form the bond is founded on the total convergence of object cathexes and narcissistic cathexes in a regressive collusion. In his consideration of the two groups, army and the church, Freud highlights the ineluctable connection between intense commitment to the group and intolerance. Freedom of thought is perverted in favour of a voluntary enslavement to the dogma and ideals of the group. The mainspring of group psychology is the non-freedom of the individual in the mass. This ideological position entails the equalisation of group members and the sectarian position goes further by subjecting everyone to belief in the group and all its thought contents without discernment, in an attachment to a mother-crowd that depends on a fundamentally fetishist belief, denial of any lack.

[6] Chouvier, B. and Morhain, Y. (2007). Position sectaire, croyance et emprise groupale. *Revue de psychothérapie psychanalytique de groupe*, 2 (49): 25–38.

23.2 The Sectarian Discourse as a Tool of Subjection and Destruction

To do justice to the heightening of affect, which, together with inhibition of thought, constitutes one of the two mechanisms of the psychology of crowds, Freud takes up the hypothesis that was put forward in 1920 by W. McDougall of a "primitive induction of emotion". The subjects in a crowd are affectively induced, emotional elements override rational data. Induction subdues reason, the capacity for deduction and differentiation, which is anaesthetised by the power of the mobilised affects. Cognitive processes are placed at the exclusive service of libidinal attachment to the group. It is this exclusivity that creates the sectarian dimension. Certain subjects will be more readily induced, by reason of their psychical predisposition and personal history, and this tendency is greatly encouraged and manipulated in the sectarian group. The utilitarian group superego annihilates individual moral judgment and the capacity for thought and judgement. The individual's own narcissistic investments are displaced onto group narcissism and affective attachment to the group takes precedence over self-preservation. The extreme case of suicide bombers illustrates the effect.

This "primitive induction of emotion" is central in mobilising individual suggestibility to subvert subjective autonomy. The subversion uses the mechanisms of a "drive for mastery", as Freud had emphasised in discussing the component of cruelty of the sexual drive in infantile sexuality: "since the obstacle that brings the drive for mastery to a halt at another person's pain – namely, a capacity for pity – is developed relatively late."[7] And he says that we are entitled to suppose that the cruel tendency issues from the drive to mastery and comes into play during the period of pregenital organisation. The need for mastery stems from a profound insecurity in respect of identity, which may characterise the psychical structure of the leader himself. Mental mastery in the sectarian discourse aims to reduce the other to a thing; it is a discourse of deceit that denies the other's humanity, when the person aspiring to mastery turns up their

[7] Freud, S. (1905). *Three Essays on the Theory of Sexuality.* S.E. 7: 123–242. J. Strachey (Trans.). London: Hogarth, 1953, p. 192. Here, "drive" ("Trieb" is substituted for Strachey's "instinct").

nose at the belief in life and the symbolic pact that makes the distinction between truth and falsehood necessary. The discourse that aims to make the other into a thing is a perverse discourse, one that assaults the other's humanity and dignity of being.

We must ask what makes such a regression, such a disintegration of the symbolic and of its humanising dimension possible? Even after progressing beyond the first stage of psychical construction, which involves an alienation in the Other, the human being remains vulnerable to a regression to this first position of being an object of the Other, in which he or she becomes an object for the mastery and unfettered *jouissance* of an all-powerful Other. This can happen at the individual level, in cases of mental subjection, and at the collective level, in wars. In sectarian mastery, the object is put in the place of the ideal ego and the mastery becomes complete. In the sectarian position, it is the group that thinks, decides and acts through the enlisted subject.

This subject is dispossessed of himself, he is no longer an agent in the tie between subjects, but is passive and is shackled by this tie. We are in a situation beyond the libidinal attachment described by Freud, in an attachment that is rather of a passionate nature, caught in a fetishist urge to ignore the captivating mastery of the maternal Other, in a denial of castration. The leader embodies the paternal function, but he plays the role of father of the primal horde—the archaic figure that Freud placed at the head of the first human group, following Darwin. The group represents the maternal element and, at the level of group ties, a veritable primal scene of belief can be extracted, symbolised in the union of leader and group. This union, this quasi-coitus between leader and group, is constantly reactivated by the regression of the subject to the powerful image of his ideal ego.

23.3 The Sectarian Discourse as a Sixth Discourse?

Could we speak of a sectarian discourse in the Lacanian sense, which might be a sixth discourse (after the fifth, capitalist discourse)?

In the sectarian process, the discourse of the leader is the only discourse that bears meaning, bears all meaning. His discourse will be the engine, for his follower, of an unlimited desire, the jouissance of which facilitates a passage to the act. This is exemplified in a book by M. Declair, a woman who was in the clutches of a sect for 10 years, and who did not hesitate to prostitute herself for the relief of brother members of the sect who felt isolated and lacking affection, by way of a "law of reciprocity" in which she felt herself indebted to the community and to the leader.[8] Idealisation is taken to the extreme, in an ideational euphoria, in the figure of the leader who alone embodies the ego ideal. Idealisation, as Melanie Klein pointed out, is a defence mechanism against separation. The leader-chief is able to incarnate in himself both the paternal and maternal figures, in a multiple gearing of the libidinal relationship of his followers to himself. This is evident in some current sects, where the leader embodies the divinity.

This opens up a new dimension of the leader, namely his relation to the sacred. The chief is bearer of the *mana* described by Mauss[9]—the obscure force inherent in the totemic emblem evoked by Freud in 1912–1913. His followers believe that he is alone in "truly communing with God". The sacred is characteristic of the religious dimension to the extent that it connects two essential emotional features: that which fascinates and that which terrifies. These are the two minimum conditions for the hypnotic relationship, Freud says, and they constitute the original essence of the group bond by establishing the sacredness of the leader and thereby reviving the infantile religiosity of the follower. This is the key to the power and to the affective and drive charge of the tie between the leader and each member of the sectarian group. It is the affective element that is at the root of religious belief. It is also because of this sacralisation that the relationship to the leader needs to be mediated. Proximity to the sacred chief has destructive effects. The chief is idolised in a maniacal enthusiasm, and this same movement is what generates fanaticism in the

[8] Declair, M. (2008). *De l'enfer à l'endroit.* Romanel-sur-Lausanne: La Maison de la Bible.

[9] Mauss, M. (1922). *The Gift: Forms and Functions of Exchange in Archaic Societies.* London: Routledge, 1990.

sectarian position. The essence of fanaticism is that the sacred flame and veneration for the leader find concrete realisation at the heart of an act.

Can the sectarian discourse be heard as the sixth discourse? "Discourse" here is to be understood as structure, as a positioning of the agents of speech (S1, S2, $ and *a*), which organise speech as a function of the places or positions that constitute it (agent, other, production, truth), but that also go beyond it insofar as it constitutes the reverse unconscious side of the social bond. In his Seminar, *The Other Side of Psychoanalysis*, Lacan specifies four major discourses which revolve in quarter turns in a logical evolution that depends upon a mutation of the discourse that precedes it: the discourse of the master, the discourse of the hysteric, the discourse of the analyst and the discourse of the university.[10]

The capitalist discourse, derived from the discourse of the master by an inversion of the positions of S1 and $ and a reversal of the direction of the arrow, is considered as a fifth discourse. How can the sectarian discourse be located in the creation of a neo-truth, and what dominant signifier does it rest upon? It seems that the sectarian discourse, just as the religious discourse and that of the analyst, rests upon the object *a*, the object most opaque to truth. Sectarian discourse would be a perversion of religious discourse. In the discourse of the analyst the object *a*, the object that is fundamentally lost, is the agent of the discourse and S2 is put in the place of truth. I would put forward this hypothesis for consideration: if we apply the displacement, which Lacan applied to the discourse of the master to arrive at the capitalist discourse, to the discourse of the analyst, the sectarian discourse would displace truth to the place of *jouissance* and $ to the place of agent, opening the flood gates to *jouissance*. This discourse is an inversion of the discourse of the analyst, where the step taken by *jouissance* is between the master signifier and the field available to knowledge in so far as it rests on truth.[11]

The sectarian discourse is apparently based on the human need to believe, the source of which Freud connects with the "oceanic feeling"

[10] Lacan, J. (2007)[1969–70]. *Seminar XVII: The Other Side of Psychoanalysis.* R. Grigg (Trans.). New York: W. W. Norton & Company.

[11] Thanks to my translator Ben Hooson and to Brigitte Lalvee for help with this formulation

that he defines in each person as "a shrunken residue of a much more inclusive – indeed, an all-embracing – feeling which corresponded to a more intimate bond between the ego and the world about it",[12] and which he judges to be reinforced by a repressed longing for the father as protector. The genesis of this need to believe articulates with the representation of God, which originates from the enigma of death, a God-affect, the god of the heart of whom Pascal speaks. From there it is but a step to thinking of God as the resurgence of the dead father, and Freud takes that step. "The recognition of the function of the Father is a sublimation that is essential to the opening up of a spirituality" Lacan says in the *Ethics* Seminar.[13]

Freud analyses the religious believer in reaction to his own Jewishness and to Jung's positions that are related to the unresolved question of the father and therefore caught in an alienation. Freud treats various "props", such as work, substitutive satisfactions provided by the life of the imagination and art, which could be extended as far as the various addictive modalities that exist today, as no more than profane outlets for this need to believe. Sophie de Mijolla[14] goes a step further in this search for the source of the need to believe, pointing to the foetus and an experience of "original vision" where there is no distinction between inside and outside. De Mijolla-Moller believes that it is not the murder of the father that is the fundamental crime in the Bible and that creates the sense of guilt, but the "sin of knowledge" in the West. This is why the Christian religion is founded a logic of forgiveness. Knowledge cannot but destroy this original vision insofar as it establishes distinctions, separations, gaps between beings, non-being in being. Psychoanalysis makes the demand for knowledge foundational for the human subject. Psychoanalysis is an experience that works towards an extension (*Erweiterung*), an expansion of consciousness in a recognition of the symbolic law but also of what escapes this law, i.e. the real, which it does not hypostasise under any divine name. This is the sense in which it is opposed to religion. To look

---

[12] Freud, S. (1930). *Civilization and its Discontents*. S.E. 21: 57–146. J. Strachey (Trans.). London: Hogarth Press, 1961, p. 67.

[13] Lacan J. (1992)[1959–60]. *The Seminar of Jacques Lacan, Book VII: The Ethics of Psychoanalysis*. London: Tavistock/Routledge, p. 181.

[14] De Mijolla-Mellor, S. (2004). *Le Besoin de Croire*. Paris: Dunod.

into what distinguishes religion from sect would require further research. But what one can say generally is that the religious discourse is based on the Universal, beginning with an absent God, and that it is based on the discourse of a leader in the place of a living God for whom parricide has not been symbolised.

24

The Logic of Disavowal in the Production of Subjectivities in the Contemporary World

Maria Izabel Oliveira Szpacenkopf

> For any way of thought to become dominant, a conceptual apparatus has to be advanced that appeals to our intuitions and instincts, to our values and our desires, as well as to the possibilities inherent in the social world we inhabit.[1]

This paper is part of a broader research project which analyses fetishism, cynicism and self-reification as categories that are easily identified by the way they operate or even the way they respond to what happens in the contemporary world, and which intervene, in an extreme way, with a particularly remarkable presence in the capitalist system. These categories

[1] Harvey, D. (2005). *Brève Histoire du Néo-libéralism.* Paris: Les Prairies Ordinairies, p. 19.

M.I.O. Szpacenkopf (✉)
Espace Analytique

D. Caine, C. Wright (eds.), *Perversion Now!*,
DOI 10.1007/978-3-319-47271-3_24

are studied in the light of the mechanism of defence called *Verleugnung* (disavowal) as understood by psychoanalysis and philosophy. Naturally, this study implies certain aspects of the concept of ideology, which in turn can be read in several ways based on different criteria throughout the history of ideas. Aspects such as false consciousness, alienation, mystification, forms of slavery, the relations of domination and exploitation, the pronouncement of what is false or true, delusion, beliefs, among others, each of which qualify and designate different ways of understanding what ideology is.

> Ideology can designate anything from a contemplative attitude that misrecognizes its dependence on social reality to an action-oriented set of beliefs, from the indispensable medium in which individuals live out their relations to a social structure to false ideas which legitimate dominant political power.[2]

Having previously studied capitalism from the perspective of ideology, I will confine myself here to the possibility of understanding its new, neoliberal aspect, which operates not only as a manager of narcissistic suffering but also in the formation of subjectivities. To do this, I will consider self-reification based on a reading of Lukács and Axel Honneth to try and illustrate how the mechanism of *Verleugnung* (disavowal) works.

The task of neoliberalism in the 1970s was to extend and rescue capitalism, which was in a state of exhaustion: to restore the power of the dominant classes, which were threatened by socialist and communist political movements. I will not discuss here how neoliberalism came into play as a project to redeem the world—at least, the economic world—but I will try to highlight certain features of this system.

According to David Harvey, "the evidence strongly suggests that the neoliberal turn is in some way and to some degree associated with the restoration or reconstruction of the power of economic elites",[3] thereby creating an institutional atmosphere which is favourable to profit. In this context, human dignity and individual freedom are respected as "central

---

[2] Zizek, S. (1994). Introduction. In S. Zizek (Ed.), *Mapping Ideology*. London: Verso, p. 3.

[3] Harvey, op. cit.

values of civilization"[4] only to the extent to which they are provided by the free market and trade. Neoliberalism wins a cultural hegemony, based on the concept of freedom, which, according to Marx, is always the freedom of capital:

> In the name of this freedom people are exploited. On behalf of this freedom they are made to suffer. On behalf of this freedom war is waged on [...] the enemies of freedom.[5]

The reference to freedom helps neoliberalism to gain legitimacy and its supporters to attain positions from which they can exercise a remarkable degree of influence on education, the media, executive boards and boards of directors, as well as on financial institutions and key state institutions, such as finance ministries, central banks, and international monetary funds charged with regulating international finance and commerce.

> Neoliberalism has, in short, become hegemonic as a mode of discourse. It has pervasive effects on ways of thought to the point where it has become incorporated into the common-sense way many of us interpret, live in, and understand the world.[6]

Through a discourse that preaches the free market and opportunity for all, the project is really focused on the enrichment of elites, contributing significantly to the increase of inequality. If everyone has to compete because everyone has the same opportunities, either the premise is not true, or a belief in the supremacy of the winners has been authorised, attributing the failure of the rest to the fact they were not "good entrepreneurs", thereby encouraging feelings of guilt, shame and humiliation. Similarly, a country in economic difficulty is a country that has failed to be competitive.

In any case, as Margaret Thatcher liked to say, there was no "no alternative"[7] and so she supported a system that entailed a change in ways

---

[4] ibid., p. 20.

[5] Denord, F. (2014). Introduction to Harvey, *Brève Histoire du Neo-liberalism*. Paris: Les Prairies Ordinairies, p. 9.

[6] ibid., p. 3.

[7] Harvey, op. cit., p. 40.

of thinking and living, as indicated by a number of her most famous comments on the nature of society: that there is "no such thing as society, only individual men and women" (she subsequently added "and their families"); that "all forms of social solidarity were to be dissolved in favour of individualism, private property, personal responsibility, and family values"; that "economics are the method, but the object is to change the soul."[8]

24.1 Disavowal and Fetishism

The theory of disavowal in psychoanalysis is closely, though not exclusively, related to fetishism and it frequently happens that when we talk about one we also talk about the other. Disavowal was theorised by Freud in 1923,[9] although the idea of its mechanism was already present in 1917.[10] In *Fetishism*[11] and the *Outline of Psychoanalysis*[12] *Verleugnung* is put forward as the fundamental mechanism of fetishism, which then has the splitting of the ego (*Ichspaltung*) as a consequence. By refusing the perception of that in reality which was unbearable, disavowal operates inside a person's ego, causing a division, a splitting of the ego, by which two different attitudes, mutually exclusive and independent, coexist. Whatever defensive steps are taken by the ego, it denies a part of the external real world or seeks to reject a drive requirement from the internal world and its success is never total or absolute and leads to psychical consequences.

In fetishism, an object is chosen to supplement and substitute for what is lacking in the mother in an effort to save the boy from castration anxiety aroused not only by the perception of the lack of a penis in the mother, but also as a way of accepting the prohibition of an excitation

[8] ibid., p. 23.

[9] Freud, S. (1923). *The Infantile Genital Organisation (An Interpolation into the Theory of Sexuality)*. S.E. 19: 139–146. J. Strachey (Trans.). London: Hogarth, 1953.

[10] Freud, S. (1914). *A Metapsychological Supplement to the Theory of Dreams*. S.E. 14: 217–235. J. Strachey (Trans.). London: Hogarth, 1957.

[11] Freud, S. (1927). *Fetishism*. S.E. 21: 147–157. J. Strachey (Trans.). London: Hogarth, 1961.

[12] Freud, S. (1940)[1938]. *An Outline of Psychoanalysis*. S.E. 23: 139–207. J. Strachey (Trans.). London : Hogarth, 1964.

in relation to this figure. This new object, the fetish, overvalued and idealised, is a bridge between truth ("I know that castration exists") and a lie ("I don't care that castration exists"). Thus, two contradictory judgments, both of them valid,[13] keep alive a system of beliefs that cannot be shaken by reality even while entailing the triumph of that reality (i.e. of castration). Freud initially presented this mechanism as the foundation of perversion, but he reformulated this later in saying that ultimately it is a part of psychical life in general, and not exclusively or specifically linked to the perverse structure.[14]

The formula eternalised by Octave Mannoni "I know perfectly well… but all the same" ("Je sais bien… mais quand-même"),[15] not only brilliantly illustrates the operation of disavowal, but also highlights the importance of the recourse to belief and how it is used in this process, emphasising that in *Verleugnung* (a mechanism of protection, rather than defence, as Mannoni says), the magical action of belief is contained in the words "… but all the same", which, in a way, make it possible to institutionalise this piece of trickery. So there is not a negation of knowledge, because knowledge and non-knowledge can coexist together. *Verleugnung* offers a paradoxical contradiction instead of the knowledge marked by forgetting, which is characteristic of repression.[16]

Neoliberalism has not been applied uniformly, but often manifests specifically national characteristics. In Chile and Argentina, for example, the use of force (a military coup) was required for its introduction. In other countries, it has been installed democratically, but requiring legitimation by popular consent, which is often obtained by arguments such as: the love of God and country; the place of women in society; fear of Communists, Socialists, immigrants—a raft of values that can be used "to mask other realities".[17] The use of such arguments recalls what Freud

[13] ibid., p. 203.

[14] Bass, A. (2000). *Difference and Disavowal: The Trauma of Eros.* Stanford University Press., deals, among other things, with resistance and rejection of interpretation in the analytic treatment, based on the theory of denial and differentiation.

[15] Mannoni, O. (2003). "I Know Well, but All the Same…" G.M. Goshgarian (Trans.). In M.A. Rothenberg, D.A. Foster & S. Zizek (Eds), *Perversion and the Social Relation.* Durham: Duke University Press, pp. 68–92.

[16] Safatle, V. (2008). *Cinismo e Falência da Crítica.* São Paulo: Boitempo Editorial, p. 165.

[17] Harvey, op. cit., p. 39.

has to say about how the fetishist deals with the absence of a penis on the female body. He calls the invention of the fetish: "a very ingenious solution of the difficulty" and "a way of dealing with reality, which almost deserves to be described as artful."[18]

24.2 Denial and Self-Reification

Honneth takes as his starting point the work of conceptualisation carried out by Georg Lukács,[19] who, based on Marxist theory, describes reification as the relationship between people in the form and character of things:

> A series of behaviours ranging from sheer egoism to the triumph of economic interests and including a lack of empathy for others.[20]

What is at issue here is the quantitative apprehension of the object and the treatment of other people as instruments, viewing their needs and characteristics from the standpoint of economic profit, which also moves in the direction of objectification. Subjects would then tend to act in social life as distant observers rather than active participants, since what is required of them is a rational, unemotional attitude, constituting what Lukács called the "second nature" of man in capitalism.[21]

Honneth proposes an understanding of reification and self-reification via the concept of recognition, signalling the presence of denial in these processes. He proposes that recognition precedes knowledge. By the age of about nine months a baby is able to distinguish the perspective of others, leading to the development of symbolic thought. A transition from first to second subjectivity, involving progress in the field of interactive behaviour, allows the child to divert his attention from the privileged

[18] Freud, S. (1938). *Splitting of the Ego in the Process of Defence.* S.E. 23: 271–278. J. Strachey (Trans.). London: Hogarth, 1964, p. 277.

[19] Lukács, G. (2000). *History and Class Consciousness: Studies in Marxist Dialectics.* Cambridge, MA: MIT Press.

[20] Honneth, A. (2007). *Reification: A Recognition-Theoretical View.* Oxford: OUP, p. 97.

[21] Lukács, op. cit.

person and address it to other objects in a creative way. The emphasis is less on cognition and more on the fact that:

> A child could not make all these advances if it had not already developed a feeling of emotional attachment to its psychological parent.[22]

This process allows us to recognise ourselves from the outset in the world of those who care for us and who, in turn, are also inserted into the world of others. This preliminary and initial recognition is what operates in the subsequent task of getting to know other people. There is therefore a prior recognition which is crucial for subsequent knowledge of objective reality.

For Honneth, reification is like amnesia, a forgetting of this prior recognition: "the reification of human beings signifies that we have lost sight of or disavowed the fact of antecedent recognition."[23] In respect of the objective world, this means that the diversity of its meanings is lost, as well as the positions of other people, the same people whom the subject previously recognised.

Similarly, self-reification would come about by forgetting a self-acceptance that was attained and that was previously founded on social practices, and would thus facilitate reified manners of self-reference, giving rise to a sense of the self as an object to be produced and sold. Such a manifestation would be expressed by the lived experience of one's own feelings and desires, but these would be apprehended on the model of an object-thing, whether passively observed or actively produced.[24]

The examples provided by the author—extracts from the social context—are situated in an institutionalised field of specialised practices of self-presentation: job interviews, coaching-type services, internet sites to find partners for romance. Such practices seek to encourage feelings and emotions that must be displayed publicly and to best possible effect, in order achieve desired goals in the form of objects to be acquired. High performance becomes the virtue *par excellence* of the candidate, so the criteria are the same as on the job market.

[22] Honneth, op. cit., p. 116.
[23] ibid., p. 134.
[24] ibid.

This position is already implicit in the trend towards commercialisation, by which everything has a price, everything can be bought or sold, since neoliberalism seeks to bring all human actions into the domain of the market.[25] So self-reification already presents itself as a manifestation of subjectivity, arising from the effort to find a solution to the invasion of irreconcilable thoughts and prejudices, finding in disavowal a solution that aids survival in such situations. Self-presentation and self-affirmation are modified as a function of institutional arrangements and needs, so that subjects accept their roles as constructions manufactured to meet the requirements of certain exploitative practices.

It is also important to highlight the existence of narcissistic suffering.[26] Our proposal is to use balance and conflict resolution based on what Freud called the *synthesis of the ego*[27] and what Lacan, in the first book of his *Seminar*,[28] calls the *identificatory and synthetic illusion of the ego* (French "moi")[29] which, in our opinion, can function as the foundation of narcissistic suffering. To model the advent of the subject on this synthesis of the ego is to strive for the presence and confirmation of identity where the negative and the unfamiliar cannot be recognised, it is to eliminate negativity and anxiety as essential elements of subjectivation. We cannot but think that a synthesis based on the ego, loaded as it must be with determinations that impose a unification will seek, as a matter of principle, to exclude any relationship with the unknown, the unfamiliar, the different, the inimical. If unwanted otherness incites the movement of the ego towards identificatory organisation in order to avoid narcissistic suffering, it also triggers strategies to avoid an even worse evil. Disavowal is one of these strategies of narcissistic defence.

---

[25] Harvey, op. cit., p. 3.

[26] Szpacenkopf, M.I.O. (2014). I have developed the theme of narcissistic suffering in an article, "Pathologie du social : La souffrance narcissique dans l'invisibilité sociale et la violence", presented at the third Espace Analytique Congress in Toulouse, and published in *Actualités de la Psychanalyse*, Paris: Érès, September 2014.

[27] Freud, S. (1926). *Inhibitions, Symptoms and Anxiety*. S.E. 20: 75–176. J. Strachey (Trans.). London: Hogarth Press, 1959, p. 117.

[28] Lacan, J. *The Seminar, Book I: Freud's Technical Papers*. J. Forrester (Trans.). Cambridge: CUP, 1988.

[29] This is Lacan's concept of the image-based formation from the mirror stage, which usurps the role of the subject in mental life.

I believe that narcissistic suffering is exacerbated by neoliberalism, to the extent that everyone has to adapt themselves and to defend a logic, in which performance is fetishised and replaces the question of individual differences. Individual differences are disavowed in deference to a declared principle of equality that seeks to go beyond singularities, homogenising them from the top down and leaving, at the bottom, a great mass of those who have been excluded, without any chance of upward mobility and afflicted by feelings of panic, fear of imminent death, and loss of control. It should also be remembered that, according to Lacan, the ego is constituted through the recognition of the other, and if I do not recognise the other, I do not access ego identification. Honneth's hypothesis rightly refers to the forgetting of an attitude that can support the perspective of the other in the sense of interpersonal communication, symbolic thought and language, but it also seems possible to think that, in Lacanian terms, due to the necessary disavowal supported by neoliberalism, I cannot address myself to the other or recognise myself in the other, since it is precisely the other that I must overcome as the one who can rob me of the possibility of "*jouissance*" ("enjoyment"), who threatens me and makes me suffer. In this way, as in the paranoid competitiveness of the mirror state—it is either me or them—the danger is to be found at once in the other. But if I disavow the other, I lose my own identity. Self-reification could then be seen as a subjective attempt to seek *jouissance* as the object of the Other, guaranteed through performance.

If, in the classical perspective, disavowal is a narcissistic solution that indicated misrecognition of female castration, the threatened synthesis of the ego will use other strategies of defence, including disavowal, to the extent that it has to live with contradictory norms. Faced with a situation that requires so much trickery on the part of the ego to enable these norms to coexist, the ego struggles for unity, at constant risk of division. In this context the issue of narcissistic suffering is increasingly relevant for all of us in contemporary society.

References

Adams, P. (1996). *The emptiness of the image: Psychoanalysis and sexual differences*. London: Routledge.

Adorno, T. W., & Horkheimer, M. (2002)[1947]. *Dialectic of enlightenment: Philosophical fragments*. G. Schmid Noerr (Ed.) & E. Jephcott (Trans.). Stanford: Stanford University Press.

Ahmed, S. (2004). Declarations of whiteness: The non-performativity of anti-racism. *Borderlands e-journal*. http://www.borderlands.net.au/vol3no2_2004/ahmed_declarations.html. Accessed 10 Feb 2016.

Aitkenhead, D. (2006). The shadow that refuses to disappear. *The Guardian*. http://www.theguardian.com/society/2006/feb/25/socialcare.familyandrelationships. Accessed 10 Feb 2016.

Alcoff, L. M. (n.d.). *Whose afraid of identity politics*. http://www.alcoff.com/content/afraidid.html. Accessed 10 Feb 2016.

Allouch, J. (2011). *L'érotique du deuil au temps de la mort sèche*. Paris: Broché.

American Psychiatric Association. (1952). *Diagnostic and statistical manual of mental disorders (DSM)*. Washington, DC: American Psychiatric Press.

American Psychiatric Association. (1968). *Diagnostic and statistical manual of mental disorders, second edition* (DSM-II). Washington, DC: American Psychiatric Press.

D. Caine, C. Wright (eds.), *Perversion Now!*,
DOI 10.1007/978-3-319-47271-3

American Psychiatric Association. (1980). *Diagnostic and statistical manual of mental disorders, third edition (DSM-III)*. Washington, DC: American Psychiatric Press.

American Psychiatric Association. (1987). *Diagnostic and statistical manual of mental disorders, third edition - revised* (DSM-IIIR). Washington, DC: American Psychiatric Publishing.

American Psychiatric Association. (2000). *Diagnostic and statistical manual of mental disorders, fourth edition, text revision (DSM-IV-TR)*. Washington, DC: American Psychiatric Publishing.

American Psychiatric Association. (2013). *Diagnostic and statistical manual of mental disorders, fifth edition* (DSM-V). Washington, DC/London: American Psychiatric Publishing.

André, S. (1993). *L'imposture perverse*. Paris: Seuil.

André, S. (2006). The structure of perversion: A Lacanian perspective. In D. Nobus & L. Downing (Eds), *Perversion: Psychoanalytic perspectives*. London: Karnac.

André, S. (2013). *Les perversions No. 2: Le sadisme*. Lormont: La Muette.

André, J., Catherine, C., & Guyomard, P. (Eds). (2015). *La perversion, encore*. Paris: Presses Universitaires de France.

Balibar, E. (2010). *Violence et civilité*. Paris: Galilée.

Bass, A. (2000). *Difference and disavowal: The trauma of eros*. Redwood: Stanford University Press.

Bataille, G. (1957). *L'érotisme*. Paris: Minuit.

Bataille, G. (1959). *Le procès de Gilles de Rais*. Œuvres complètes X. Paris: Gallimard, 1987.

Bellmer, H. (2005). *The doll*. London: Atlas Press.

Blanchot, M. (1963). *La Raison de Sade*. In *Lautréamont et Sade*. Paris: Minuit.

Bond, H. (2009). *Lacan at the scene*. Cambridge, MA: MIT Press.

Boothby, R. (1991). *Death and desire*. New York/London: Routledge.

Brousse, M. H. (2002). Ravage and the desire of the analyst. In *Almanac of psychoanalysis III, the logical time of ravishment* (pp. 67–73). Rehovot: GIEP.

Butler, J. (1990). *Gender trouble: Feminism and the subversion of identity*. London/New York: Routledge.

Butler, J. (2005). *Vie précaire : Les pouvoirs du deuil et de la violence après le 11 septembre 2001*. Paris: Broché.

Castanet, H. (1992). *Regard et perversion. A partir des Lois de l'Hospitalité de Pierre Klossowski*. Nice: Z'éditions.

Castanet, H. (1999). *La perversion*. Paris: Anthropos.

Castoriadis Aulagnier, P. (1967). La perversion comme structure. In *L'inconscient 2*, La perversion. Paris: PUF.

Chaperon, S. (2012). *Les origines de la sexologie (1850–1900)*. Paris: Payot.

Chinese Society of Psychiatry. (2001). *The Chinese classification and diagnostic criteria of mental disorders, third edition (CCMD-3)*. Jinan: Chinese Society of Psychiatry.

Chouvier, B., & Morhain, Y. (2007). Position sectaire, croyance et emprise groupale. *Revue de psychothérapie psychanalytique de groupe, 2*(49), 25–38.

Clavreul, J. (1980). The perverse couple. In S. Schneiderman (Ed.), *Returning to Freud: Clinical psychoanalysis in the school of Lacan*. New Haven: Yale University Press.

Combahee River Collective. (1977). History is a weapon: Combahee River Collective Statement. http://historyisaweapon.com/defcon1/combrivercoll.html. Accessed 10 Feb 2016.

Dachet, F. (2008). *L'innocence violée?: le petit Hans Herbert Graf: devenir metteur en scène d'opéra*. Paris: Unebévue.

De Mijolla-Mellor, S. (2004). *Le Besoin de Croire*. Paris: Dunod.

de Sade, D. A. F. (1986–1991)[1797]. *Histoire de Juliette*. Œuvres Complètes, tome 8. Paris: Gilbert Lely.

Dean, T. (2006). Lacan meets queer theory. In D. Nobus & L. Downing (Eds), *Perversion: Psychoanalytic perspectives*. London: Karnac.

Dean, T. (2008). The frozen countenance of the perversions. *Parallax, 14*(2), 93.

Declair, M. (2008). *De l'enfer à l'endroit*. Romanel-sur-Lausanne: La Maison de la Bible.

Deleuze, G., & Sacher-Masoch, L. (1994). *Coldness and cruelty and venus in furs*. New York: Zone Books.

Denord, F. (2014). Introduction to D. Harvey, *Brève Histoire du Neo-liberalism*. Paris: Les Prairies Ordinairies.

Desanti, J. T. (1983). L'obcène ou les malices du signifiant. In *The Dado syndrome : Dado's virtual anti-museum*. Available from http://www.dado.virtual.museum/dado-artwork-desanti.php.

Diamond, D. (2005). Narcissism as a clinical and social phenomenon. In J. S. Auerbach, K. N. Levy, & C. E. Schaffer (Eds), *Relatedness, self-definition and mental representation: Essays in honor of Sidney J Blatt*. New York: Brunner-Routledge.

Dollimore, J. (1991). *Sexual dissidence: Augustine to Wilde, Freud to Foucault*. Oxford: Clarendon Press.

Dor, J. (2001). *Structure and perversions*. S. Fairfield (Trans.). New York: Other Press.

Evans, D. (1996). *An introductory dictionary of Lacanian psychoanalysis*. London: Verso.

Fairbairn, R. W. D. (1952a). Endopsychic structure considered in terms of object-relationships. In *Psycho-analytic studies of the personality*. London: Routledge.

Falzeder, E. (Ed.). (2002). *The complete correspondence of Sigmund Freud and Karl Abraham 1907–1925*. C. Schwarzacher (Trans.). London/New York: Karnac.

Farage, N. (2015). I'm taking on the establishment and they hate me for it. *Spiked Online*. http://www.spiked-online.com/newsite/article/im-taking-on-the-establishment-and-they-hate-me-for-it/16758#.Vml5j14zpQK. Accessed 10 Feb 2016.

FIIMG. (2015). Queer: Excitable speech on tinternet. http://fiimg.com/2015/04/07/queer-excitable-speech-on-tinternet/. Accessed 10 Feb 2016.

Fink, B. (1995). *The Lacanian subject*. Princeton/Chichester: Princeton University Press.

Fink, B. (1997a). *A clinical introduction to Lacanian psychoanalysis: Theory and technique*. Cambridge, MA/London: Harvard University Press.

Fink, B. (1997b). *A clinical introduction to Lacanian psychoanalysis*. Cambridge/London: Harvard University Press.

Fink, B. (2003). The use of Lacanian psychoanalysis in a case of fetishism. *Clinical Case Studies, 2*(1), 50–69.

Fondation du Champ Freudien. (1990). *Traits de perversion dans les structures cliniques*. Paris: Navarin.

Foucault, M. (1975). Sade, sergent du sexe. In *Dits et écrits* (Vol. 2). Paris: Gallimard, 1984.

Foucault, M. (1978a). Sexual morality and the law. http://www.geocities.ws/foucault_on_age_of_consent/. Accessed 10 Feb 2016.

Foucault, M. (1978b). *The history of sexuality. Volume 1: An introduction*. R. Hurley (Trans.). New York: Random House.

Foucault, M. (1989). *Archaeology of knowledge*. A. M. Sheridan Smith (Trans.). London: Routledge.

Foucault, M. (2013). *La grande étrangère. A propos de littérature*. Notes des éditeurs. Paris: EHESS.

Freud, S. (1897). Letters 55, 69, 75, 125 from Freud's correspondance with W. Fliess. In *Pre-psychoAnalytic publications and unpublished drafts. S.E.* 1 J. Strachey (Trans.). London: Hogarth, 1953.

Freud, S. (1905). *Three essays on the theory of sexuality. S.E.* 7: 123–242 J. Strachey (Trans.). London: Hogarth, 1953.

Freud, S. (1909a). *Analysis of a phobia in a five- year-old boy. S.E.*10: 5–149 J. Strachey (Trans.). London: Hogarth Press, 1953.

Freud, S. (1909b). *Notes upon a case of obsessional neurosis. S.E.*10: 151–318 J. Strachey (Trans.). London: Hogarth Press, 1953.

Freud, S. (1910). *The future prospects of psycho-analytic therapy. S.E.*11: 139–152 J. Strachey (Trans.). London: Hogarth Press, 1955.

Freud, S. (1912). *Recommendations to physicians practising psychoanalysis. S.E.* 12: 111–120 J. Strachey (Trans.). London: Hogarth Press, 1955.

Freud, S. (1913). *On beginning the treatment. S.E.* 12, 121–144 J. Strachey (Trans.). London: Hogarth Press, 1955.

Freud, S. (1914). A metapsychological supplement to the theory of dreams. *S.E.* 14: 217–235 J. Strachey (Trans.). London: Hogarth, 1957.

Freud, S. (1915). *Instincts and their Vicissitudes. S.E.* 14: 109–140 J. Strachey (Trans.). London: Hogarth, 1957.

Freud, S. (1916–17). Introductory lectures on psycho-analysis. *S.E.* 16 J. Strachey (Trans.). London: Hogarth, 1963.

Freud, S. (1918). *The taboo of virginity (Contributions to the psychology of love III). S.E.* XI: 191–208 J. Strachey (Trans.). London: Hogarth, 1957.

Freud, S. (1919). *'A child is being beaten': A contribution to the study of the origins of sexual perversions. S.E.* 17: 175–205 J. Strachey (Trans.). London: Hogarth, 1955.

Freud, S. (1921). *Group psychology and the analysis of the ego. S.E.* 18: 65–144 J. Strachey (Trans.). London: Hogarth Press.

Freud, S. (1923). *The infantile genital organisation (An interpolation into the theory of sexuality). S.E.* 19: 139–146 J. Strachey (Trans.). London: Hogarth, 1953.

Freud, S. (1925). *Some psychical consequences of the anatomical distinction between the sexes. S.E.* 19: 248–258 J. Strachey (Trans.). London: Hogarth, 1961.

Freud, S. (1926). *Inhibitions, symptoms and anxiety. S.E.* 20: 75–176 J. Strachey (Trans.). London: Hogarth Press, 1959.

Freud, S. (1927). *Fetishism. S.E.* 21: 147–157 J. Strachey (Trans.). London: Hogarth, 1961.

Freud , S. (1928). *Analyse d'une Phobie Chez un Petit Garçon de Cinq Ans (Le Petit Hans)* M. Bonaparte (Trans.). *Revue Française de Psychanalyse, 2*(3), 411–540.

Freud, S. (1930). *Civilisation and its discontents. S.E.* 21: 64–148 J. Strachey (Trans.). London: Hogarth Press, 1961.

Freud, S. (1933). Why war? *S.E.* 22: 195–216 J. Strachey (Trans.). London: Hogarth Press, 1964.
Freud, S. (1938). *Splitting of the ego in the process of defence. S.E.* 23: 271–278 J. Strachey (Trans.). London: Hogarth, 1964.
Freud, S. (1940)[1938]. *An outline of psychoanalysis. S.E.* 23: 139–207 J. Strachey (Trans.). London: Hogarth, 1964.
Freud, S. (1954). *Cinq psychanalyses*. Paris: Presses Universitaires de France.
Freud, S., & Breuer, J. (1895). *Studies in Hysteria* N. Luckhurst (Trans.). London: Penguin, 2004.
Gallagher, C. (2010). The Founding Act, the Cartel and the riddle of the PLUS ONE. *The Letter: Irish Journal for Lacanian Psychoanalysis, 44*(Summer), 1–31.
Goux, J. J. (1991). Lacan Iconoclast. In A. Leupin (Ed.), *Lacan and the human sciences*. Lincoln/London: University of Nebraska Press.
Graf, M. (1942). Reminiscences of Professor Sigmund Freud. *Psychoanalytic Quarterly, 11*(4), 465–476.
Halperin, D. (1995). *Saint Foucualt: Towards a gay hagiography*. Oxford: Oxford University Press.
Harari, R. (2002). *How James Joyce made his name: A reading of the final Lacan*. New York: Other Press.
Harvey, D. (2005). *Brève Histoire du Néo-libéralism*. Paris: Les Prairies Ordinairies.
Hénaff, M. (2014). *Violence dans la raison ? Conflit et cruauté*. Paris: Essaie.
Hewson, B. (2015). How "recovered memories" fuelled the paedo panic. *Spiked Online*. http://www.spiked-online.com/newsite/article/how-recovered-memories-fuelled-the-paedo-panic/16850#.Vml77V4zpQK. Accessed 10 Feb 2016.
Honneth, A. (2007). *Reification: A recognition-theoretical view*. Oxford: Oxford University Press.
Isay, R. A. (2009). *Becoming gay: The journey to self-acceptance*. New York: Vintage Books.
Israël, L. (1996). *La jouissance de l'hystérique, Séminaire 1974*. Paris: Arcanes.
Jadin, J. M. (1997). *André Gide et sa perversion*. Paris: Arcanes.
Jallon, H. (1997). *Sade. Le corps constituant*. Paris: Michalon.
Jelinek, E. (1988). *The piano teacher*. J. Neugroschel (Trans.). London: Serpent's Tail.
Kaplan, L. J. (2006). *Cultures of fetishism*. New York: Palgrave-Macmillan.
Kernberg, O. F. (1975). *Borderline conditions and pathological narcissism*. New York: Jason Aronson.

Kinsey, A. (1948). *Sexual behavior in the human male*. Bloomington: Indiana University Press.

Kohut, H. (2009). *The analysis of the self.* Chicago: University of Chicago Press.

Krafft-Ebing, R. (1886). *Psychopathia sexualis: Eine klinisch-forensische Studie* (1st ed.). Stuttgart: Enke.

Lacan, J. (1957–8). *Seminar, Book V: Formations of the unconscious* C. Gallagher (Trans.). http://www.lacaninireland.com/web/published-works/seminars/

Lacan, J. (1958a–9). *Le Séminaire, Livre 6: Le désire*, http://staferla.free.fr/S6/S6.htm. Accessed 10 Feb 2016.

Lacan, J. (1958b–9). *Seminar, Book VI: Desire and its interpretation* C. Gallagher (Trans.). http://www.lacaninireland.com/web/published-works/seminars/

Lacan, J. (1960–1). *Seminar, Book VIII: Transference* C. Gallagher (Trans.). http://www.lacaninireland.com/web/published-works/seminars/

Lacan, J. (1961–2). *Seminar, Book IX: Identification* C. Gallagher (Trans.). http://www.lacaninireland.com/web/published-works/seminars/

Lacan, J. (1966a)[1949]. Le Stade du miroir comme formateur de la fonction du Je, telle qu'elle nous est révélée dans l'expérience psychanalytique. In *Écrits 1* (Sélection). Paris: Seuil.

Lacan, J. (1966b)[1957]. L'Instance de la lettre dans l'inconscient ou la raison depuis Freud. In *Écrits 1* (Sélection). Paris: Seuil.

Lacan J. (1966c)[1958]. Jeunesse de Gide ou la lettre et le désir. In *Écrits (Sélection)*. Paris: Seuil.

Lacan, J. (1966d)[1953]. Fonction et Champ de la parole et du langage en psychanalyse. In *Écrits 1 (Sélection)*. Paris: Seuil.

Lacan, J. (1966e)[1962]. Kant avec Sade. In *Écrits (Sélection)*. Paris: Seuil.

Lacan, J. (1968–9). *Seminar, Book XVII: From an other to another/The other side of psychoanalysis* C. Gallagher (Trans.). http://www.lacaninireland.com/web/published-works/seminars/

Lacan, J. (1972–3). *Seminar, Book XX: Encore* C. Gallagher (Trans.). http://www.lacaninireland.com/web/published-works/seminars/.

Lacan, J. (1974–5). *Le Séminaire, Livre XXII: R.S.I. Ornicar?* 5, 37–46.

Lacan, J. (1975–6). *Seminar, Book XXIII: Joyce and the Sinthome* C. Gallagher (Trans.). http://www.lacaninireland.com/web/published-works/seminars/.

Lacan, J. (1977)[1953]. The function and field of speech and language in psychoanalysis. In *Ecrits: A selection* A. Sheridan (Trans.). New York: W. W. Norton & Company.

Lacan, J. (1978)[1954–1955]. *Le séminaire, Livre 2 : Le Moi dans la théorie de Freud et dans la technique de la psychanalyse*. J.-A. Miller (Ed.). Paris: Seuil.

Lacan, J. (1980)[1955–6]. On a question preliminary to any possible treatment of psychosis. In *Ecrits: A selection* A. Sheridan (Trans.). London: Routledge.

Lacan, J. (1986)[1959–60]. *Le séminaire, Livre VII : L'Éthique de la psychanalyse.* J.-A. Miller (Ed.). Paris: Seuil.

Lacan, J. (1988)[1953–4]. The *Seminar, Book I: Freud's papers on technique.* J.-A Miller (Ed.) J. Forrester (Trans.). Cambridge: Cambridge University Press.

Lacan, J. (1990a)[1964]. Founding Act (*Acte de foundation)* in *Television/A challenge to the psychoanalytic establishment*. D. Hollier, R. Krauss, & A. Michelson (Trans.). London/New York: W. W. Norton & Company.

Lacan, J (1990b). In Fondation du Champ freudien (Ed.), *Traits de perversion dans les structures cliniques.* Paris: Navarin.

Lacan, J. (1991)[1953–4]. *The seminar of Jacques Lacan, Book I: Freud's papers on technique.* J.-A Miller (Ed.). J. Forrester (Trans.). New York: W. W. Norton & Company.

Lacan, J. (1992)[1959–60]. *The seminar of Jacques Lacan, Book VII: The ethics of psychoanalysis.* J.-A. Miller (Ed.) & D. Porter (Trans.). London: Routledge.

Lacan, (1994a)[1956–7]. *Le séminaire, Livre IV : La relation d'objet et les structures freudiennes.* J.-A. Miller (Ed.). Paris: Seuil.

Lacan, J. (1994b)[1964]. *The four fundamental concepts of psycho-analysis.* A. Sheridan (Trans.). Harmondsworth: Penguin.

Lacan, J. (1995). Spring awakening S. Rodríguez (Trans.). *Analysis, 6*, 34.

Lacan, J. (1998)[1957–8]. *Le Séminaire, Livre V : Les formations de l'inconscient.* J.-A. Miller (Ed.). Paris: Seuil.

Lacan, J. (2001)[1960–1]. *Le Séminaire, Livre VIII : Le transfert* (2ème édition). J.-A Miller (Ed.). Paris: Seuil.

Lacan, J. (2005)[1975–6]. *Le Séminaire, Livre XXIII: Le Sinthome.* J.-A. Miller (Ed.). Paris: Seuil.

Lacan, J. (2006a)[1968–9]. *Le Seminaire, Livre XVI : D'un Autre à l'Autre.* J.-A. Miller (Ed.). Paris: Seuil.

Lacan, J. (2006b). Beyond the pleasure principle. In *Écrits: The first complete edition in English* B. Fink (Trans.). London: W. W. Norton & Company.

Lacan, J. (2006c). Kant with Sade. In *Écrits: The first complete edition in English* B. Fink (Trans.). London: W. W. Norton & Company.

Lacan, J. (2007a)[1969–70]. *The seminar, Book XVII: The other side of psychoanalysis* R. Grigg (Trans.). New York: W. W. Norton & Company.

Lacan, J. (2014). *The seminar of Jacques Lacan, Book X: Anxiety.* J.-A. Miller (Ed.) & A. Price (Trans.). London: Polity.

Lanteri-Laura, G. (1979). *Lecture des perversions. Histoire de leur appropriation médicale.* Paris: Masson.

LaPlanche, J., & Pontalis, J. B. (1973). *The language of psychoanalysis* D. Nicholson-Smith (Trans.). New York: W. W. Norton & Company.

Lebrun, J. P. (2007). *La Perversion Ordinaire*. Paris: Denoël.

Lebrun, J. P. (2011). *Un monde sans limite: Suivi de Malaise dans la subjectivation*. Toulouse: Érès.

Left Unity. (2014). Crime and justice policy. http://leftunity.org/crime-justice-policy/. Accessed 10 Feb 2016.

Lichtenstein, T. (2001). *Behind closed doors: The art of Hans Bellmer*. Berkeley/New York: University of California Press International Center of Photography.

Lukács, G. (2000). *History and class consciousness: Studies in Marxist Dialectics*. Cambridge, MA: MIT Press.

Mannoni, O. (1969). *Clefs pour l'imaginaire ou l'Autre Scène*. Paris: Seuil.

Mannoni, O. (2003). I know well, but all the same… G. M. Goshgarian (Trans.). In M. A. Rothenberg, D. A. Foster & S. Zizek (Eds)., *Perversion and the social relation* (pp. 68–92). Durham: Duke University Press.

Masson, C. (2000). *La Fabrique de la poupée chez Hans Bellmer: Le "faire-œoeuvre perversif", une étude clinique de l'objet*. Paris: Harmattan.

Mauss, M. (1922). *The gift: Forms and functions of exchange in archaic societies*. London: Routledge.

Mazaleige-Labaste, J. (2014a). *Les déséquilibres de l'amour. La genèse du concept de perversion sexuelle, de la Révolution française à Freud*. Paris: Ithaque.

Mazaleige-Labaste, J. (2014b). *Les déséquilibres de l'amour. La genèse du concept de perversion sexuelle, de la Révolution française à Freud*. Paris: Ithaque.

Melman, C. (2005). *L'homme sans gravité*. Paris: Denoël.

Melman, C. (2010). *La nouvelle économie psychique*. Toulouse: Erès.

Metz, C. (1985). Photography and fetish. *October*, Autumn, 81–90.

Miller, J.-A. (1996). On perversion. In R. Feldstein, B. Fink, & M. Jaanus (Eds), *Reading seminars I and II: Lacan's return to Freud*. Albany: State University of New York Press.

Miller, J.-A. (2008). Extimity. In *The Symptom, 9*(Fall). http://www.lacan.com/symptom/. Accessed 13 Aug 2015.

Millot, C. (1996). *Gide Genet Mishima. Intelligence de la perversion*. Paris: Gallimard.

Money, J. (1988). *Gay, sraight and in-between: The sexology of erotic orientation*. New York: Oxford University Press.

Nobus, D. (2003). Lacan's science of the subject. In J. M. Rabaté (Ed.), *The Cambridge companion to Lacan*. Cambridge: Cambridge University Press.

Nobus, D. M. (2009). Perversion as symptom: On defining the sexuality of the other. *Analysis, 15*, 21–30.

Nobus, D., & Downing, L. (Eds.). (2006). *Perversion: Psychoanalytic perspectives*. London: Karnac.
Parker, I. (2005, June 1). *Cartels in Lacanian Psychoanalysis*. Paper given at the founding meeting of Manchester Psychoanalytic Matrix.
Pommier, G. (2009). Des Perversion polymorphes de l'enfant à la perversion proprement dite. *Revue La Clinique Lacanienne, 16*, 233–246.
Preciado, B. (2000). *Manifeste contra-sexual*. Paris: Balland.
Rey-Flaud, R. (2002). *Le Démenti pervers: le refoulé et l'oublié*. Paris: Aubier.
Rosario, V. A. (1997). *The erotic imagination: French histories of perversity*. New York/Oxford: Oxford University Press.
Rose, L. (1988). Freud and fetishism: Previously unpublished minutes of the Vienna psychoanalytic society. *The Psychoanalytic Quarterly, 57*, 147–166.
Rose, B. A. (1996). *Jekyll and Hyde adapted: Dramatizations of cultural anxiety*. Westport: Greenwood Press.
Roudinesco, E. (2007). *La part obscure de nous-mêmes : Une histoire des pervers*. Paris: Albin Michel.
Roudinesco, E. (2009). *Our dark side: A history of perversion*. Cambridge: Polity.
Roudinesco, E., & Plon, M. (2006). *Dictionaire de la Psychanalyse*. Paris: Fayard.
Roughton, R. E. (1995). Overcoming antihomosexual bias: A progress report. *The American Psychoanalyst, 29*(4), 15–16.
Roughton, R. E. (2002). The international psychoanalytical association and homosexuality. *Journal of Gay and Lesbian Psychotherapy, 7*(1/2), 189–196.
Safatle, V. (2008). *Cinismo e Falência da Crítica*. São Paulo: Boitempo Editorial.
Schaffner, A. K. (2011). *Modernism and perversion: Sexual deviance in sexology and literature 1850–1930*. Basingstoke: Palgrave Macmillan.
Seymour, R. (2015). The guilt of the abused. *Lenin's Tomb*. http://www.leninology.co.uk/2015/03/on-guilt-of-abused.html. Accessed 10 Feb 2016.
Skeat, W. (1888). *An etymological dictionary of the English language*. Oxford: Clarendon.
Soler, C. (2003). The paradoxes of the symptom in psychoanalysis. In J. M. Rabaté (Ed.), *The Cambridge companion to Lacan*. Cambridge: Cambridge University Press.
Soler, C. (2014). *Lacan: The unconscious reinvented*. London: Karnac.
Spivak, G. (2014). Herald exclusive: In conversation with Gayatri Spivak. *Dawn*. http://www.dawn.com/news/1152482/herald-exclusive-in-conversation-with-gayatri-spivak. Accessed 10 Feb 2016.
Stein, R. (2005). Why perversion? 'False love' and the perverse pact. *The International Journal of Psycho-Analysis, 86*, 775–799.

Swales, S. (2012). *Perversion. A Lacanian psychoanalytic approach to the subject*. New York/Hove: Routledge.

Szpacenkopf, M. I. O. (2014). Pathologie du social : La souffrance narcissique dans l´invisibilité sociale et la violence. In *Actualités de la Psychanalyse*. Paris: Érès.

Taylor, S. (2000). *Hans Bellmer: The anatomy of anxiety*. Cambridge, MA: MIT Press.

Thompson, B. (1994). *Sadomasochism: Painful perversion or pleasurable play?* London: Continuum.

Thurston, L. (Ed.). (2002). *Re-inventing the symptom: Essays on the final Lacan*. New York: Other Press.

Thurston, L. (2004). *James Joyce and the problem of psychoanalysis*. Cambridge: Cambridge University Press.

Uvsløkk, G. (2011). *Jean Genet. Une écriture des perversions*. Amsterdam/New York: Rodopi.

Vadolas, A. (2009). *Perversions of fascism*. London: Karnac.

Valas, P. (2012). Freud et la Perversion I_II_III [Online]. Available from http://www.valas.fr/IMG/pdf/Freud_et_la_perversion_I_II_III.pdf.

Verhaeghe, P. (2001a). Perversion I: Perverse traits. *The Letter, 22*, 59–75.

Verhaeghe, P. (2001b). Perversion II: The perverse structure. *The Letter, 23*, 77–95.

Verhaeghe, P. (2004). *On being normal and other disorders*. New York: Other Press.

Verhaeghe, P. (2006). Enjoyment and impossibility: Lacan's revision of the Oedipus complex. In J. Clemens & R. Grigg (Eds), *Jacques Lacan and the other side of psychoanalysis: Reflections on seminar XVII*. Durham: Duke University Press.

Verhaeghe, P. (2015). *Contemporary madness does not make sense*. Unpubl. Lecture delivered at CFAR 3.5.2015.

Webb, P., & Short, R. (1985). *Hans Bellmer*. London: Quartet.

Weber, S. (1991). *Return to Freud: Jacques Lacan's dislocation of psychoanalysis*. Cambridge/New York: Cambridge University Press.

Welldon, E. V. (1988). *Mother Madonna Whore*. London: Karnac.

Wittig, M. (1973). *Le corps lesbian*. Paris: Minuit.

Wittig, M. (1980). *The straight mind. Feminist Issues, 1*(1), 103–111. 10.1007/BF02685561.

Wood, M. J. (1999). New life for an old tradition: Anne Rice and Vampire literature. In L. G. Heldreth & M. Pharr (Eds.), *The blood is the life: Vampires in literature*. Bowling Green, Wisc: Bowling Green State University Popular Press.

Wood, H. (2014). Working with problems of perversion. *British Journal of Psychotherapy, 30*(4), 422–437.

World Health Organisation. (1992). *The ICD-10 classification of mental and behavioural disorders: Clinical descriptions and diagnostic guidelines*. Geneva: World Health Organisation.

Zizek, S. (1994). Introduction. In S. Zizek (Ed.), *Mapping ideology*. London: Verso.

Zürn, U. (1994). *The man of Jasmine*. M. Green (Trans.). London: Atlas Press.

Index

Note: Page numbers followed by "n" denote notes.

D. Caine, C. Wright (eds.), *Perversion Now!*,
DOI 10.1007/978-3-319-47271-3

I

J

K

L

GPSR Compliance
The European Union's (EU) General Product Safety Regulation (GPSR) is a set of rules that requires consumer products to be safe and our obligations to ensure this.

If you have any concerns about our products, you can contact us on

ProductSafety@springernature.com

In case Publisher is established outside the EU, the EU authorized representative is:

Springer Nature Customer Service Center GmbH
Europaplatz 3
69115 Heidelberg, Germany

www.ingramcontent.com/pod-product-compliance
Lightning Source LLC
Chambersburg PA
CBHW050522240926
51846CB00003B/657
* 9 7 8 3 3 1 9 8 3 6 9 6 6 *